Queer
African
Cinemas

D1572032

A CAMERA OBSCURA BOOK

A series edited by Lynne Joyrich, Patricia White, Lalitha Gopalan, Bliss Cua Lim, Homay King, Tess Takahashi, Constance Penley, and Sharon Willis

Queer
African
Cinemas

LINDSEY B. GREEN-SIMMS

Duke University Press *Durham* 2022

Library of Congress Cataloging-in-Publication Data
Names: Green-Simms, Lindsey B., [date] author.
Title: Queer African cinemas / Lindsey B. Green-Simms.
Description: Durham : Duke University Press, 2022. | Includes
bibliographical references and index.
Identifiers: LCCN 2021022864 (print)
LCCN 2021022865 (ebook)
ISBN 9781478015406 (hardcover)
ISBN 9781478018018 (paperback)
ISBN 9781478022633 (ebook)
Subjects: LCSH: Homosexuality in motion pictures. | Homosexuality and
motion pictures—Africa. | Gays in motion pictures. | Motion pictures—
Africa—History and criticism. | BISAC: PERFORMING ARTS / Film / History &
Criticism | SOCIAL SCIENCE / LGBTQ Studies / General
Classification: LCC PN1995.9.H55 G744 2022 (print) |
LCC PN1995.9.H55 (ebook) | DDC 791.43/653—dc23
LC record available at https://lccn.loc.gov/2021022864
LC ebook record available at https://lccn.loc.gov/2021022865

Cover art: Still from Wanuri Kahiu's *Rafiki*, 2018.

To those for whom
queer African cinema
is lifesaving

Queer African Cinemas has been over a decade in the making. The project began, albeit in a different iteration, when I was a postdoctoral fellow in Women's Studies at Duke University in 2009–2010. There I had the opportunity to present and develop some of my thoughts on the two films that would become the basis for my first chapter. I am therefore very much indebted to formal and informal feedback and conversations with Jennifer DeVere Brody, Tina Campt, Rey Chow, Ranjana Khanna, Negar Mottahedeh, and Charles Piot, as well as Brian Goldstone, Ignacio Adriasola Muñoz, and many of the graduate students and other fellows there at the time, all of whom helped to set this book into flight. The postdoctoral fellowship at Duke also funded my first research trip to Nigeria in the summer of 2010. There, I met up with the formidable Unoma Azuah and conducted many interviews with Nollywood filmmakers, distributors, audiences, and censors that have helped me to understand the multiple complexities of gay-themed Nollywood films. I want to thank Patricia Paulina Bala, Andy Chukwu, Kabat Esosa Egbon, Dakore Egbuson-Akande, Dickson Iroegbu, Emem Isong, Afam Okereke, and Ikechukwu Onyeka for granting me interviews. After watching almost two dozen films together, Unoma and I wrote up some of our findings from this trip in an article titled "The Video Closet: Nollywood's Gay-Themed Movies" published in *Transition*, and I am incredibly grateful for Unoma's continued support and conversations, as well as to all of those who have engaged with that article.

Throughout the years many people have read different iterations or sections of these chapters and offered valuable advice and feedback. These people include Grant Andrews, Elisabeth R. Anker, Wendy Belcher, Carli Coetzee, Carmela Garritano, Lalitha Gopalan, Stephen Groening, Kenneth Harrow, Jonathan Haynes, Onokome Okome, Taiwo Adetunji Osinubi, and Katrien Pype.

In the fall of 2019, the College of Arts and Sciences at American University funded a book incubator workshop that enabled me to bring in Naminata Diabate, Rudolf Gaudio, Z'étoile Imma, Jeanne-Marie Jackson, and Robert McRuer for an incredibly lively and fruitful discussion of the manuscript in progress. My arguments and close readings are undoubtedly stronger because of the thoughtfulness and generosity of these colleagues.

I have also been lucky to have a wonderful set of Africanist friends and colleagues who nourish me intellectually and help me think more broadly about African cultural texts and whose conversations I have been missing very much during the COVID-19 pandemic. These brilliant humans include Moradewun Adejunmobi, Shola Adenekan, Susan Andrade, A. B. Brown, Matthew H. Brown, Eleni Coundouriotis, Ashley Currier, Esther de Bruijn, Lindiwe Dovey, Ainehi Edoro, Jordache Ellapen, Rosalind Fredericks, Joshua Grace, Anne Gulick, Jennifer Hart, MaryEllen Higgins, Neville Hoad, Cajetan Iheka, Tsitsi Jaji, Keguro Macharia, Zethu Matebeni, Carmen McCain, John McCall, Brenna Munro, Laura Murphy, Stephanie Newell, John Nimiss, S. N. Nyeck, Matthew Omelsky, Samantha Pinto, Ato Quayson, Connor Ryan, Lily Saint, Stephanie Bosch Santana, Stephanie Selvick, Bhakti Shringarpure, April Sizemore-Barber, Nathan Suhr-Sytsma, T. J. Tallie, Phyllis Taoua, Noah Tsika, Paul Ugor, and Ann Elizabeth Willey, as well as the colleagues already listed in the paragraph above and the many, many more who make conferencing so meaningful. And since my days as an undergraduate at the University of Michigan, Frieda Ekotto's writing, mentorship, and friendship have been invaluable.

Parts of this book were presented at talks and conferences at Pratt Institute, Johannes Gutenberg University, Empire State College, University of Michigan, Princeton University, Yale University, University of the Witwatersrand, North-West University in Potchefstroom, University of Western Ontario, and University of South Carolina as well as at annual meetings of the African Literature Association, the African Studies Association, and the American Comparative Literature Association. I am indebted to all those who invited me, listened to me, and asked important questions of me.

I would also like to thank my incredibly supportive and inspiring colleagues in the Literature Department at American University: Amanda Berry, Fiona Brideoke, Kyle Dargan, Erik Dussere, Dustin Friedman, Stephanie Grant, Despina Kakoudaki, David Keplinger, Keith Leonard, Sarah Marsh, Jeffrey Middents, Marianne Noble, Patricia Park, Deborah Payne, Dolen Perkins-Valdez, David Pike, Richard Sha, Anita Sherman, Kathleen Smith, Rachel Louise Snyder, David Vasquez, Linda Voris, Melissa Scholes Young, and Lily Wong, along with the wonderful team in Writing Studies and my many interlocutors across campus. And a very special thanks goes to David Pike and Richard Sha, who have helped tremendously with grant applications, tenure letters, and overall scholarly advice. I am quite fortunate to teach alongside such talented and dedicated people. I am also grateful to the many students at American University who have taken African film and literature courses with me over the years and who have shared their keen observations and insights on the material. A special shout-out goes to Alejandro Hirsch Saed for helping with the filmography at the end of this book and for sharing my love of the Nest Collective.

The intellectual scope of this project would not have been possible without my research trips to the continent over the past several years. I am therefore very grateful for funding provided by the American University Faculty Research Support Grant, the American University Mellon Grant, and the College of Arts and Sciences International Travel Grant. In Nigeria, I want to thank Pamela Adie, Olumide Makanjuola, Asurf Olesyi, and Tope Oshin for taking the time to talk to me about their filmmaking endeavors and some of the challenges of queer filmmaking in Nigeria. And a special thanks to my research assistant Kuro Fred who made sure Lagos traffic and pouring rain (and subsequent midday wardrobe changes) did not thwart our endeavors. (Thanks, too, to Olumide and to Jude Dibia for a lengthy Zoom conversation about *Walking with Shadows*.) In Uganda I am very grateful to Kamoga Hassan, the fearless organizer of the Queer Kampala Film Festival, as well as to George Barasa (who was visiting from Kenya), Clare Byarugaba, Vincent Kyabayinze, Qwin Mbabazi, Pepe Julian Onziema, and Peter Yiga for the lovely and helpful conversations. And in Kenya, I want to thank Frances Aldous-Worley, Jim Chuchu, Neela Ghoshal (whom I now get to see more frequently in DC), Aida Holly-Nambi, Ken Kabuga, Wanuri Kahiu, Neo Musangi, Njoki Ngumi, Mwangi Njagi, Immah Reid, and Selly Thiam. And I want especially to express my deep gratitude to those who made the 2018 Out Film Festival in Nairobi such an incredible experience: Jackie Karuti and Muthoni Ngige, the festival curators; Susanne Gerhard and Anisha Soff at the Goethe Institute; Kevin Mwachiro, who can be credited with helping to inaugurate the festival and who also organized a wonderful four days in Nairobi; and Godiva Akullo, Mildred Apenyo, Dionne Edwards, Gloria Kiconco, and Rachael Ray Kungu, who provided much laughter and continue to provide inspiration. I am also grateful to Bradley Fortuin II and the LEGA-BIBO crew, along with Anthony Oluoch, who took the time to talk to me during my quick trip to Gaborone for the Batho Ba Lorato film festival in 2019. My experience at the February Lecture Series in Potchefstroom, South Africa, was also very valuable in shaping my understanding of queerness in post-apartheid South Africa, and I thank Chantelle Gray van Heerden and Wemar Strydom for organizing the conference as well as Mel Chen, Hardus Ludick, Sreddy Yen, and a fabulous group of conference attendees for the wonderful conversations and companionship. I am also very appreciative of Makgano Mamabolo for a lengthy Zoom chat as I was putting the final touches on the book that helped me to better understand the complexities of filmmaking, production, and distribution in South Africa. And before this book was even a glimmer of an idea, a trip to Ghana in 2007, funded by the Harold Leonard Film Fellowship at the University of Minnesota, gave me the opportunity to meet Socrate Safo, whose film *Jezebel* I discuss in chapter 1, and Serena Dankwa, whose incredible scholarship has helped me think more deeply about what constitutes queerness in postcolonial Africa. I am very grateful to both of them.

As I was working through the revisions of *Queer African Cinemas*, I was also putting together a special issue of the *Journal of African Cultural Studies* on "The Possibilities and Intimacies of Queer African Screen Cultures" with Z'étoile Imma. I want to thank Z'étoile, as well as all of the contributing authors (Grant Andrews, A. B. Brown, Lyn Johnstone, Gibson Ncube, Kwame Edwin Otu, and Lwando Scott) and the editor, Carli Coetzee, for the opportunity to think through so many different ways that queer African screen media can create new intimacies and possibilities.

Funding for the homestretch of writing was provided by a National Endowment for the Humanities summer grant, for which I am incredibly grateful. Wendy Belcher and Tsitsi Jaji deserve an extra thanks for their help with way too many grant applications. I want, too, to thank Elizabeth Ault for guiding me through this journey, along with the many other people who put so much care and effort into this book at Duke University Press. And this book owes so much to the two anonymous reviewers whose rigorous and thoughtful engagement pushed me to clarify and deepen the arguments.

Earlier versions of sections of chapters 1 and 2 appeared as "Occult Melodramas: Spectral Affect and West African Video-Film" in *Camera Obscura: Feminism, Culture, and Media Studies* 27, no. 2 (80) (2012): 101–8; "Hustlers, Home-Wreckers, and Homoeroticism: Nollywood's *Beautiful Faces*" in *Journal of African Cinemas* 4, no. 1 (2012): 59–79; "The Video Closet: Nollywood's Gay-Themed Movies" (coauthored with Unoma Azuah) in *Transition* 107, no. 1 (2012): 32–49; and "'Outcast Orders' and the Imagining of a Queer African Cinema: A Fugitive Reading of *Karmen Geï*" in *The Companion to African Cinema*, edited by Kenneth Harrow and Carmela Garritano (Hoboken, NJ: Wiley/ Blackwell, 2019), 194–215. A short section of the introduction appeared in an earlier version in "Queer African Cinema, Queer World Cinema" in *College Literature: A Journal of Critical Literary Studies* 45, no. 4 (2018): 652–58. And earlier reviews of the films *Ifé*, *Under the Rainbow*, and *Rafiki* appeared on the blog *Africa Is a Country*—much thanks to Sean Jacobs, too, for making that blog such a dynamic and queer-friendly space.

Finally, I want to express my deepest gratitude to the Simms, Greenberg, and Green-Simms crews for their continued love, support, and encouragement. My family has always meant everything to me, and my parents, Debra and Stuart, and sisters, Kimberly, Carly, and Alexandra, have all modeled how to work hard while always making time for the people they love. I would not be who I am today without all of them. (A special thanks to my mom, too, for giving me the confidence and desire to travel on my own.) And I am lucky to have an extended queer family too—you all know who you are and how much you mean to me. Much of the research and traveling for this book was done when my two boys were babies and toddlers. I am grateful to my mother-in-law, Barbara Greenberg, who came up to help with childcare when I traveled, as well as to Lourdes, our amazing nanny, who made much of my productivity possible during those early years. I could not have done any of this alone. And, of course, there is always Amy, always the love of my life, who has been my unwavering partner in queer life-building for the past two and a half decades.

Introduction

Registering Resistance in
Queer African Cinemas

In their Nairobi apartment, Liz and Achi, two women who have lived together as a couple for three years, sit on a couch watching a news broadcast. Their expressions are deadpan. They barely blink. Liz moves her hand slightly so that it rests on Achi's upper arm. It is 2014 and the voice from the television, that of Kenyan politician Irungu Kang'ata, explains in a matter-of-fact tone that there has been a recent promotion of gay activities (or what he calls "gayism"), in Kenya and Africa as a whole, that he finds concerning (figures 1.1 and 1.2).[1] He notes that people go to hotels and have demonstrations supporting "gayism" and that there have been "situations where some writers have gone publicly saying that they are gays," referring to the coming out of the famous Kenyan author Binyavanga Wainaina, who published "I Am a Homosexual, Mum" online in early 2014. But what seems to anger Kang'ata the most is that the Kenyan government has failed to do anything to stop these things from happening. He calls upon the police to arrest those promoting "gayism" in Kenya and notes that if the police do not take action, the law allows for "citizens' arrest of gays." Midway through the broadcast, Achi gets up and walks into another

FIGURES I.1 AND I.2. Stills from *Stories of Our Lives* (2014). Liz and Achi (*top*) watch Irungu Kang'ata (*bottom*) on the television in their living room.

room, where she begins applying lipstick. Moments later Liz, recognizing the couple's vulnerability, follows Achi and asks, "What do we do?"

This is how "Each Night I Dream," the last of five vignettes in the film compilation *Stories of Our Lives*, begins. I begin my discussion of queer African cinemas with "Each Night I Dream" because of the way that it imagines the quiet and loud, public and private, and hopeful and fearful ways of resisting and evading state-sanctioned homophobia that are at the heart of many of the queer-focused African films and videos I examine in this book. *Stories of Our Lives* was made in 2014 by members of the Nest Collective, a Nairobi-based arts collective, and directed by the Nest Collective member Jim Chuchu, whose original music also provides the film's soundtrack. Though it has received many accolades and awards, the film was, in some ways, an accidental film. The Nest Collective had been working on a book of the same name, collecting stories from queer-identified people around the country, and decided to turn a few of the stories into short films to show to the community of people they had interviewed. They filmed sparsely in black and white using a single Canon DSLR video camera. One of these shorts was shown to a curator of the Toronto International Film Festival, who asked if the Nest Collective could make more vignettes for a feature-length film. The collective agreed, and *Stories* was slated to show in Toronto before the film was even finished. The first four vignettes reflect the stories they had collected, either as a direct dramatization of a person's stories or as a composite of several stories in order to show the many different lived experiences of queer Kenyans. (The first vignette is about two high-school girls separated by their school principal; in the second, a gay man outruns a homophobic friend; in the third, a farm worker confesses his love to his sympathetic but straight best friend; and in the fourth, a Kenyan researcher in London hires a white male prostitute for himself.) But at the last minute the collective decided that a fifth short they had filmed did not work well in the collection, and, rather than making another one from the stories they had gathered, they created "Each Night I Dream," a film that, to me, perfectly captures so many of the multiple and conflicting and intimate forms of resistance found in queer African cinemas and discussed throughout this book.[2]

After asking Achi what to do about the threat of the citizens' arrests advocated by Kang'ata, Liz begins to narrate "Each Night I Dream" from off-screen, explaining how she and Achi have always kept a low profile and have never expressed intimacy outside of the walls of their shared apartment. But as Liz lies awake next to a sleeping Achi, she tells the audience about her constant anxiety: "Every night I wonder what we will do when they come for us. Will we fight or will we run?" At first, she envisions fighting, and the camera cuts to Liz and her friends staring down an angry mob (figure 1.3). Then she contemplates the possibility of running and becoming a fugitive, wondering out loud what they would take with them as the camera shows them grabbing a framed photo of themselves, embracing affectionately, and leaving with little else. Liz also wonders where they would run to, noting that all the countries around them have worse conditions for LGBTQ citizens.[3] And then she fantasizes about running away to an island of their own, a safe haven to which "everyone who needed to run could go." At this point, a chanted, dreamlike song (composed by Chuchu) begins to play, and the two girlfriends are shown

FIGURE I.3. Still from *Stories of Our Lives* (2014), showing Liz's vision of what it would be like if she and her friends were to physically fight homophobic violence.

dancing and walking in slow motion on their island as bubbles float across the screen (figure 1.4). Achi dances with a sparkler, and they both have glitter on their faces as they kiss playfully on the cheek and smile. Like several of the other vignettes in *Stories of Our Lives*, "Each Night I Dream" demonstrates the persistence of pleasure in queer lives, the "thinking, imagining, and creating [of] queer African pleasure itself" (Munro 2018, 664) even as it is under threat.

But as the island fantasy ends, Liz also considers the possibility that fleeing might not be feasible, that hiding might be a better option. She then recalls a traditional Gĩkũyũ myth, in which it is possible to change one's sex by walking backward around a Mũgumo tree seven times.[4] Liz imagines herself walking around the tree and coming home as a boy. When police officers come to their door, presumably to arrest them for homosexuality, Liz responds, "You think I'm a woman?" and then drops her pants to prove that she is not. The crowd gathered behind the police gasps and she shuts the door on them. The film then leaves Liz's fantasy sequence and returns to the present, back to Liz lying awake next to Achi and back to the footage of Kang'ata on television talking about how "gayism" is not African. In light of the traditional gender-bending story Liz has told about the Mũgumo tree, Kang'ata's claims—that queerness "is against our culture, against our tradition, against all the religious belief"—ring hollow, though they are no less dangerous for that.

In the final segment of the short, Liz muses on the absurdity of saying that African people are un-African, a refrain often used by homophobic politicians.

FIGURE I.4. Still from *Stories of Our Lives* (2014), showing Liz's dream of an island where she and Achi could escape and live freely.

She looks down, examining her hands, turning them over, and asks, "If we are not African, then what are we?" She offers one possible answer: "Maybe we are aliens. Maybe we come from a place where gender and sexuality are silly ideas. Primitive ideas. Maybe we came here to find out what it's like to be human. And maybe it's time for us to go back home." The camera then cuts to a shot of the stars, taking the viewer farther and farther into the universe as the soundtrack overlays multiple indistinct, staticky voices. Then a male voice takes over, narrating the last minute of the vignette as the camera continues to pan out into the universe. Though few outside the queer activist and artist community in Kenya would identify it, the voice is that of Anthony Oluoch, a prominent activist who has worked for several queer African organizations, including Pan Africa ILGA, Kaleidoscope Trust, and Gay Kenya Trust, and who was the cohost of the podcast *Kenyan Queer Questions* and, more recently, of the podcast *Padded Cell*. In his deep, resonant, and calmly confident voice, Oluoch delivers the following monologue:

> There's a law in this country that says that a man and another man are not allowed to express love. This law justifies violence, evictions, being excluded by your family, being blackmailed, being harassed by the police, losing your job, and many other things. I want to live in a place where I'm allowed to love who I want to love. I want to live in a place where my life is not constantly monitored and I have to justify how I live it. This is my country, and as a Kenyan I want to live here. I would not want to run

away. I am a homosexual and I am a proud homosexual and I have never felt ashamed of who I love. . . . All of us are different. All seven billion of us on this planet are different. But all of us need love.

When he is done talking, the screen goes black, and as the credits roll, the dreamlike chanting music from the island returns. This final monologue of the film imagines a journey not just to outer space but also to a Kenya where queer people would not in fact want to run away, a Kenya that activists like Oluoch and artists like the Nest Collective are trying to create, so that queer Kenyans can stay and live on and love whom they please without shame. It is, given the realist documentary news footage that opens the vignette, a decidedly defiant and even abstract way to conclude an anthology of films highlighting multiple stories about the challenges of queer love and intimacy in Kenya. But what this ending demonstrates is that, although Liz dreams of all the worst-case scenarios, queer African cinema can also register dreams for different possible presents and futures, presents and futures that are often even in conversation with more traditional and fluid understandings of gender and sexuality. Here, then, I follow Elena Loizidou who, expanding our ideas of what might be considered political resistance, writes that "we can think of the dream (its experience and a recounting) as an extension of the political actions of demonstration and protests, tracking the *flight* to freedom" (2016, 125). In this way, the final shots of the stars and constellations show that *Stories of Our Lives*, despite its documentary foundations, should be understood not in terms of a singular or concrete visibility project but as a film that illuminates planetary dreams in which there is "a kernel of political possibility within a stultifying heterosexual present" (Muñoz 2009, 49). Or, as Z'étoile Imma and I write of queer African screen media more broadly, the vignettes as a whole "offer us a new visual language, one that speaks in terms less invested in explicit narratives of resistance and domination, but instead enacts visions of interaction, touch, and longing which anticipate African queerness as possibility and belonging" (Green-Simms and Imma 2021, 5).

But just as it is important to highlight *Stories of Our Lives'* investment in love, pleasure, and imaginative possibilities, it is no less essential to underscore how the film records and tracks the increased fear, anxiety, and vulnerability many queer Africans were experiencing both in Kenya and across the continent at this particular historical moment, as public outings, violent attacks, and calls to further criminalize homosexuality were proliferating in many African countries in the first decades of the twenty-first century. For instance, in 2014 when Kang'ata was delivering his hateful message on television in Kenya and actively trying to strengthen the country's antihomosexuality laws (which he was not successful in doing), Nigeria's draconian Same Sex Marriage Prohibition Act (SSMPA), first introduced in 2006, had just been signed, emboldening many Nigerian citizens to lure and attack queer people. Only a month after Nigeria's law was signed, so too was Uganda's Anti-homosexuality Act (AHA). Like Nigeria's SSMPA, the AHA was many years in the making and likewise based on British colonial law. And though Uganda's law would be overturned later that year because it passed without the necessary quorum, the antigay violence it unleashed and encouraged persisted. Likewise, Ayo Coly (2019, 44) notes that in Francophone Senegal, political leaders also "engaged in a performance of virile postcolonial African nationhood" that aimed to show the world that they too could resist emasculation by embracing antigay rhetoric. Indeed, the increase in antigay rhetoric in the first two decades of the twenty-first century, even when not accompanied by calls to further criminalize homosexuality, affected many queer Africans across the continent.

What I want to emphasize, then, is that Stories of Our Lives, like many of the films discussed in this book, registers the upsurge in homophobia that swept up many African countries in the first decades of the twenty-first century and, at the same time, attempts to find alternatives to the violent heteronormativity that continually threatens hopes of queer belonging and life-building. But what is important for the purposes of this book is that the films discussed here do so by indexing multiple and sometimes conflicting or even opaque or muted forms of resistance and refusal—forms that include loving, touching, fighting, running away, staying put, staying quiet, taking refuge in customary practices, and dreaming of otherworldly possibilities—that are often practiced from a position of vulnerability. What I argue in this book is that queer African cinemas articulate forms of resistance that cannot be understood through narrow understandings of resistance as visible or audible strategic opposition to the status quo. Here, I follow Judith Butler, Zeynep Gambetti, and Leticia Sabsay (2016, 6), who argue in their introduction to Vulnerability in Resistance that resistance needs to be understood outside of the context of "masculinist models of autonomy," that it needs to be understood as drawing from vulnerability and not mutually opposed to it, and that it must be tracked across its different and conflicting registers.

Moreover, as I suggest throughout Queer African Cinemas, if one is to understand all the complexities of resistance in queer African cinema, one needs to look both at and beyond the text and to the politics of production, consumption, and distribution. For instance, Stories of Our Lives was banned in Kenya in large part because of its hopeful ending. According to Chuchu and fellow Nest

Collective member and cowriter Njoki Ngumi, the Kenyan Film Classification Board thought that the end of the film was too positive, too progay, and told the Nest Collective that if they wanted the film to be shown in the country they needed to either drop the final vignette or change it. The Nest Collective, however, stood their ground, and the film was censored in Kenya. George Gachara, who was listed as the producer, was arrested for filming without a license. The charges against him were eventually dropped, but if the Nest Collective violated the ban and showed the film in Kenya or uploaded it to the internet, the government said they would pursue charges.[5] In this case, the Nest Collective not only made a resistant film but at the same time faced a growing resistance to queerness and queer expression in Kenya. They kept the ending they wanted but also chose to comply with the law and not risk the safety of their members by screening or uploading the film, even though this meant that the film is nearly impossible for Kenyans to see unless they are able to access it internationally or obtain a smuggled copy.[6] These complex decisions and maneuvers by the Classification Board and the Nest Collective—each practicing and pushing back against the other's practices of resistance—show that resistance does not follow any neat or discernible path, that it is never as simple as simply showcasing forms of agential resistance or celebrating transgression against power.

Though I begin my discussion here with *Stories of Our Lives*, a film made by a director who identifies as queer about the lived experiences of queer Kenyans, it is important to note that while the Nest Collective's film anthology embodies so many of the different forms of resistance that I see in queer African cinemas more broadly, it is not necessarily typical of the films discussed. The films and videos I examine throughout *Queer African Cinemas* come from a range of African countries, all with their own cinematic traditions, aesthetic practices, political histories, and sets of censorship regulations that determine not only the types of queer stories that are told but also how the films circulate locally, regionally, and globally. Moreover, what I am calling queer African cinemas in this book are not only films made by queer filmmakers or their allies. In fact, many popular films that portray queer characters, especially those emerging from West African video film traditions like Nollywood, are structured as cautionary tales intended to warn audiences against the dangers or threats of homosexuality. It has indeed been a challenge to put the types of films that queer Africans have largely found to be homophobic, films that often resist projects that make queer African lives habitable, next to life-affirming films like *Stories of Our Lives*. But it is precisely this juxtaposition that has helped me to understand how all queer African films, regardless of why they were made or who made them, invite an understanding of resistance as a messy process that entails both opposing and consenting to forms of power, that involves fearing for the worst but dreaming of the best, and that sometimes demands slow or imperfect forms of negotiation. In this way, the films discussed in this book do not pit a "noble, heroic subaltern" against a "corrupted, malicious state," to borrow the phrasing of Ebenezer Obadare and Wendy Willems (2014, 9) in their introduction to the collection *Civic Agency in Africa: Arts of Resistance in the 21st Century*. Rather, each film I discuss here—and I examine a range of audiovisual output across the continent that includes avant-garde films, realist dramas, popular melodramas, occult films, and a music video—reveals how the types of resistance in queer African cinemas are always multilayered, always determined by a complex entanglement of racial, gendered, and sexual identities and national politics as well as by conventions of genre and format and modes of circulation. But it is my contention that paying attention to these multidirectional vectors of resistance makes palpable the way that the precarities and vulnerabilities of queer African life exist alongside modes of survival, practices of care, and aspirational imaginaries.

Queer and African and Cinemas

I situate this project within the emerging and burgeoning field of queer African studies. Though there is still some debate about the applicability of the term *queer* to same-sex practices and desires in Africa, it has been the case that, at least for the past decade, the word *queer* has been widely used by those on the continent as a mode of thinking through and about diverse, nonconforming African sexualities and of challenging heteronormative assumptions. As Zethu Matebeni, a leading South African sociologist, curator, and filmmaker, and Jabu Pereira, director of the Johannesburg-based LGBTI+ media advocacy organization Iranti, write in their preface to *Reclaiming Afrikan: Queer Perspectives on Sexual and Gender Identities*, the use of *queer* is "understood as an inquiry into the present, as a critical space that pushes the boundaries of what is embraced as normative" (2014, 7). But Matebeni and Pereira also understand that the term *queer*, like the acronym LGBTI (lesbian, gay, bisexual, transgender, intersex) that it often stands in for, has the potential to conflate very different types of people and to reinforce invisibilities within the broader queer community. They also make clear that *queer* should be applied not just to twenty-first-century identities and that gender nonconformity in different forms has existed on the African continent for centuries, despite false claims that it is un-African. Thus, Matebeni and Pereira use the space-making and boundary-pushing term *queer* to acknowledge many forms and local categories of nonheteronormative sexual identities while emphasizing that it is far from perfect and that it has much work still to do. The Ugandan intellectual and activist Stella Nyanzi articulates some of this work when she argues that queer inquiry in Africa must take on a "two-pronged approach, namely queering African Studies on the one hand, and Africanising Queer Studies on the other hand" (2015a, 127). Taiwo Adetunji Osinubi (2016, xiv) writes in his introduction to the first queer-focused special issue of *Research in African Literatures* (RAL) in 2016 that the question now is "less about the applicability of queer and more about the already-existing applications of queer in Africanist research."

This, of course, does not mean that *queer* is a universally accepted term. As Serena Dankwa argues in *Knowing Women: Same-Sex Intimacy, Gender, and Identity in Postcolonial Ghana,* her study of intimate friendships between working-class women in Ghana, many people who engage in same-sex practices in Africa are uncomfortable with or unfamiliar with the language of sexual identity (e.g., *queer, gay, bisexual, lesbian*) that is more common in larger cities and activist or "Afropolitan" circles. Although she judiciously avoids using the term *queer* to describe people who would not use it to describe themselves (preferring instead to underscore the multiple and sometimes ambiguous ways same-sex-desiring women "know" each other), Dankwa, like the thinkers above, also recognizes the strategic usefulness of *queer* in literary and activist spaces across the African continent. While not ideal, part of the appeal of the term *queer* is that it can be more flexible as well as more inclusive of indigenous same-sex practices that fall outside of "gay" identities and that it can, despite its association with Euro-American spaces and identities, provide theoretical tools that unsettle rigid, Western understandings of sexual identities (Dankwa 2021, 24, 37). My own position follows the scholars above: despite its imperfections, the term *queer* is useful in naming both a range of nonheteronormative sexualities and the critical possibilities and openings they afford.

But what exactly constitutes queer African cinema? While the African literary scene has seen several queer-identified African authors—such as Binyavanga Wainaina, Jude Dibia, Unoma Azuah, Kevin Mwachiro, Frieda Ekotto, Frankie Edozein, Akwaeke Emezi, and Romeo Oriogun—making public statements, going on book tours, or publishing work that explicitly challenges homophobia, the same cannot be said of the African film scene. Feature films about queer African characters tend not to be made by people who publicly identify as part of the queer African community. Many, in fact, are not made by Africans at all, and some are made by African filmmakers who make films to depict homosexuality as a threat to the social order. Unlike queer African writing, queer African films often run into problems with national censorship boards that determine what can and cannot be said or shown. In their wonderfully ambitious and carefully argued book *Queer Cinema in the World*, Karl Schoonover and Rosalind Galt address this challenge with regard to queer cinema throughout the world. Citing the limitations of narrow definitions that reduce queer cinema to productions by or explicitly for queer people, the authors prefer a model that is more capacious and that is free from Western cultural presumptions about what a gay director or gay audience might look like. Schoonover and Galt (2016, 14) argue for an approach that does not "determine in advance what kinds of films, modes of production, and reception might qualify as queer or do queer work in the world," and they set out to answer an equally capacious question: Given that queer world cinema is such an open-ended category, "where in the world is queer cinema?" Their response takes them to queer film festivals in New York and India and Botswana, and to video stores, BitTorrent sites, underground DVD markets in Iran and Egypt, and, of course, to sites such as YouTube and Vimeo. Such an itinerary allows them to leave open the definition of cinema, claiming that it is "a space that is never quite resolved or decided" (3), and to sidestep the tangled debates about how one defines world cinema. Rather, they opt for a discussion of a queer cinema that "enables different ways of being in the world" and "creates different worlds" (5), and they focus on "cinema's unique role in sustaining and making evident queer counterpublics" (2).

Because the categories of "queer" and "cinema" can encompass so many different forms, I follow Schoonover and Galt in keeping the definition of the terms as capacious as possible. Additionally, one must always keep in mind that "the invention of Africa" by colonialists, as V. Y. Mudimbe puts it, means that "Africa" as an epistemological object of knowledge is also always a bit unresolved. This means that I am working with several terms—*queer*, *Africa*, and *cinema*—that are all multiply and sometimes arbitrarily determined and boundless. However, because one of the goals of this book is to think particularly and regionally about queer African cinema and the politics of place, I argue that in order to understand the world of queer African cinema, one must pay attention not only to the porousness of categories but also to the various material and political challenges faced by African audiences and African filmmakers in a global world. In other words, while Schoonover and Galt (2016, 30) privilege films that partake in "worlding," a term that is necessarily diffuse, a more specific set of questions arises when trying to define queer African cinema, especially considering the paucity of publicly queer-identified film-makers and the role of state censorship boards in trying to limit or prohibit films with queer African content. My aim, then, is to attend to the unique complexities and challenges of filmmaking, exhibition, and distribution in Africa, complexities that sometimes make it difficult to fit queer African cinema neatly into broader projects of "worlding" and creating queer world cinema counterpublics.

In order to understand the particularities and specifics of queer African cinema, I would like to begin by outlining three main categories into which it can be grouped: 1) international art films; 2) popular melodramas made for local audiences; and 3) documentaries by and about queer African communities. International art films, or those feature films that primarily circulate at global film festivals, are oftentimes the most visible and well-known queer African films to both local and global audiences. Though there were a few Senegalese films in the 1970s that had minor queer characters, as well as a few relatively obscure anti-apartheid films with queer content made by white South Africans in the 1980s, it is Mohamed Camara's *Dakan* (1997) that is most often considered the first global African feature film about homosexuality. *Dakan* is a Guinean film about two teenage boys, Sory and Manga, who fall in love, are separated by their parents, and then reunite. The film premiered at the Cannes Film Festival as part of the Director's Fortnight and went on to tour at primarily international gay film festivals. In 1998 it won the Los Angeles Outfest award for "OUTstanding International Narrative Feature" and then opened in French cinemas the following year. Though the film screened at the French-Guinean cultural center in Guinea as well as at the 1999 FESPACO (Panafrican Film and Television Festival of Ouagadougou)—Africa's most famous film festival, which occurs every other year in Burkina Faso—almost all of its accolades were received abroad, where international Black audiences had a much more positive reaction to the film than audiences based on the continent. Four years after *Dakan* was released, *Karmen Geï* (2001), a Senegalese version of Bizet's opera *Carmen* in which Karmen's lovers are both male and female (see chapter 1), was selected at major film festivals such as Cannes, the Toronto International Film Festival, Sundance, and the New York African Film Festival. It also screened for about six weeks in Dakar but was eventually banned after the theater was stormed by two to three hundred people wielding machetes who threatened to burn the theater down. Though the protest was technically over the use of a Mouride (Sufi Muslim) holy song during the scene in which Karmen's female lover is buried in a Catholic cemetery—and not over the first-ever depiction of African lesbian sex on screen—*Karmen Geï*, like *Dakan*, was primarily viewed by Western rather than African audiences.

Between 2001 and 2014 the only queer African-made films to receive major international attention were South African films. These films included John Greyson's *Proteus* (2003), a historical drama about a love affair between two male prisoners on Robben Island in the early eighteenth century; Shamim Sarif's historical drama *The World Unseen* (2007), about two South African women of Indian heritage who fall in love in Cape Town in the 1950s; and Oliver Hermanus's *Skoonheid* (2011), about a closeted Afrikaner man who attempts to rape his friend's son, a film which I discuss at length in chapter 3. These films toured internationally but were also screened throughout South Africa, where both homosexuality and same-sex marriage are legal and where cinema has played an important role in post-apartheid queer activism.

Then, in 2014, *Stories of Our Lives* became the first East African queer film to screen at international film festivals. It won multiple awards, but its censorship in Kenya, its country of origin, foreshadowed the fate of many queer African films that followed in the years after. In 2018 the South African film *Inxeba*, titled *The Wound* in translation (see chapter 3), and Kenyan Wanuri Kahiu's film *Rafiki* (see chapter 4) were, likewise, blocked in their own countries while simultaneously racking up international awards. After protests at early screenings of *Inxeba* in South Africa, the film was given an 18-and-over rating and pulled from theaters, though the filmmakers were eventually able to overturn the rating and return the film to the theaters. Kahiu also challenged her government in court, but *Rafiki* was permitted to screen in Kenya for only seven days, the exact length of time a film must screen in its country of origin to be eligible for an Oscar, before it was banned again. And while many queer African films do screen in South Africa, which with the release of three more queer art films in 2018–19—*Kanarie*, *The Harvesters*, and *Moffie*—is seeing a noticeable growth in queer filmmaking, outside of South Africa it is often difficult to see a queer African film screening in an African theater unless it is exhibited at a local festival, in which case the film is screened only one or two times total. Furthermore, while a few of these films, like *Inxeba*, can occasionally become available on Netflix, which is an increasingly popular way to stream movies across the continent, many are available only on Amazon Prime, to which the vast majority of Africans do not have access. And many, like *Stories of Our Lives*, *Karmen Geï*, and *Dakan*, are not available on any streaming services. (*Karmen Geï* and *Dakan* are, however, available on Kanopy, a streaming service accessible through university libraries.) In fact, while attending a queer film festival in Nairobi I met an actor from *Stories of Our Lives* who had not himself seen the film as a finished product. Illegal downloading is, of course, sometimes a possibility, and pirated copies do occasionally pop up on YouTube for limited periods of time. (As of early 2020, there has also been an increase in queer African films available to rent on YouTube.) Nevertheless, for most of the twenty-first century, the African films that typically screened at film festivals across the world, the ones that would be most readily identifiable as queer African cinema and accessible to viewers in the West, have often been difficult to find for viewers based on the continent.[7] This means that the queer African films that are most explicitly designed to counter the dehumanization of queer Africans are often unable to create counterpublics in their countries of origin.

However, the situation is quite different for the second category of films mentioned above. While African filmmakers and audiences in the twentieth century often complained about the difficulty of circulating and distributing celluloid feature films on the African continent (in this sense, queer films faced many of the same challenges of African film in general), the advent and increasing popularity of video films in Anglophone Africa shifted much of the discussion. In the late 1980s and early 1990s, Nigerian and Ghanaian filmmakers began to change the model for the production, distribution, and circulation of African film. While African celluloid films, primarily from Francophone countries, were often funded by a combination of national and foreign governments and, even when not about taboo topics, were more readily circulated to international audiences, Nigerians and Ghanaians were making what would be called Nollywood (or in the case of Ghana, Ghallywood/Ghanawood) films that were self-financed movies explicitly for local audiences. The stories were embedded in popular culture and based on local rumors or moral expectations and often centered around family melodramas. Using inexpensive video technologies (first VHS, then VCD and DVD), these West African filmmakers created an industry and model of filmmaking that was hugely popular across the continent. In Nigeria, and, to a much lesser extent, Ghana, filmmakers aiming to make melodramatic stories with wide, local appeal have capitalized on the salacious topic of homosexuality.[8] But in these films—with the exception of the handful of Nigerian films produced by human rights organizations such as The Initiative for Equal Rights (TIERS) or The Equality Hub—homosexuality is always condemned, blamed on occult spirits, overly strict parents, unfaithful spouses, or greedy individuals who enter homosexual cults as a way of acquiring wealth. And, as a result, homosexual characters are always either punished with death or imprisonment—or saved by Jesus. By and large, for most of this century (though this is beginning to change) the African depictions of same-sex desire that are the most easily available across Africa (i.e., that do not require a subscription to Amazon, Netflix, or Kanopy and that might screen for free on television, YouTube, or be available for purchase in market stalls) are those that pathologize homosexuality and that will be approved by censors who work for governments that condemn it.

The third category of film I consider here—documentary films by or about those in the African LGBTQ community—have, again, historically been those that are more likely to circulate internationally than locally. On the global stage, this category was initially dominated by Western-made films whose primary goal has been to offer global audiences a glimpse of queer African life. Laurent Bocahut and Philip Brooks's *Woubi Cheri* (1998), about the Ivoirian queer and trans communities; Katherine Fairfax Wright and Malika Zouhali-Worrall's *Call Me Kuchu* (2012), about slain Ugandan gay rights activist David Kato; Shaun Kadlec and Deb Tullman's *Born This Way* (2013), about the underground queer community in Cameroon; and Jonny von Wallström's *The Pearl of Africa* (2016), which follows a Ugandan trans woman as she undergoes surgery and relocates to Kenya, are some of the most well-known documentaries. Many of these documentaries, all of the ones just listed, have screened at international film festivals and have been available to stream on Amazon or Netflix. Unoma Azuah (2018, 11) argues that these Western-made documentaries have played an important role in highlighting the courageous battles being fought by African activists, and that "the issue of who shoots the movies may not be as significant as whose story is being told." But it is difficult to tell the impact that these films have on what Azuah calls the "re-education" of homophobic publics when, in many cases, the documentaries do not screen in the countries where they are filmed. This seems to be especially true in Uganda, which has drawn a considerable amount of media and documentary attention. For instance, several activists I spoke to in Uganda seemed frustrated that the film *Call Me Kuchu*, which won over a dozen awards globally, was not screened to the Ugandan queer community at large or to their allies. And, to make matters worse, Uganda had, the year before *Call Me Kuchu's* release, been the subject of a BBC documentary called *The World's Worst Place to Be Gay* (2011), a film that Kwame Edwin Otu scathingly describes as a homophobic safari in which "queer people are perceived as *endangered species* in dire need of rescue" (Otu 2017, 127, emphasis in original). There are, of course, exceptions: *The Pearl of Africa*, for instance, screened to a large crowd at the inaugural 2016 Queer Kampala International Film Festival and was well received by the audience, including many of those in the trans community. Though there is much to say about these Western-produced documentaries and though one might include them in the category of queer African cinema, I wish to bracket this subset of films for the purposes of this study in order to focus on the type of audiovisual material being produced on the continent itself.

And, indeed, many queer Africans have been documenting their own stories, engaging in what the renowned South African photographer and visual artist Zanele Muholi calls "visual activism," a method of activism Muholi (2013, 170) uses to mark the "resistance and existence" of Black lesbians. Since the end of apartheid, many South Africans have produced films about their experience during and after the struggle. Zackie Achmat and Jack Lewis's *Apostles of Civilised Vice* (1999), which documented white, Black, and colored South African queer histories, and Beverley Ditsie's film about her friendship with the famous gay anti-apartheid activist Simon Nkoli, *Simon and I* (2001), were some of the first, but many have followed.[9] Ditsie continues to make documentaries about Black lesbian life and activism—her more recent films include *The Commission: From Silence to Resistance* (2017) and *Lesbians Free Everyone: The Beijing Retrospective* (2020)—as do filmmakers such as Zethu Matebeni and Busi Kheswa, who made *Breaking Out of the Box* (2011). And Muholi directed *Enraged by a Picture* (2005) and *Difficult Love* (2010), both of which document their pathbreaking photography and have screened around the globe as well as at festivals in Africa. More recently, the South African nonprofit organization STEPS produced a beautiful coming-out documentary about a young trans man from the Kingdom of Lesotho called *I Am Sheriff* (2017) that screened at Batho Ba Lorato, Botswana's queer film festival, as well as at the Zanzibar International Film Festival. And, likewise, the organization Iranti continues to make short documentaries about queer life in South Africa and released a film about the decriminalization of homosexuality in Botswana called *There Is Power in the Collar* (2020).

In Nigeria, TIERS made the documentary *Veil of Silence* (2013) on the eve of the signing of the Same Sex Marriage Prohibition Act, and though several years went by before another queer Nigerian documentary was made, activist Pamela Adie launched *Under the Rainbow* in 2019, a visual memoir about her life as a lesbian in Nigeria, through her organization The Equality Hub. (And after finding documentary filmmaking so fulfilling, Adie went on the following year to produce a short fiction film titled *Ifé* about a lesbian couple on a three-day date in Lagos.)[10] Also in 2020, Harry Itie, founder of the Lagos-based LGBT+ media platform The Rustin Times, released *Defiance*, a documentary that highlights the voices of young queer creatives and advocates in Nigeria. Additionally, in Uganda, queer activists have been especially keen to represent their own stories. *And Still We Rise* (2015), about the impacts and forms of resistance that have emerged in the wake of Uganda's Anti-homosexuality Act, was codirected by Richard Lusimbo, a researcher and documentation manager for Sexual Minorities Uganda (SMUG), and the Canadian professor Nancy Nicol; Pepe Julian Onziema, program director of SMUG, made the documentary *See Me As* (with Tim McCarthy and Deus Kiriisa) that features interviews with allies and members of the queer community and that was made specifically for the community itself; and East African Visual Artists made *Resilience Diaries* (see chapter 4), about Uganda's trans community, and several other films documenting queer Ugandans' lived experiences, including during the COVID-19 pandemic, that are made with local rather than international audiences in mind. In Kenya, the queer digital media organization None on Record has produced short video documentaries that are posted on their website and has also moved into podcast production with their award-winning podcast *Afro-Queer*.[11] And Peter Murimi's documentary, *I Am Samuel*, which follows the life of a queer Kenyan man over the course of five years, premiered at several major film festivals in 2020. Likewise, filmmaker Aiwan Obinyan released the short documentary *Kenyan, Christian, Queer* (2020), about the first LGBTI church in Kenya which was featured in executive producer Adriaan Van Klinken's book of the same name. The list of African-made queer documentaries (even if they are sometimes coproductions) continues to expand at such a rate that it is no longer the case that the West is the sole, or even prime, producer of queer African documentary content.

Until the first decade and a half of the twenty-first century, these three categories existed with relatively little crossover. But, slowly, the categories are beginning to blend into one another. For instance, in Nigeria, TIERS, a human rights organization, has begun to produce fictional Nollywood films (see chapter 2) that appeal to local audiences but have a more global reach, thereby straddling the first two categories of cinema. In 2019 TIERS collaborated with producer Funmi Iyanda to make *Walking with Shadows*, an adaptation of Jude Dibia's novel of the same name, which became the first Nigerian queer film to premiere internationally when it screened at the British Film Institute Film Festival. The work of TIERS and other queer media organizations producing dramatic content in Africa also indicates that visual activism is no longer to be associated with the documentary mode alone. Even a film like *Rafiki*, an independent art film that Kahiu intended to be a simple story about young love in Kenya, is now also, because of the censorship imbroglio which caused Kahiu to sue the government, tied to the work that activists are doing to create a more open Kenya. At a screening of *Rafiki* in Washington, DC, Kahiu told the audience that what has surprised her most about the trajectory that her film has taken was that it has thrown her into the role of an activist rather than just a filmmaker. And even before *Rafiki*, the music video for "Same Love (Remix)" by the Kenyan collective Art Attack (see chapter 4) became linked to larger censorship debates. When the video was posted on YouTube and the Kenyan Film Classification Board attempted to force Google to remove it, George Barasa of Art Attack, on whose life the video was based, became a key opponent of the Board and its subsequent attempts to censor the internet in Kenya. What seems to be happening now is that just as activists are producing art films, art directors are making films that are more explicitly linked to activist efforts.

Likewise, African activists are increasingly working to create spaces where queer audiences can come together to watch both African films from across the continent and global queer films. For many years the Out in Africa South African Gay and Lesbian Film Festival, which ran from 1994 to 2014, was the only queer film festival on the continent, and though the lion's share of their films were non-African, they were increasingly able to screen and fund African films (see chapter 3).[12] In 2011 they were joined by the Durban Gay and Lesbian Film Festival, and the same year an organization called Gay Kenya Trust, in conjunction with the Swiss embassy and Kenya's Goethe Institute, began to host the Out Film Festival (OFF) in Nairobi, the first queer African film festival outside of South Africa. In 2013, Lesbians, Gays and Bisexuals of Botswana (LEGABIBO) began organizing the Batho Ba Lorato (People of Love) Film Festival in Gaborone, a festival that began in the living room of the activist Caine Youngman and that now takes place at a mainstream movie theater in a busy Gaborone mall. In 2016, the queer Ugandan filmmaker Kamoga Hassan, who made his own docudrama called *Outed* (2015), inaugurated the Queer Kampala International Film Festival (QKIFF), a festival that unfortunately was raided by the police in 2017 and has not yet resumed. And in 2017, Zimbabwean activists organized The Rainbow 263 Film Festival, a two-day event that was part of a weeklong "Queer University" program that taught filmmaking to interested people in the queer community. Film festivals also often include panel presentations on an array of topics and have (as I discuss in chapters 3 and 4) been spaces where films provide the occasion for activism, education, queer sociality, and affective community engagement. Likewise, they often provide opportunities for Africans to see queer films that are difficult to access or that are banned in nearby countries.

Throughout *Queer African Cinemas*, my focus is largely on the films in the first two categories discussed above: internationally circulating art films, including those made by NGOs, and popular, more locally bound melodramas—though I do often bring African-made documentaries into the discussion and do readily acknowledge the porousness of these categories. My primary goal, however, is to emphasize the meaning-making and experimental possibilities of fictional works and to highlight how the creative and imagined stories that are told by and about queer African citizens register the multiple and sometimes contradictory contestations of queer resistance in a global world. I also suggest that discussions of what constitutes queer African cinema cannot be severed from discussions of the spaces in which these films may or may not circulate. I am not claiming that a film must be seen by a queer African audience to be considered queer African cinema, but I am claiming that in order to understand the messy forms of resistance I outline in this book, one cannot think about these films existing in a void without audiences. I therefore concentrate specifically on films made on the African continent, and it is important to note that I not only leave out Western-made films, I have also set aside films that are about queer Africans living in the West as these films do not have to contend with state censorship or concern themselves with local audiences in the same way as those that circulate on the continent do. Diaspora films—films like *Rag Tag* (2006), *Sex, Okra and Salted Butter* (2008), *Unspoken* (2013), or *Reluctantly Queer* (2016)—while certainly not unaffected by events on the continent, do, I argue, navigate different geopolitical realities. This book is therefore a sustained examination of queer fictional films and videos that have come out of the continent during the first two decades of the twenty-first century and that reflect and participate in the unprecedented homophobia that exists concurrently with an unprecedented resistance to it. Of course, the films I examine in this book are not at all monolithic, and neither, for that matter, are the countries from which they come. In fact, I have deliberately chosen to highlight the plurality of African cinemas in my title and to attend to the similarities and differences of different nations and regions in each of the four chapters of the book. I am therefore not trying to prescribe any forms of resistance; nor am I attempting to fit the films I discuss into any particular model of oppositional cinema or political liberation. Rather, I want to call attention to the ways that queer African films, whether intentionally or not, animate layered and sometimes contradictory, sometimes mundane modes of resistance, as well as to how these films, in turn, mobilize the affective formations and emotional lives that reside inside these layers.

Registers of Resistance

Because this project is interested in the different national or regional queer cinematic practices across the African continent, it is important to note that my concerns are not necessarily the same as those of scholars examining cultural production in the global North. Indeed, queer studies scholars, who have by and large been located in and focused on the global North, have often aimed their criticism at mainstream LGBTQ movements that frame their goals in terms of assimilation, marriage equality, and a liberal progressive agenda. As Rahul Rao (2020, 2) remarks in his wonderful study of queer temporality in postcolonial Uganda and India, "Salutary as its critiques have been, we need to consider the extent to which queer theory's determination to stand askew to the progressive march of time has been shaped by its geopolitical provenance in the contemporary United States." Thinking through Jasbir Puar's work on what happens when liberal rights are granted to queer people, Rao notes that the question Puar asks—i.e., "What happens when 'we' get what 'we' want?"—is very different from the questions asked when the focus is on queerness in the postcolonial global South. Rao argues that a different set of questions emerges when attention is turned to ongoing queer postcolonial struggles that are often marked by feelings and temporalities of dissatisfaction rather than to "a critique of the progressive triumphalist temporalities of queer liberalism" (10). And it is within these ongoing struggles—struggles that, as Rao reminds, are often marked by temporal tensions and frictions rather than discernible forward, backward, or sideways temporalities (27)—that I wish to situate the plural and very much ongoing forms of resistance at work in queer African cinemas.

One of the aims of this project, as mentioned above, is to articulate an expansive understanding of the concept of resistance that encompasses multiple and sometimes conflicting forms that include but also extend well beyond overt political acts. This capacious understanding of resistance reflects the way I see the term being deployed by queer artists and activists on the continent and also, I argue, foregrounds localized forms of creativity and life-building. In the Nigerian anthology and social media campaign #HowIResist, for instance, queer Nigerians articulate forms of resistance that include writing, flourishing, finding self-acceptance, letting go of heteronormative ideals, waking up and living, detaching, and persevering. Likewise, in the introduction to *Meanwhile . . . Graphic Short Stories about Everyday Queer Life in Southern and East Africa*, an anthology of comics written by a group of queer African youth called the Qintu Collab, two members, listed simply as Talia and Alex, argue that queer African stories of resistance should be situated in the heterogeneous "imperfect present." The Qintu Collab uses the title *Meanwhile* to indicate how in their lives—just as in comic books, where the caption *meanwhile* is often used—events are often concurrent rather than strictly linear. Resistance, for these writers, might mean resistance to Western narratives of queerness, but Talia and Alex also insist on seeing "resistance as a more mundane, indeterminate and ongoing endeavor" (Qintu Collab 2019, n.p.). They write, "Across the continent churches and politicians are crowing about queerness being an import, legislators are deliberating over decriminalizing same-sex sex, and across the world the continent is portrayed as hostile and homophobic; *meanwhile* every day, all over the continent, there are a myriad [of] queer moments—the look, the gesture, the smile, the touch, the first date, the break-up convo, the text, the selfie" (my italics). In other words, the forms of resistance practiced by queer African storytellers and everyday citizens are not always positioned as agential forms of mastery or political action: they do not always easily fit neatly into a progressive political agenda (or even a more radical critique of that agenda), and sometimes they might not be immediately discernible as narratives of subversion. As the Qintu Collab implies, resistant practices might hover in a moment of indeterminacy, existing in a *meanwhile* and in an ongoing present that contains multiple and sometimes contradictory ways of resisting oppression or rejection.

In their collection *Vulnerability in Resistance* Butler, Gambetti, and Sabsay suggest that one way to decenter a resistance that is often conceived of as autonomous, and often masculinist or paternalistic, is by privileging rather than dismissing vulnerability. In their introduction, they ask, "What in our analytical and political frameworks would change if vulnerability were imagined as one of the conditions of the very possibility of resistance? What follows when we conceive of resistance as drawing from vulnerability . . . , or part of the very meaning or action of resistance? What implications does this perspective have for thinking about the subject of political agency?" (Butler, Gambetti, and Sabsay 2016, 1). I find these questions to be key to broadening understandings of resistance, and I add the following: What happens when intimacy, pleasure, small gestures of unruliness, practices of survival and fleeing, or even of negotiation, are imagined as conditions or resources for resistance? What happens when we see resistance not as the opposite of subordination and complacency but as something that is entangled with it? What happens when we take seriously the Qintu Collab's framing of resistance as something that might be routine or vague, as something that hovers in the spaces of the meanwhile? My position is that when we disengage resistance from its progressive teleology and its binary relations (to subordination, to domination, to vulnerability, etc.) we can better attend to all of the imperfect forms of adaptation, life-building, and belonging that more indeterminate forms of resistance make possible and that exist alongside the necessary work of overt and strategic po-litical organizing.[13]

What I propose in this book is a way of reading queer African cinemas for different and sometimes conflicting *registers of resistance*, and I take this phrase to mean several things at once. At the most basic level, this book, like all forms of queer African cinema more broadly, can be seen to register queer African existence at a moment when it is sometimes denied or seen as un-African. But I also use the phrase to describe the practice of registering, as in taking inven-tory or recording, the different types of resistance that exist within the texts and subtexts of different films and different modes of African cinema. As in my reading of "Each Night I Dream," in which I identified different forms of re-sisting homophobia—forms that include love, pleasure, violence, fantasy, and fugitivity—here I attend to the indexical function of cinema. In other words, I offer this book up as a register of different films and the plural practices of resistance they make palpable as works of art, even when those forms of resis-tance might be contradictory or imagined or incomplete.

But I also understand the word *register* to indicate the different vocal or sonic ranges, or registers, that in Saidiya Hartman's (1997, 13–14) words, "occur below the threshold of formal equality and rights" but that nevertheless "gesture toward an unrealized freedom." In her book *Listening to Images*, Tina Campt (2017, 9) advocates a way of "attuning our senses to other affective frequen-cies" that "quiet" forms of art, like vernacular photography in her case, reg-ister. Though cinema is certainly not quiet—at least not the films discussed here—and though the sonic ranges are expressed through very audible frequen-cies, I want to make the case that lower frequencies, or registers, and inaudi-ble expressions of interiority are also part of resistant practices and present in many queer African films.[14] For instance, silence becomes one of the many modes of speaking back and speaking out in the film *Vibrancy of Silence: A Discussion with My Sisters* (2018), in which the queer Cameroonian director Marthe Djilo Kamga and the queer Cameroonian producer Frieda Ekotto team up to discuss the complexities of being a Cameroonian woman artist. In the producer's statement, Ekotto states that the film is intended to create a visual archive of African women's creative work, of their goals, their achievements, their hopes, their dreams, and their struggles. But at the same time that they contend that creating an archive is a way of marking that which is "sayable," the filmmakers also insist on recognizing the "vibrancy of silence," the ability of silence also to vibrate or reverberate or resonate, and to take part in com-municating these desires, vulnerabilities, and aspirations. In the section of the film where Ekotto, who also published the first African Francophone lesbian novel, talks about her own work, she says, "I think I was born a rebel. . . . I no longer am, I'm more settled in my way of thinking because I've understood that it's not by screaming that we're going to change anything. You just have to operate differently." For Ekotto, these quieter modes of operating differently, these ways of reflecting, thinking, and being at a lower frequency, are just as important as the public utterances, the screaming, that defy a long history of invisibility. And indeed, as Nyanzi (2015b, 190) argues, silence can often act as a powerful "collective language of some queer communities particularly in the Global South" where louder forms of protest might not be possible or advisable given safety concerns. What Ekotto and her film express are not only this collective language of silence, but also how that silence becomes a quiet mode of transformation and potential. Part of what I do in this book, then, is to listen—often literally, as cinema provides the occasion for this—for these below-the-threshold forms of resistance, forms of resistance that vibrate more subtly, sometimes through music, sometimes through inaudible gestures that communicate inner desires and fears, sometimes through intimate gestures or touches, and sometimes through modes of being that might not even register as clear or celebratory resistance.

Moreover, just as resistance can operate at different frequencies, so too can it register different meanings. While resistance is often assumed to be transgressive or in opposition to power, it can often mean the exact opposite. In *The Caribbean Postcolonial: Social Equality, Post-Nationalism, and Cultural Hybridity*, Shalini Puri provides a useful parsing of the contradictory meanings of resistance, reminding us that resistance does not simply mean an opposition to or the undoing of the status quo. Puri (2004, 108) points out that *resistance* has another meaning as well, one relating to its "psychoanalytic connotation," in which the patient, often unconsciously, refuses to allow thoughts that might be disruptive to his or her conscious mind. In other words, in psychoanalysis, resistance is used to preserve rather than to dismantle the status quo—the mind resists that which it finds to be unacceptable or damaging (108). And, indeed, this allows us to see how *resistance* can be used colloquially to describe situations when dominant institutions or people in power resist that which they find to be disruptive. The ambiguity and ambivalence inherent in the term *resistance* lead Puri to favor the term *opposition* and to focus on the often complex and labor-intensive process of transforming more diffuse forms of resistance into intentional opposition.[15] But it is precisely this ambiguity that I find productive, not for the sake of ambiguity or ambivalence as intrinsically superior to concrete action, but because resistance as an everyday practice is often ambiguous for queer citizens or allies who might find simple acts of loving or dreaming to be resistant or who might, at times, uphold the very norms they at other times resist. But registering both of these conflicting definitions of resistance together, as confusing as it might seem to say that resistance can mean both opposition to the status quo and opposition to changing it, helps to forestall any romanticized or unencumbered understandings of resistance. In fact, characters in many of the films I discuss in this book occasionally perform both types of resistance simultaneously, as they might express homophobic or misogynist or racist sentiments at the same time that they contest structures of oppression.

Moreover, because of the multiple ways resistance is performed in many queer African films, different audiences might have very different perceptions of the type of resistance they are watching. And this brings me to the final way I use the term *registers of resistance*: to indicate the way that the resistance might mentally register, or make sense, to a particular audience member. One person, for instance, might see a film portraying the struggles of a queer character as resisting the official line that homosexuality is un-African. Another person might see the struggles of that same character, especially if the character faces social or legal repercussions for being queer, as resisting a gay rights agenda that seeks to normalize homosexuality. Indeed, in my discussion of Nollywood film, I discuss how there is often much public debate about whether a film is homophobic because a queer character is arrested or killed off or whether the film promotes homosexuality because it shows that queer character finding pleasure or even love. But even in art films intended to critique homophobia or to validate queer love, performances of resistance might register differently for different audience members. For instance, when I interviewed Chuchu about *Stories of Our Lives*, he mentioned that, at a screening of the film for friends and family in Kenya before the film was banned, the mother of one of the actresses pointed to the fact that because the lesbian character her daughter portrayed was suspended from school, the film beautifully portrayed the negative consequences of being gay. To this audience member, the film resisted the normalization of queer love, which was not, of course, the takeaway the Nest Collective had intended. What I am suggesting here, then, is that in order to attend to the complex social landscapes that the queer characters and queer subjects must navigate, it is important to acknowledge not only the dual meanings of resistance present in queer African cinemas but also the different ways resistance might register to different audiences.

Of course, the risk here is that if resistance is seen as both for and against the status quo, as both public and private, loud and quiet, it loses any meaning at all. But the claim I am making is that depicting queerness or even queerness in general is not inherently oppositional and that resistance is not only about triumphantly overcoming something or about gathering in public or even about coming out. Indeed, it is quite possible, as I will explore in the chapters that follow, to be both resistant (in the transgressive sense of the word) and complicit with the status quo at the same time.[16] If all of this means that resistance as a keyword becomes murky and less explicitly attached to counterhegemonic practices, then that is because the films that I discuss throughout this book, films that come from very different traditions and are made by filmmakers with very different agendas, reflect the many contradictory registers of resistance, registers that complicate any simple binary between subversive and oppressive. But the point of *Queer African Cinemas* is not to celebrate murkiness. Rather, what I try to do is to understand how one can both acknowledge it as the reality of the present and also not allow it to become an obstacle to imagining new freedoms and possibilities.

Throughout this book I examine films by and about queer African citizens that, like "Each Night I Dream," simultaneously document the pain inflicted on queer persons and invite a listening for and thinking through what Ashon Crawley (2017, 23), building on work in Black studies, calls "otherwise possibilities." But if I am to pay serious attention to the emotional labors and complex ethics of resistance and to the fact that resistance might also be a conservative gesture, it must be understood that the opening up of possibilities is also often accompanied by resistance to the otherwise. Crawley writes, "Otherwise is a word that names plurality as its core operation, otherwise bespeaks the ongoingness of possibility, of things existing other than what is known, what is grasped" (24). Understanding resistance as something that can create as well as block this operation of ongoing possibility allows me to leave behind the question of whether something is a good or bad representation of queer Africans or whether a portrayal is resistant or homophobic. It is not that I am uninterested in these discussions—in fact, I believe very strongly that it is politically and socially necessary to have hopeful and positive representations of queer life no matter where one is located. But for the purposes of this book I am less interested in a project that decides what is positive or negative or what should or should not be labeled resistant and more interested in understanding what types of frameworks and narratives become available when one imagines vulnerability, or pleasure and intimacy, or quieter modes of operating differently, or negotiating as practices of and resources for resistance. In other words, rather than pitting progressive, transgressive resistance against oppressive homophobia, I am interested in exploring all of the various registers in between.

Afri-queer Fugitivity

One of the ways to categorize the registers of resistance that rest in the middle range between heroic agency and denial of gay existence and rights is through what I call Afri-queer fugitivity, a fugitivity that can be seen in the different forms of fleeing, escape, and past/future reimaginings in "Each Night I Dream" as well as in many of the other films discussed in this book. Fugitivity is a concept used primarily by a broad range of scholars who theorize African American practices of escape and evasion as they flee from and imagine alternatives to the different types of enslavement and captivity that mark Black life in the United States. In her book on the sounds of Black, queer eccentricity, Francesca Royster (2012, 12) describes the fugitive as "the artistic impulse to escape the constraints of the objectification and social death of slavery—but also to never fully escape its embodied lessons." James Edward Ford III (2015, 110) writes that "one can define fugitivity as a critical category for examining *the artful escape of objectification*," and he emphasizes that fugitivity and the "act of fleeing" foster "alternative spaces, ethics, and structures of feeling in the name of being otherwise" (Ford 2014, n.p.). But as Matthew Omelsky writes, thinking through Fred Moten's highly influential work on fugitivity, Black fugitivity is not only an American experience or ethos: "If Moten identifies the conditions that engender Black fugitive life as a 'global phenomenon,' then indeed fugitivity names that desire to flee the confines not just of the nineteenth-century southern plantation or the contemporary American carceral state, but of colonial and postcolonial regimes that have suppressed Black life globally" (Omelsky 2020, 56). Omelsky therefore urges consideration of the specificities of African fugitivities. In *Queer African Cinemas*, I point specifically to an Afri-queer fugitivity, an African and queer fugitivity that inhabits a certain slipperiness, that dreams of lives unencumbered by state-sanctioned homophobia, that breaks or evades rules, and that flees from constraints by mobilizing past, present, and future imaginaries. I have chosen the prefix *Afri-* rather than *Afro-* because—much like the writer Nnedi Okorafor (2019), who rejects the application of the term *Afrofuturism* to her African-focused work—I find that the prefix *Afro-* often, though certainly not always, signals associations with African American rather than African life when circulating in a North American context. While Okorafor replaces *Afrofuturism* with *Africanfuturism*, I have chosen the shortened *Afri-queer* both for ease and because, when said out loud, its sonic resonance with the word *Africa* implies a queering of Africa.[17]

I understand Afri-queer fugitivity to be at work across a range of queer African writing, advocacy work, and creative expression. I recognize an Afri-queer fugitivity, for instance, in Binyavanga Wainaina's *We Must Free Our Imaginations*, a six-part video documentary he released on YouTube three days after he published "I Am a Homosexual, Mum," which he referred to as the lost chapter to his memoir. In his video, Wainaina, whose writing and activism have inspired much queer artistic expression across the continent, urges Africans to escape a neocolonial mentality, to shed submissiveness, and to reclaim African traditions that will help to reimagine new futures. Likewise, I see Afri-queer fugitivity in the African LGBTI Manifesto, drafted in Nairobi in 2010 and published anonymously by activists from across the continent, that opens by stating, "As Africans, we all have infinite potential. We stand for an African revolution which encompasses the demand for a re-imagination of our lives outside neo-colonial categories of identity and power" ("African LGBTI Manifesto/Declaration" 2013, 52). The manifesto calls for the celebration of complex sexual identities and ties "erotic justice" to economic, environmental, and racial justice, demanding "total liberation" and noting the "endless possibilities" that exist (52). In this way, Afri-queer fugitivity articulates a form of queerness that, in the words of José Esteban Muñoz (2009, 96), whose work on queer futurity influences my thinking throughout this book, is "about a desire for another way of being in both the world and time, a desire that resists mandates to accept that which is not enough." In this sense, and at its most basic level, Afri-queer fugitivity is about resisting the limitations of the present by searching for something that can surpass it.

But I also want to emphasize that Afri-queer fugitivity marks the way that constraints of the past and present continue to hold sway even as one escapes them. This can be seen quite poignantly in Zethu Matebeni's (2011) documentary *Breaking Out of the Box* (codirected by Busi Kheswa). The film begins with a poem by the late Buhle Msibi juxtaposed with Zanele Muholi's photographs of Black lesbian couples (see figures 1.5–1.7):

Today I break this box I have lived in for being black
I break this box that said to me I can't
Today I break this box I have been left in for being a woman
. . . .
Today I break this box that I have been forced to live in for being
homosexual
This box that said I am un-African
This box that said I am abnormal.[18]

Today I break this box
I have lived in for being black

I break this box
I have been left in
for being a woman

Today I break this box
that I have been forced to live in
for being homosexual

FIGURES 1.5–1.7. Stills from *Breaking Out of the Box* (2011), juxtaposing Buhle Msibi's poetry with Zanele Muholi's photographs of Black South African lesbians in the opening images of the documentary.

The film then focuses on six Black South African lesbians. They discuss the sexual fluidity that has always existed within African cultures, the difficulty of being gay during the anti-apartheid struggle, and the way in which the invisibility and vulnerability they felt during apartheid mirror how they feel as lesbians today. But they also discuss how they are now artists, athletes, organizers, and role models in their communities. In this way, the women describe their ability to break free from many of the constraints they face while also, as Royster says, never leaving behind their embodied lessons. As the film ends, the last lines of Msibi's poem appear on screen: "I break all the boxes / And free as a bird I fly to the great blue sky above." The film speaks to the forms of patriarchy, racism, and homophobia that objectify and contain, but also to the histories of defiance—the breaking of boxes—and the imaginations of freedom of Afri-queer people. *Breaking Out of the Box* therefore illustrates perfectly an Afri-queer fugitivity that suggests an otherwise to despair and submissiveness while still marking the violence and pain that sometimes permeate queer African stories.

Though Afri-queer fugitivity is a leitmotif in many of the films I discuss in this book, I want to be clear that not all films with queer African subjects contain scenes of Afri-queer fugitivity. Some do. Some do not. And those that do might, at the same time, circulate in some publics as warnings against expressions of queerness, or might wind up being complicit with other forms of oppression or structural violence, including homophobia. Moreover, sometimes moments of escape or flight are blocked for various reasons. Sometimes flight becomes physically or emotionally impossible. Sometimes, as Nyanzi (2014, 38) writes of an otherwise joyful 2014 Ugandan Pride event at Lake Victoria, one is surrounded by armed policemen who cut off all possible escape routes. Sometimes, as is the case with the vignette "Run" from *Stories of Our Lives*, a character who runs and becomes a fugitive in order to escape homophobic violence decides to stop running, to stay put. Therefore, while Afri-queer fugitivity is a useful lens through which to view the multiple yearnings for escape and the practices of refusal of many queer characters in the films under discussion, I want to underscore that it is not the only one and that it is complicated by the often contradictory registers of resistance addressed above.

My intention is to place Afri-queer fugitivity into a larger constellation of practices of resistance and refusal that, like queerness itself, sometimes fails to properly align with expectations, or fails to be directly legible. But I also find Afri-queer fugitivity to be a productive way to think about the particular forms of temporality expressed in many of the films, forms that, as I have been suggesting, might not fit into linear narratives of rights or progress. As Tavia Nyong'o (2018, 10) writes in his profound study of the polytemporality of Black, queer world-making, "The *kind* of fugitive time that allows for access to something beyond and for the emergence of the virtual is not just ordinary, everyday time." Fugitive time, in other words, allows for models of temporality that are not about overcoming and moving forward but about unpredictability, anticipation, and imagining an elsewhere, an otherwise past or future. As the queer Kenyan blogger and intellectual Keguro Macharia (2013b) writes, "Fugitivity is seeing around corners, stockpiling in crevices, knowing the un-rules, being unruly, because the rules are never enough, and not even close. . . . Fugitivity is time-distorting, multiplying and erasing, making legion and invisible." Afri-queer fugitivity therefore provides a valuable way to think about queer African cinemas as a whole, despite the very different politics that exist in the body of work I discuss: the films I examine do not fit into any familiar historically or politically progressive (or regressive) sequence; they do not spell out what queer protest looks like or what it will lead to; and they do not dwell strictly in the homophobia of the present. Rather, collectively, these films gesture both to lives negated and to lives in the process of being remade and reenvisioned.

Lineup

This book consists of four chapters, each of which reads practices of resisting homophobia alongside practices, like censorship or the pathologizing or killing off of queer characters, that reproduce homophobia or that resist an otherwise. Each chapter, then, reaches out to different sites to understand the multiple complexities and registers of resistance. In chapter 1, "Making Waves: Queer Eccentricity and West African Wayward Women," I look at two West African films that are emblematic of the first two categories of films discussed above: Joseph Gaï Ramaka's *Karmen Geï* (2001) and the four-part Ghanaian video film *Jezebel* (2007–8) by Socrate Safo, two films in which the titular queer female character is linked to the African water spirit commonly known as Mami Wata. Using Saidiya Hartman's (2019) concept of waywardness, I discuss how, despite the very different positions the two filmmakers seem to take on the acceptability of queerness, both films simultaneously create openings for, and highlight the limits of, women's sexual agency and willful errantry. I also articulate how Mami Wata provides a blueprint for indigenous forms of queerness and decolonized forms of knowing that are improvisational—that allow for an Afri-queer fugitivity—and that suggest ways to "make waves," to disrupt the status quo with an uncontainable waywardness. This chapter therefore suggests how queer African cinema in its different modes can be both an "ongoing exploration of what might be" and an enactment of "the entanglement of escape and confinement" (Hartman 2019, 228).

While chapter 1 highlights formal readings, chapter 2, "Touching Nollywood: From Negation to Negotiation in Queer Nigerian Cinema," takes a more national and historical approach, tracing representations of queerness in Nigerian video films over the past two decades. Despite the fact that Nollywood provides the largest archive of gay-themed popular culture on the continent, with dozens of films depicting same-sex relationships, very little has been written about these films in the very rapidly expanding field of Nollywood studies. The Nollywood industry, because of its impressive growth and adaptability and wide, pan-African appeal, is often lauded for its ability to speak to African moral values. But when Nollywood films take on the topic of homosexuality, these values tend to be aligned with a morality that sees homosexuality as a threat to the family and the nation, providing a conundrum for scholars like me who want to take African popular culture seriously on its own terms and not force it into Western paradigms and value systems. This chapter, following Nyanzi's proposal for queering African studies, is therefore an effort to queer Nollywood studies and to model a way of reading queer-themed Nollywood films that does not discount their complexities and cultural context but, at the same time, holds them accountable for participating in a public discourse that was supportive of the Same Sex Marriage Prohibition Act (SSMPA) of 2014. The first half of the chapter looks at the body of Nollywood films leading up to the SSMPA, arguing that even though these films contradict state discourses denying the existence of homosexuality in Nigeria, they also move and touch audiences by figuring the homosexual as an object of fear. In the second half of the chapter, however, I turn my attention to the TIERS-produced films mentioned above and discuss how queer activists have strategically utilized Nollywood aesthetics and conventions to touch audience's emotions in a way that challenges the morality of homophobia itself. Here, I argue that TIERS practices what Obioma Nnaemeka (2004) refers to as "nego-feminism," a strategy that makes use of negotiation and give-and-take and is grounded in African values and morals.

Chapter 3, "Cutting Masculinities: Post-apartheid South African Cinema," also takes a national approach but focuses on three films in particular: Oliver Hermanus's *Skoonheid*, John Trengove's *Inxeba*, and Christiaan Olwagen's *Kanarie*, all of which, like the vast majority of South African queer feature films, center on queer male desire. Unlike Senegal, Ghana, and Nigeria, where homosexual acts are illegal, South Africa has the continent's most progressive laws on same-sex relations and even legalized same-sex marriage as early as 2006. But despite these laws, homophobia still persists—as do the colonial and patriarchal structures that created it. Each of the three films that I examine highlights the complex and ongoing entanglement between homophobia, race, masculinity, and class in South Africa. Here, I return to the concept of *the cut*, a term I use in chapter 1 to discuss forms of escape and rupture. However, in this chapter I use the term more broadly to think not only about moments of breaking away or cutting away in the cinematic sense, but also to think about that which is left out or cut out, that which is cut short, that which cuts through, and that which is literally cut or wounded. What I argue is that reading these three films for the multiple forms of cutting they perform calls attention to the ways in which globally circulating queer male South African feature films simultaneously break away from and are contained by hegemonic racial and gendered structures.

My final chapter, "Holding Space, Saving Joy: Queer Love and Critical Re-silience in East Africa," turns to two Kenyan works—Art Attack's "Same Love (Remix)" music video and the feature film *Rafiki*—but examines them along-side queer art and activism in neighboring Uganda and in the context of queer film festivals in Nairobi and Kampala. Unlike chapters 2 and 3, which high-light the trajectory of queer cinema in Nigeria and South Africa, respectively, the goal here is not so much to produce a history of queer Kenyan cinema, a history that would include a very small handful of films, but rather to think through the complexities of queer African counterpublics that exist in coun-tries like Kenya, where queer art is censored, and countries like Uganda, where queer gatherings and safe spaces have been violated by police. What I articu-late here is a way of thinking about queer film and queer film festivals as enact-ing what I call a "critical resilience," a resilience that does not just repeat and reproduce neoliberal mantras of overcoming and enduring, but that embraces modes of survival and imaginative acts that are nonlinear and nondismissive of vulnerability, tenderness, and defeat. I use the phrase *critical resilience* to in-dicate modes of resistance and survival that intersect with the complexities of inner life and that often exist, as Hartman suggests, as everyday practices that exist below the threshold of overt opposition. Here, I think alongside thinkers like Macharia, who emphasizes the hard work and daily practice that it takes to resist the psychological devastation of homophobia, and Darieck Scott, who discusses how the wounds of colonialism and racial and sexual oppression can serve as tools or models of political transformation. This chapter is therefore just as much about tracing current queer cinematic practices as it is about mapping their aspirations and the critical potential they anticipate. Like all the chapters in this book, "Holding Space, Saving Joy" contains present participles in its title. I use this part of speech, these verbs expressing continuousness, to highlight the ongoingness of feelings and actions that queer African cinemas capture and to point toward the entanglement of pasts, presents, and futures that my reading practices bring to the fore.

The range of countries discussed here—Senegal, Ghana, Nigeria, South Af-rica, Kenya, and, to a lesser extent, Uganda—is admittedly limited and skewed toward Anglophone countries (with the obvious exception of Senegal) as well as toward those countries with more robust economies and film industries.[19] But, by and large, these are the countries that have produced queer feature films and videos in the twenty-first century, at least at the time of my writing. (I do also return to the 1997 Guinean film *Dakan* in a short coda concluding the book.) The concentration on these countries in particular does not, of course, mean that queer creative life and media production do not exist elsewhere in

Africa, or that there have not been queer or queer-themed films that are under the radar or impossible for me to access. But my particular focus is indicative of the way that cinema, which requires a certain amount of capital, equipment, and technical know-how—not to mention distribution networks—is more concentrated and visible in certain African countries, especially in Nigeria and South Africa, by far the continent's two largest producers of media content. I have tried, then, to address many of what I would call the major queer feature films and videos that have been made on the continent, while also acknowledging that there are many films and audiovisual materials—YouTube videos, web series, short films, documentaries, diaspora films, and so on—that also make up queer African screen media.

Throughout this book, I employ methodologies from several different disciplines in order to highlight, as Lindiwe Dovey (2015, 3) suggests, that "the value and meaning of films are contingent on their contexts of distribution, exhibition, and reception." I have interviewed many of the filmmakers discussed in this book, especially those who have not been widely interviewed by media outlets, and I have tried to include their perspectives, anecdotes, and aspirations. I have also met with and interviewed activists, queer film festival organizers, censors, and queer audiences based in the countries discussed and have attended queer film festivals in Nairobi, Kampala, and Gaborone. But, at the end of the day, this is not an ethnographic project. My focus is on the films themselves, on their formal structures, on the meanings and ambivalences they produce as fictional texts, and on the ways they circulate and resonate and register different meanings for different people.

It is also important to acknowledge that I write from a particular vantage point. I am trained as a film and literary theorist and postcolonialist. I have the privilege of a tenured position at an American university (one named, in fact, "American University"). My position has provided me access to books, articles, and films that are often not available on the African continent. It has also provided me with funding to attend conferences and to travel internationally; it has provided me with a mobility that has essentially made this book and its multiple sites of inquiry possible. But my subject position and geographic location also limit me: I am an outsider looking in, a non-African and non-Black scholar who does not live or work in Africa and who has not made films or worked as an activist. This is why what I offer here is not intended to be prescriptive, nor is it intended to be definitive or encyclopedic. What I provide are a set of readings and a model of reading that I think can be useful to scholars, activists, and filmmakers—or to anyone, for that matter—interested in thinking about queer cinematic practices, ethics of resistance, and the different challenges, strategies, and queer cinematic histories across the African continent. Though I have been studying and thinking about African cinema for almost two decades, I have tried to approach this project, and will continue to do so, with a sense of humility, with a readiness to listen and to acknowledge my mistakes and flaws. I am incredibly grateful to the people who have met with me, talked to me, hosted me, answered my questions, and engaged in conversations and exchanges of ideas. I see *Queer African Cinemas* as a necessarily incomplete and imperfect continuation of this dialogue that, I hope, will open up more questions than it answers.

Making Waves

Queer Eccentricity and West
African Wayward Women

In an article titled "Impossible Africans," the queer Cameroonian political scientist S. N. Nyeck (2008, 6) argues that, within mainstream African discourse, queer African subjects are considered to be "impossible" or unimaginable, not because homosexual desire itself is seen to be impossible but because queer Africans are considered to be noncitizens, or misnomers, held somewhere in suspension, somewhere in the shadows of the state and the social institutions that support it. Nyeck therefore calls for a focus on queer eroticism—an eroticism which names the "network of relational behaviors, ideas, aspirations, emotions, common socio-economic and political dreams" of (impossibly) queer Africans—and which seems to be precisely what political and social institutions find threatening (6). In the early years of West African queer cinema, that is, the first decade of this century, erotically threatening queer figures were almost exclusively figured to be women. (Though West Africa's first queer film, the 1997 film *Dakan*, focused on two teenage boys, gay men did not appear again in West African cinema until 2010, with the exception of minor subplots in a few Nigerian films.) But the ways these erotic noncitizens were imagined and treated on screen was often dependent on whether the film came from Francophone or Anglophone Africa. In West African Francophone cinema, which tends be art or "auteur" cinema, nonconforming women are often used to critique the postcolonial state, and women's sexual agency in general, along with the threat it poses to an often corrupt state, is often celebrated on screen. However, in the popular West African Anglophone video film tradition centered in Nigeria and Ghana, films are often tied to Christian, and more often specifically Pentecostal, worldviews, and women's erotic agency or nonconformity, at least in the first decade of the 2000s, was often presented as spiritually and morally dangerous to the heterosexual family.[1] But what I suggest is that in their depiction of queerness these two cinematic traditions converge in unexpected ways, offering insights into the often messy links between women's queer eccentricity, West African spiritual traditions, and the resistant practices of Afri-queer fugitivity. I begin *Queer African Cinemas* with a formal study of one film from each of these film traditions—Joseph Gaï Ramaka's Senegalese art film *Karmen Geï* (2001) and Socrate Safo's four-part Ghanaian video film *Jezebel* (2007–8)—in order to foreground the different ways that some of the earliest queer West African films focused their attention on women's sexuality and on its ability to upset the state, in the case of *Karmen Geï*, and the family, in the case of *Jezebel*.

Perhaps one of the most widely written-about African films, *Karmen Geï* is an adaptation of Prosper Mérimée's 1845 novella *Carmen*, which was famously turned into an opera by Georges Bizet in 1875. In both Mérimée's and Bizet's versions, Carmen, a Gypsy and outlaw in southern Spain, seduces the officer Don José, who destroys his career for Carmen and joins her fellow bandits. But when Carmen turns her affections to a bullfighter (Escamilo in the opera, Lucas in the novella), Don José murders Carmen. *Karmen Geï*, the first African adaptation of the story, follows this basic plot with one major change: in the original *Carmen*, and in most of the eighty-some filmic adaptations, Carmen is caught in a love triangle between two men; in Ramaka's version, Karmen loves both men and women.[2] In all *Carmens*, Carmen is an outsider and outlaw, a wayward woman, who challenges the status quo. In *Karmen Geï* this remains the case: throughout the film Karmen, a queer, drug-smuggling free spirit, performs her opposition to patriarchy, the national bourgeoisie, and compulsory heterosexuality and links her struggles to French colonial oppression and to the transatlantic slave trade. But here, Ramaka connects Karmen to a long line of historical and divine resisters and calls Karmen the daughter of the water spirit Kumba Kastel. Ramaka's *Karmen* therefore has the same discourse on love, resistance, and freedom that is the hallmark of all global Carmen stories, but here it becomes both a localized discourse and a queered discourse, one, I argue, that is embedded in the improvisational jazz and drumming score that connects the film to a transatlantic Black fugitive imagination and a critique of the postcolonial state.

Jezebel is also a remake, but it is a remake of one of Safo's earlier films, *Women in Love* (1996). *Women in Love* is about a woman, Julie, who is struggling to make her clothing shop successful in her coastal Ga neighborhood of Accra and who seeks the advice of a well-to-do, single friend. The friend sends Julie to a priestess who takes her to the beach and initiates her into a cult that worships a lesbian water spirit. Julie quickly becomes quite successful, acquiring her own mansion and Mercedes-Benz, but her wealth comes with a condition: she may never again sleep with a man, and any woman whom Julie sleeps with may also never again sleep with a man under penalty of going mad. In other words, Julie's choice to join the cult is a direct threat to heterosexual reproduction. When I met Safo in Accra in 2007, just as he was preparing to begin filming *Jezebel*, he proudly and without prompting—I was actually working on an entirely different project at the time and did not know about his queer films—showed me *Women in Love* on a small monitor in his minivan. He told me that he wanted to remake *Women in Love*, his most popular film, because he knew that the production values were substandard and that with all the development in technology he was confident that he could do better. The film, to him, presented a true story of how lesbians obtain wealth through secret networks, and he knew his audiences would be keen to see a sleeker version of the film. *Jezebel*, the multipart remake and expansion of *Women in Love*, keeps the same story line but is full of digital special effects that Safo had mastered in the decade that separated the two films: in the new version the water spirit materializes out of thin air and transforms into a human, the Mercedes-Benz is replaced with a yellow Hummer emerging from a morphing fireball, and good and evil spirits fight each other with breaths of fire and Bible shields. In the end, Christian forces prevail and Jezebel is defeated.

As can be seen from just these brief descriptions, many things separate *Karmen Geï* and *Jezebel*, but in addition to the differing content of the two films, they also have incredibly different forms. *Karmen Geï* is an avant-garde film whose generic categorization has confounded critics, who have called it a "quasi-musical," a "musical drama," a "musical comedy," or even a "dance review" (Dovey 2009, 221).[3] Moreover, though it follows the basic story line of *Carmen*, Ramaka cares very little for conventional plot, often favoring cuts and breaks over linearity. Ayo Coly (2016, 399) writes that "the elliptical structure of the film, although critiqued by some reviewers, obeys the logistics of a queer assemblage. . . . The film constructs Karmen as an irruption, an unplanned event whose occurrence interrupts, diverts, redirects, and confounds." And the film is certainly a celebration of this irruption.

Jezebel, on the other hand, is paradigmatic of a genre of West African video film that, in my earlier article on the film, I call the occult melodrama. The occult melodrama is a genre that was most popular in the early years of video film (i.e., the 1990s and early 2000s) and can be understood as one that introduces an occult presence—almost always one that promises wealth to postcolonial subjects who have been left out of the formal economy—as a way to depict what Brian Larkin (2008, 186) calls the "negation of morality." In occult films, figures that negate morality are linked to the devil or to various spirits who almost always present a threat to the monogamous heterosexual family but who are, by the end of the film, neatly contained and subdued by Christian forces. Therefore, while *Karmen Geï* proliferates and indeed celebrates the queer disruption and eccentricity that Coly argues are actually intrinsic to postcolonial Senegal, *Jezebel*, like West African video film more broadly, positions such disruptions as precisely that which must be eliminated so that social order can be restored.

But in both films audiences can take pleasure in the queer eccentricity of Karmen and Jezebel as they watch love triangles unfold and can root for non-virtuous women with ties to the spiritual world. And in *Karmen Geï* as well as in *Jezebel*, queer possibilities and futures are simultaneously displayed and cut short (both films end with the death of the titular characters), and resistance is registered in multiple ways. What this chapter provides is not an accounting or contrasting of Senegalese and Ghanaian queer cinema, categories that would contain hardly any films other than those already mentioned. In fact, when they were released, *Karmen Geï* and *Jezebel/Women in Love* were almost singular within their national contexts for their depiction of same-sex desire between women—and remain so, as they were made before the uptick in homophobic rhetoric across the region that shifted public discourse on the topic.[4] Furthermore, it is not my intention to position these as paradigmatic queer African films: both films, made by cisgender heterosexual males, certainly have their limits and flaws. The purpose of this chapter is to demonstrate how films from different cinematic traditions can both limit and open the otherwise possibilities of what Nyeck refers to as impossible African queerness. Therefore, what I emphasize here are practices of reading that show how queer African cinemas can resist or interrupt the constraints of the present and simultaneously reinforce those constraints.

I refer to Karmen and Jezebel as wayward women to highlight how both women exhibit a willful unruliness that disrupts and strays from expected forms of social respectability and that cannot be captured in terms of legible oppositional strategies. In *Wayward Lives, Beautiful Experiments: Intimate Histories of Social Upheaval*, a superbly rendered history of African American women's everyday gestures of defiance at the beginning of the twentieth century, Saidiya Hartman (2019) offers the following meditation on *wayward* as a sort of keyword:

> Wayward, related to the family of words: errant, fugitive, recalcitrant, anarchic, willful, reckless, troublesome, riotous, tumultuous, rebellious and wild. To inhabit the world in ways inimical to those deemed proper and respectable, to be deeply aware of the gulf between where you stayed and how you might live. . . . Waywardness articulates the paradox of cramped creation, the entanglement of escape and confinement, flight and captivity. Wayward: to wander, to be unmoored, adrift, rambling, roving, cruising, strolling, and seeking. To claim the right to opacity. (228)

While my archive is clearly quite different from Hartman's, to me this "entry," as Hartman calls it, on waywardness and its paradoxes helps to articulate the ways that both Karmen and Jezebel, queer women who intentionally cause the state and the heterosexual family trouble, are uncontainable and, at the same time, constantly in danger of being captured and contained. Moreover, as Hartman argues, to be wayward means to be not entirely of this world or in this world: waywardness "traffics in occult visions of other worlds and dreams of a different kind of life. Waywardness is an ongoing exploration of what might be; it is an improvisation . . . when there is little room to breathe" (2019, 228). And, as I shall demonstrate below, Karmen's and Jezebel's particular forms of waywardness—Karmen's dominated above all by improvisation, Jezebel's by her occult unknowability—are mirrored in the formal structures and cinematic language of the films that bear their names.

What I also want to suggest, though, is that this waywardness, one coupled with the type of queer eroticism Nyeck describes, opens up new, decolonized forms of knowing, forms that operate outside of the Europatriarchal frameworks that have disavowed the queer eccentricities that are often embedded in African indigenous understandings. As the Ugandan feminist Sylvia Tamale (2020, 29) reminds us, "The process of colonization erased, suppressed and demonized all Indigenous non-Western knowledge systems. In particular, knowledges of women (e.g., alchemist wise women), of 'peasants' and working classes, and of the 'pagans' or earth-centered religion worshippers were all subjugated and criminalized." What Tamale advocates for is a form of decolonization or "breaking free" that makes use of African-centered feminist practices, practices that make space for queerness and that see queerness as intrinsic to local cultural beliefs, in order to create frameworks outside of dominant ways of knowing (2020, 30, 39). What I find in Karmen and Jezebel, then, are characters whose eccentricity or "empowering oddness" (Peterson 2001, xii) model ways of being and knowing that depend on local practices of rebelliousness as well as occult, or what I describe below as spectraphilic, ways of operating differently.[5] In this sense, to say that these two films make waves does not mean that they make visible or audible any particular trajectory of resistance but, rather, indicates how their slippery and unruly water spirit protagonists subtly disturb Eurocentric, linear, rational, or heteropatriarchal structures of power.

Karmen and the Fugitive Impulse

There has perhaps always been something a little queer about Senegalese cinema. For instance, as early as the 1970s Ousmane Sembene, often considered to be the father of Black African cinema, included a *gorjigeen* in his film *Xala* (1975), a film that critiques the postcolonial nation through an extended allegory about the main character's curse of impotence. *Gorjigeen* is a Wolof term that is now used to describe homosexual men but which literally translates as "man-woman" and which was, at the time *Xala* was made, a fairly neutral description of gender-nonconforming men who were integrated into Senegalese society. Not at all pathologized, the gorjigeen often performed roles like the one in Sembene's film, who was the master of ceremonies at an elite wedding (Coly 2019, 30, 34).[6] In this sense, there was nothing particularly radical about the inclusion of the gorjigeen in Sembene's realist cinema. Queer minor characters likewise appeared in films by the more avant-garde Senegalese filmmaker Djibril Diop Mambety. Kenneth Harrow, in his essay "The Queer Thing about Djibril Diop Mambety: A Counterhegemonic Discourse Meets the Heterosexual Economy" (2001), discusses queer characters in two of Mambety's films. Namely, he looks at Charley in *Touki Bouki* (1973), the wealthy gay man whom the main characters rob, and two castrati in *Hyenas* (1992) who accompany the character of Lady Ramatou when she returns to take her revenge on a village that expelled her as an unmarried pregnant teenager. Harrow argues that what makes Mambety's work queer is not so much these minor characters but rather their inclusion in films that openly revolt against the hegemony of a heterosexual economy, a point that might equally apply to Sembene's *Xala*, which is a film about many forms of postcolonial impotence. Ivy Mills, in a brilliant revisiting of Harrow's essay, locates the queerness of Mambety's films in the discourse of the hyena (*Touki Bouki* means "hyena's journey") and in the subversive sexuality that the animal represents in Wolof oral traditions (Mills 2019). But despite these precedents, *Karmen Geï* is the first and thus far the only Senegalese film to depict same-sex intimacy itself and the first and only with an explicitly queer protagonist. It is also the first African Francophone film to portray love between two women. In other words, though queerness existed in Francophone African cinema—and was often associated with critiques of state power—*Karmen Geï* was, and still is, unparalleled in its context.[7] In this sense, I read *Karmen Geï* as a break, as a cut and departure from what came before, that itself participates in the very Afri-queer fugitivity that defines its protagonist.

As the opening credits of *Karmen Geï* roll, the audience can hear the saxophone of the African American jazz musician David Murray playing over a chorus of Senegalese sabar drumming. The music continues as the first image of the film appears: Karmen Geï is seated and smiling between two of the drummers, her legs spread apart and her black *boubou* draped to reveal her thighs that open and close to the rhythm (figure 1.1). A reverse shot reveals that Karmen is smiling at Angelique, a lighter-skinned woman dressed in a khaki uniform who sits off to the side and who watches Karmen lustfully.

FIGURE 1.1. Still from *Karmen Geï* (2001). Karmen performs for the prison warden, Angelique, in the courtyard of Kumba Kastel prison in the opening sequence of the film.

Murray's saxophone recedes into the background as the drumming picks up and the camera pans out to show the full ensemble of drummers and a circle of cheering, clapping women, some of whom have joined the drummers by keeping the rhythm on overturned plastic buckets. Karmen stands up and moves to the center of the circle where she dances for the crowd and then moves toward Angelique. Placing Angelique's closed legs in between her own open, gyrating legs, Karmen reveals her silver waist beads and red-orange *sous-pagne*, a provocative undergarment. Karmen then puts one finger under Angelique's chin and guides Angelique to a standing position and the two dance an intimate sabar duet as the circle around them tightens (figure 1.2).[8] A high-angle shot shows Karmen and Angelique in the midst of the dancing crowd (figure 1.3), and then, as the sound of the saxophone returns, the camera pans out to reveal prison guards positioned in a circle above the crowd. Suddenly, the audience becomes aware that the dancing women, including Karmen, are prisoners and that Angelique is their warden. A whistle blows, and the women are herded back to their cells. As the camera pans out farther, the audience can see that the courtyard where the women were dancing is both a fictional prison, with guards positioned in panopticon style, and the real House of Slaves on Gorée Island where slaves, from the fifteenth to the mid-eighteenth centuries, were housed before being taken across the Atlantic.

FIGURE 1.2. Still from *Karmen Geï* (2001). Angelique (*front*) and Karmen perform an intimate sabar dance in front of the other prisoners.

FIGURE 1.3. Still from *Karmen Geï* (2001). Women prisoners gathered in the courtyard of Kumba Kastel prison begin to return to their cells.

Once back in the cell, Karmen leads the other women in call-and-response singing as they celebrate Karmen's successful seduction of the warden. When night falls Karmen is led to Angelique's quarters (figure 1.4), and images of intertwining limbs and sensual gyration fill the screen in the first-ever depiction of same-sex intimacy between women in African cinema. As the women make love and a soft piano plays on the soundtrack, the camera cuts back to the other prisoners who are tapping out a slow rhythm with spoons against the prison bars. The next morning Angelique, who knows better than to keep Karmen locked up, sets Karmen free. (And though Karmen will have several other love interests in the film, it is perhaps this act that leads Karmen to declare that Angelique is the one she loved the most.) As the jazz score and saxophone pick up again, Karmen flees the prison and Gorée, running down the dark passageway of the prison, kissing one of the guards goodbye, and leaving the House of Slaves for the open air and sunshine.[9] But unlike the slaves that were taken from Gorée, Karmen heads toward freedom rather than away from it. Karmen's artful jog down the dark prison corridor—her literal escape from captivity—and subsequent emergence into the sunshine, into freedom, are therefore a paradigmatic fugitive moment. And though the setting of Kumba Kastel prison in the House of Slaves links Karmen to the dark history of transatlantic slavery, throughout the film Karmen continually sheds constraints and refuses to

FIGURE 1.4. Still from *Karmen Geï* (2001). Angelique disrobes and approaches Karmen in the lovemaking scene before Karmen is set free.

be bound by anyone else's desires or rules. She works against sexual norms, she criticizes the state, she rejects any form of love that objectifies her, and she engages in piracy and smuggling while also rejecting the financial gains they bring her. Here, and throughout the film, I read Karmen's practices of refusal, as well as her creative, Afri-queer waywardness, as part of a global Black fugitive imagination that explores and improvises other, often opaque, ways of being and knowing when, as Hartman (2019, 228) says, "there is little room to breathe."

For Fred Moten (2007, 44) fugitivity is not simply about fleeing or escaping but is also an aesthetic impulse, one that is linked to the "profound discourse of the cut," a discourse I find to be key to understanding the particular forms of disruption that Karmen enacts. The *cut* is both a musical term and a cinematic term. In music, the cut refers to "an abrupt, seemingly motivated break" from a series (Snead 1992, 220). For James Snead, the cut is a key feature of Black musical forms and provides one way to distinguish African and African American forms of music, with their rhythms and patterns of repetition, from the goal-oriented "accumulation and growth" of European music (220). In film, the cut refers to the splicing together of two different scenes and the transition between two different times and places. In the opening scene that I just described, the musical cuts and the cinematic cuts work together to create a fugitive structure of feeling. As Snead writes, "In jazz improvisation, the 'cut' . . . is the unexpectedness with which the soloist will depart from the 'head' or theme and from its normal harmonic sequence or the drummer from the tune's accepted and familiar primary beat" (222). And when attuned to the frequency of the score, the audience can register Murray's saxophone's or the lead drummer's departure from the theme and then their return to it. But Karmen herself also enacts a cut. When she dances for Angelique or leads the call-and-response or escapes from prison, she is the soloist who departs from the group, who breaks from the ensemble that surrounds her.

Moreover, once Karmen escapes from Gorée, there is another cut, one that cuts through the established orders and logical sequences. As Karmen flees the island, her silhouette running toward the ocean, the sounds of the sabar drums heard in the opening dance scene rejoin the soundtrack. The next image is a cut to a medium shot of a sabar drummer leading a rhythm for a happy couple—Corporal Lamine Diop and Majiguene—who then enter their wedding celebration. Angelique, not in uniform, trails the couple and sits behind them. A griot begins to praise the couple, but suddenly, the lights turn off and a spotlight shines on Karmen, who dances for the crowd. Karmen pauses her dance, silences the drummers, and begins a chant-like speech addressed to the wedding couple and the state officials seated behind them. "Let Kumba Kastel's spirit appear," she says, evoking the name of the water goddess who watches over Gorée Island (and for whom the prison is named). She continues: "Your rifles cannot bring me down. The eagles soar through the sky. Ramatou the little bird flies under his wings. You are evil. I say you are evil. You've swallowed up the country. We'll eat your guts." When the drumming picks up, she begins to dance, strips off a piece of cloth from under her boubou and tosses it to Lamine, who lustfully sniffs the fabric, much to his bride's dismay. Majiguene steps up to challenge Karmen in a dance duel but Karmen, who has the crowd's support, tosses Majiguene to the ground. Lamine, who has now been seduced by Karmen, is reprimanded and ordered to arrest Karmen. As Karmen is being arrested she repeats, "You've swallowed up the country, but it will stick in your throat." The repetition of this line, Karmen's critique of a corrupt postcolonial state whose representatives (Angelique and Lamine) are undone by their attraction to Karmen, shows Karmen's determination to disrupt the order of things. Lamine leads Karmen away in ropes, but Karmen sings him a love song and easily escapes from him, again artfully (though obliquely) fleeing toward her freedom.

While both the opening sequence of the film and the wedding sequence begin with dancing and drumming and end with Karmen's escape, the cinematic cut from the first sequence to the second privileges interruption over continuity: the order that is disrupted or cut is both the official order of the state and the order, or logic, of the film. It is not quite clear what Karmen is doing at the wedding, why this seems to be her first stop after she leaves prison, whether she knows the couple, or what, if anything at all, Angelique has to do with Karmen's presence at the wedding. Karmen simply appears and none of these questions are ever answered. Eventually, Lamine (the Don José equivalent) falls madly in love with Karmen and neglects his duties. Karmen, however, does not return Lamine's love and, after allowing him to join her crew of smugglers, encourages him to go back to his fiancée. At the end of the film, as at the end of all Carmen stories, the scorned Lamine kills Karmen, an event predicted in Karmen's visions of death and painted-face ghosts throughout the film. But the plot of *Karmen Geï* is certainly not linear or straightforward as cuts, breaks, and musical sequence seem to determine much of the form and content. In this way, Karmen's errant disruptions and irruptions—her critiques of state power, her literal disruption of a heterosexual marriage, her disregard for conventions, and her fugitive spirit—are enacted in the film's cinematic syntax, just as much as in its jazz score.

Another way of putting this is that the film's structure, like its jazz soundtrack, puts into practice the waywardness and eccentricity that Karmen herself embodies. But I also suggest that there is a way in which Karmen's movements themselves—her dancing, her lovemaking, her fleeing—register as below-the-threshold practices of freedom that require her to learn how to maneuver and make space, or waves, inside existing structures. In this way, I understand Karmen's movements (along with the songs that accompany them) as being enabled in part by what Moten (2007, 33) sees as the "practice of rhythmic flexibility" in jazz that is tied to what he calls the fugitive law of movement. Moten explains this connection via Charles Mingus's concept of "rotary perception," a concept that I think sheds light on the relation and play between freedom, movement, and structures in *Karmen Geï*. Moten elaborates and quotes from Mingus's autobiography *Beneath the Underdog*:

> If you get a mental picture of the beat existing within a circle you're more free to improvise. People used to think the notes had to fall on the centre of the beats in the bar at intervals like a metronome, with three or four men in the rhythm section accenting the same pulse. That's like parade music or dance music. But imagine a circle surrounding each beat—each guy can play his notes anywhere in that circle and it gives him a feeling he has more space. The notes fall anywhere inside the circle but the original feeling for the beat isn't changed. If one in the group loses confidence,

somebody hits the beat again. The pulse is inside you. (quoted in Moten 2007, 38)

Minna Salami (2020) notes that these types of circular musical structures—she describes the hip-hop tradition known as a cypher, where emcees come together to share their rhythms in a circle—originated in call-and-response elements that traveled from different locations in Africa to various parts of the diaspora. And, like Moten, Salami finds the circle to be an apt way of describing how individuals express themselves in a group to which they are bound: "In the cypher, everyone brings their unique rhymes and styles, and each emcee is cheered on by the others. Participants are aware that, while there may be playful competitiveness, the variety of styles and voices only enriches the cypher as a whole" (92). What Salami and Moten both seem to be describing are circles of musicians, grooving and improvising, where no single individual is self-sufficient, where there are freedom and departure from the structure but also a responsibility to others in the circle and to a "rhythmic, de-centering preservation of structure" (Moten 2007, 39).

With this in mind, I see a type of cypher or rotary perception in the opening scene of *Karmen Geï* that is indicative of the fugitive law of movement at work throughout the film. Karmen sits, then stands, in the center of a circle surrounded by sabar drummers, drumming prisoners, and guards. She performs a solo and then brings in Angelique for a duet. She dances in the center of a courtyard, itself a circle, guarded by cannons and by more guards who watch from above. When the guards blow the whistle, the circle collapses: discipline and linearity cut the seductive improvisation, and the prisoners are herded down a tight, dark hallway into their cells, back to captivity. But as Mingus says above, "Each guy can play his notes anywhere in that circle and it gives him a feeling he has more space," a freedom of movement and flight. In *Karmen Geï* the circles formed in the opening sequence create space—they "teach and transform" (Salami 2020, 92)—and make new fugitive structures both for the soloist and for those who have kept the beat with her. Notably, though, they do not always prevent recapture or reintegration back into the structures from which the soloist wants to break. As Alexander Weheliye (2005, 63) puts it, "While the cut or break deviates from the main theme or primary beat, it does so only in dialogue with these forces."

Moreover, once the inmates are back within their cell another "practice of rhythmic flexibility" emerges: the call-and-response that celebrates Karmen's seduction of Angelique as a collective triumph. Karmen chants, "Where does it go?" and the women respond, "Wherever you like." Karmen then sings, "It goes here," and the women repeat, "Wherever you like." Though it is clear that the women are praising Karmen, the subtitled English translation does not make much apparent sense. However, in Wolof the women are chanting the words *asaaloo* and *asabombe*, words that have important meaning in Wolof folklore. Babacar M'Baye (2011, 120) writes, "Pamela Munro and Dieynaba Gaye say that the word *asaaloo* means 'to throw (something desirable) up in the air or away so that someone in a group can get it,' while the term *asabombe* is the response that the audience offers to the person who gives away things." Moreover, M'Baye explains, "This song is part of the large repertoire of under-explored African oral poetry that is known as *taasu*. . . . *Taasu* poetry is often expressed through a language that connotes desire and pleasure while having a covert subtext of opposition and belligerence against the established power or men" (120). Though it is Karmen who has seduced the warden, Karmen who leads the call-and-response, and Karmen who will gain her freedom, Karmen has also thrown something up in the air for the group to get. What that something is remains unclear, but it is something, it would seem, that is cause for celebration and hope, something that can resist, mock, and parody the existing social order through local cultural practices. This is why the women tap on the bars during Karmen's lovemaking scene: they are part of the circle she breaks from and is bound to, keeping the beat, registering the soloist's departure.

Later in the film, yet another musical sequence indicates how Karmen is keeping the beat for a long line of ancestral spirits to which she remains linked. After Lamine is imprisoned for failing to bring Karmen in to the authorities, Karmen and her band of smugglers break Lamine out of jail. On the run from the law, Karmen visits her mother's restaurant with Lamine. When the police arrive and demand to search Ma Penda's establishment, they are chased out by the musician Massigi, another one of Karmen's love interests. The patrons of the restaurant become a chorus that circles around the police and accuses them of "scheming and dealing" and disrespecting their mothers. After the police leave, Ma Penda orders the party to continue and Murray, who is physically present in this scene, begins to play his saxophone while the patrons celebrate the return of Karmen Geï, singing, "You've suffered so long but you've always had hope. Tell me you're here so I can hope again." But in order to understand the type of hope that Karmen represents, one must note that the song Massigi and the patrons sing to the police links Karmen to other Senegalese heroines, such as the women of Nder who burned themselves rather than being taken by Islamic invaders in 1820; or Aline Sitoé Diatta, queen of the Casamance region in Southern Senegal from 1940 to 1942, who was arrested and deported when she tried to prevent children from being taken by the French to fight in World War II (Dovey 2009, 248); or the water goddesses Mame Njare and Kumba Kastel. While Karmen flees and breaks free from the law, she is linked—through music, through call-and-response singing—to the rebellious Senegalese women who broke from established structure, who are bound together by a radical fugitive impulse, and who, through both their willful unruliness and subsequent suffering, all embody "the entanglement of escape and confinement" (Hartman 2019, 228).

The Contamination of Genre

What I have been arguing in my reading of Ramaka's film is that Karmen's queerness and waywardness are registered not only through her nonconforming sexuality but also through the way she both disrupts and inhabits certain structures in unruly ways. And, again, my focus is not simply the character of Karmen but also the eccentric structure of the film itself, a structure that borrows much from the improvisational and fugitive impulses of jazz and African musical forms. However, within a Senegalese context, what was most unsettling and disruptive was neither queer sexuality nor jazz but a different form of music: a holy song, or *khassaïd*, that was sung by Massigi during the funeral of the lonely and heartbroken Angelique, who drowned herself in the sea after Karmen's departure. In fact, after the film had been showing for about six weeks in Dakar, a *fatwa* was issued against the film by Serigne Moustapha Diakhaté, a high-ranking cleric in the Mouride Muslim brotherhood and the host of a religious radio show (Nelson 2011, 76). Though Diakhaté had not seen the film, he was incensed upon hearing that the funeral procession for Angelique, a "lesbian" and Catholic, was combined with a khassaïd of the Mouride founder Cheikh Amadou Bamba. The day after the fatwa was issued, between two hundred and three hundred Mourides and Baye Fall (members of a Mouride subgroup) stormed the theater where *Karmen Geï* was playing and, wielding machetes, swords, and clubs, threatened to burn it down. As Abdoulaye Babou of the Alliance of Forces of Progress stated, "The use of a poem of Cheikh Amadou Bamba . . . to accompany the burial of a lesbian in a Catholic cemetery is blasphemous" (quoted in Nelson 2011, 76).[10] Ramaka and his wife, the actress who plays Karmen, were out of the country at the time, but when they returned they received threatening phone calls (Nelson 2011, 76). In response, the government banned the film and impounded copies, and, despite Ramaka's efforts, *Karmen Geï* was not shown again in Senegal.

Though there was a confluence of factors contributing to the fatwa and subsequent censoring of the film, it seems that the argument that finally won out, according to the journalist Mari Maasilta, was that of verisimilitude. As Steven Nelson (2011, 79) puts it, "[The Mourides] argued that the meeting of Islam and Christianity, of a khassaïd and a lesbian who had committed suicide, of homosexuality at all, were somehow inauthentic representations, somehow not accurate social or religious depictions, in short, somehow not real."[11] While the Mourides could have criticized the explicit dancing at the beginning of the film, the lovemaking between Karmen and Angelique despite Senegal's laws (rarely invoked at that time) against homosexuality, or the scene of Angelique masturbating, these were not, in fact, their focus. They also did not seem to object to depictions of drug smuggling or the attacks against state power at a time when that power was held by a fellow Mouride, President Abdoulaye Wade. In a letter to the newspaper *Mouers*, Diakhaté demanded the removal not of any of these other potentially objectionable scenes but simply of the khassaïd itself, which he said is not to be used for entertainment purposes and was a threat to public security (Maasilta 2007, 265). In other words, what Diakhaté seems to have found the most egregious was the contamination of the genre of the khassaïd, a genre that is supposed to be, in a word, pure. Though the articulated argument might have been about verisimilitude, the real issue, it seems, had to do with various forms of pollution set off by an "improper" use of the khassaïd. Misuse of the khassaïd was a violation of a form (the holy song) that was queered in multiple ways: literally associated with a queer body and also made to signify beyond its primary, intended meaning. The fact that in French, spoken throughout Senegal, the word for gender and genre is the same (*genre*) adds multiple meanings to the queer blurring of *genre* that the khassaïd instantiated.

Interestingly, in a letter published in two local papers, Professor Madièye Mbodji defends the film by arguing that it depicts religious tolerance, a tolerance that is part of the very fabric of Senegalese society. Mbodji says that Ramaka had been influenced by an event ten years before he made the film in which a group of Baye Fall sang khassaïds at the funeral of a Catholic person (Maasilta 2007, 266). Mbodji counters the claim of inauthenticity by claiming that an event like the one in the film did indeed happen. For both Mbodji and Diakhaté, the khassaïd at a Catholic funeral contaminates, but to different ends: for one, contamination is a utopian vision of Senegalese cosmopolitanism and tolerance; for the other it equals a dangerous unraveling. It is also quite possible that Ramaka uses the poem by the anticolonial resister and spiritual leader Cheikh Amadou Bamba to infuse the film with what Bamba referred to as a "Sufi attitude" that was critical of hierarchal power regimes and that delegitimized "colonial power authority by emphasizing the moral power of the oppressed" (Packer 2019, 62) and to highlight Sufi beliefs about the moral legitimacy of the marginalized. In this sense, the khassaïd, like the rest of the soundtrack, is central to the film's politics and aesthetics, to the way it destabilizes hierarchies, linearity, and rules of law and genre and creates a space of fugitivity within the very structures of Senegalese culture.

"Tomorrow Is Another Day"

Though my reading of *Karmen Geï* thus far has been one that focuses on Karmen's defiance and Afri-queer fugitivity, several critics have pointed out that the film's liberationist politics are far from perfect. Carmela Garritano (2003, 159), for instance, writes that Karmen "becomes pure spectacle" who "never frees herself from the male gaze of the camera." Frieda Ekotto (2007, 75–76) reminds readers that Ramaka "could have changed the musical's narrative by keeping Karmen alive to continue her mission of liberating herself and other women" and notes that both Karmen and Angelique, the two characters who threaten the order and normativity of Senegalese society, wind up "erased." My own students, when I taught the film in a class on "Black World Cinema and Resistance," pointed out that Karmen seems to abandon her friends in prison, never trying to free them. I take these claims seriously and offer them here as an attempt to temper a euphoric reading of the film. I have been referring to Karmen and the film as "eccentric," a word that refers both to Karmen's unconventional practices and to her empowering uncontainability, but as Francesca Royster (2012, 15) notes, eccentricity offers "freedom of movement in an otherwise constraining situation." And as Ekotto and Garritano make clear, this "constraining situation" remains, despite the film's disruptive politics and form. *Karmen Geï* was, after all, literally constrained by the state in Senegal.

But *Karmen Geï* does indeed "make waves," as Karmen says of herself. In a scene toward the middle of the film, Karmen and Massigi are on the beach across from Gorée when Karmen picks up a flag from a fishing boat and starts waving at the ocean. Massigi asks her whom she is waving to, and Karmen responds, "My women, Massigi. And my jailer. They're there. Just there. In that lousy prison." Massigi smiles, seemingly understanding Karmen's feelings for Angelique, and says, "You're really quite a woman." Karmen replies, "No more than the others, Massigi. Only they don't show it. So as not to make waves." That Karmen should choose to frame her eccentricity and resistance in terms of making waves is important on at least three different levels. First, it is a reminder that throughout the film Karmen is linked to the water goddess Kumba Kastel, of whom she is said to be a descendant. Kumba Kastel is a local incarnation of the transatlantic Mami Wata spirit (Mami Wata is pidgin English for "Mother Water"), who is known as a seductress of both men and women and who can bring wealth, as Karmen brings to her fellow smugglers, as well as madness and death, as Karmen brings to Lamine and Angelique. Moreover, as M'Baye (2011, 118) notes, Kumba Kastel, which is also the name of the prison itself, "is an important force in Karmen's revolutionary struggle since she provides her with ambiguous identities and a dual capacity to do good and evil at once." In this sense, Karmen's resistance is linked to the ambiguous waves made by the water spirit herself. Second, the metaphor of the wave also perfectly captures the very way in which Karmen's disruption registers. A wave might constitute a disturbance, an unsettling, a breaking point even, but it is still part of the ocean, part of what is contained within. The cut or break Karmen makes, as is the case with Mingus's rotary perception, is made from within the system: it creates space and room but "the original feeling for the beat isn't changed." Finally, in this scene with Massigi on the beach, Karmen makes waves, but her gaze is toward a horizon, toward her lover and friends in the distance, and toward what is not yet visible. In this sense, I would like to suggest Karmen's/Karmen Geï's queerness is, as José Esteban Muñoz (2009, 11) suggests of queerness in general, "always on the horizon."

I therefore read Karmen's death as a failure by Ramaka to imagine another possibility for this queer Carmen, as Ekotto suggests, and, at the same time, as a gesture toward a "forward-dawning futurity" (Muñoz 2009, 1), one that might be otherwise. In the final sequence of the film, Karmen and Lamine approach each other in the catwalks above the stage where the famous griot Yandé Coudu Sène is singing over the sabar drummers. As the sound of Sène and the drummers fade out, Karmen sings to Lamine, "Love is a rebellious bird and no one can tame it. . . . Love isn't a business deal. If you want to kill me do it quickly and do it well. Tomorrow is another day." Lamine stabs Karmen as Sène's voice reemerges from the stage below, and Karmen falls to the ground. The visuals then fade to wobbly images of colorful painted faces lining a street, the same vision of death that Karmen had seen earlier in the film when reading her cards with her dear friend Samba and when being chased through the market by Lamine. The audience is reminded that Karmen has been marked by death and associated with ancestors and unearthly spirits throughout the film, that what Hartman (2019, 228) calls "the occult visions of other worlds" have never been in opposition to Karmen's waywardness but a very extension of its paradoxes of flight and captivity.

Moreover, Karmen's final, enigmatic line—"Tomorrow is another day"— points to the otherwise possibilities Karmen enacts throughout the film and recalls the hope that is sung about in Ma Penda's restaurant. If read within the context of Sufi spirituality, the line may also suggest that Karmen's reward for enduring hardship and suffering will come tomorrow, or in the afterlife. And though Karmen does not explicitly articulate allegiance to Bamba, Bamba's khassaïd sung by Massigi at her lover's funeral might gesture toward a Sufi understanding of "resistance not as an external attempt to affect change, but, rather, as the process of societal transformation from the individual soul outward" and might be another way of understanding the waves that Karmen makes, both in life and in death (Packer 2019, 64).[12] Once Karmen dies, she joins the ghosts and the painted-faced dead, and in the final image and final act of friendship, Samba carries Karmen's corpse, wrapped simply in fabric, to the cemetery on the island of Joal. As Samba carries Karmen, Sène can be heard on the soundtrack singing about Karmen, rejoined once more by the sabar drummers. The music exceeds the image, and the final cut skips the rhythm "back to another beginning which we have already heard" (Snead 1992, 221). Karmen is both contained—no longer a threat to order—and that which cannot be contained, as the music of Sène carries her story onward, haunting the film like the images of the painted dead but also implying that "tomorrow is another day," perhaps one that is open to new, queer horizons but also, perhaps, one in which making waves can go only so far.

A Mami Wata Story

Much like *Karmen Geï*, Safo's *Jezebel* is a film that makes waves, that resists and disrupts the status quo with wayward and eccentric forms of being, despite the fact that, very much unlike *Karmen Geï*, *Jezebel* is a film that on its most obvious level positions itself as a resistance to queerness. As I have noted above, *Jezebel* is both a remake and an expanded version of Safo's popular film *Women in Love*, a film that was, to my knowledge, one of the first Black African films ever to depict lesbianism.[13] Like Karmen, Jezebel—the name of both the film and a character—is the local incarnation of a Mami Wata spirit, and, as was also the case in *Karmen Geï*, this spirit is the source of a queer eccentricity that threatens social order. Mami Wata, whose name we can hear chanted in the *Jezebel* theme song, is typically portrayed as a mermaid spirit, but she can change shapes, genders, and identities at any given moment, and she often takes on different forms and myths in various local contexts. Although visual images of mermaid-like water deities first appeared in Africa thousands of years before recorded contact with Europeans, many scholars suggest that modern Mami Wata stories originated in the fifteenth century, the first era of intensified international trade between Africa and the West. However, Tobias Wendl (2001) argues that the contemporary religious cult of Mami Wata was enabled and shaped by the modern, photographic image and its transnational mobility. He argues that the images of Mami Wata seen today seem to be related to a poster brought to Nigeria by British colonialists in the early twentieth century. The image, reprinted in England and India and sold in West African markets, was a studio photograph of a Samoan snake-charmer woman taken in Hamburg in 1885. By the 1930s, the poster was delinked from its original context and commonly referred to as Mami Wata throughout West Africa, the Caribbean, and the Americas (Wendl 2001). Contemporary video images of Mami Wata, which are certainly not unique to Safo's films, owe much to the nonfixity and technological transportability of Mami Wata's image.

Little has been written specifically about Mami Wata's queerness, but a few works do allude to West African beliefs that Mami Wata is associated with nonconforming or "eccentric" sexuality. In *The Forger's Tale*, an account of the English poet and novelist John Moray Stuart-Young, who became a wealthy palm oil trader in Eastern Nigeria in the early 1900s, Stephanie Newell (2006) discusses how Stuart-Young came to be known as one of Mami Wata's wives. What Newell uncovers is how Stuart-Young, who slept with Igbo men, lived alone without family, and engaged in odd activities like building and rebuilding structures, came to be honored and accepted within the community. One of the reasons for this acceptance, she argues, is because he was widely understood to be a spouse of Mami Wata:

> Alongside his reclusive lifestyle, such "eccentric" activities sent loud and clear signals to the Igbo community, and Stuart-Young rapidly earned his third and most important local name . . . as a votary of the water spirit Mami Wata.
>
> Mami Wata (or Mammy Water) is a powerful spirit throughout West Africa, but her precise characteristics are as slippery as the fish scales on her tail. Intimately connected with the rise of international slavery and external trade along the rivers, she is known to be surrounded by Eke snakes and to "marry" chosen mortals to whom she brings great wealth. No man can be her husband, however, so her male spouses are often considered to be her "wives." Apart from this, she is a plural and shifting force, signifying different things in different places and times and along different West African rivers. Such fluidity makes it especially difficult to obtain historically accurate information about how Mami Wata was interpreted in the early twentieth century, for her meanings cannot simply

be extrapolated from the contemporary Nigerian narratives and shrines in which she currently appears. (Newell 2006, 100)

As Newell's analysis suggests, because Mami Wata is a figure typically associated with the seductions of fortune and wealth and with the inscrutable origins of consumer goods brought from elsewhere (Fabian 1997, 24), Stuart-Young's foreignness and his rise to wealth in Igbo-land therefore gave further credence to the rumors that he was one of her spouses. What Newell argues is that Stuart-Young's supposed marriage to Mami Wata made it "possible for this single, childless, boy-loving man" to live a queer life without any social repercussions (Newell 2006, 106). His homosexuality, then, did not signify a particular identity but was "simply one of several signs of a spiritual association with the water deity" (102).

In her memoir *Embracing My Shadow*, Unoma Azuah (2020) describes how she, as a young lesbian in Eastern Nigeria in the mid-1980s, was also widely understood to be a spouse of Mami Wata. However, here homosexuality was seen as a sin, albeit one that could be eliminated with the removal of the Mami Wata spirit. Azuah recounts her experience with a local pastor who tried to release the spirit in front of Azuah's church congregation. The pastor took Azuah by the neck and yelled,

> Water spirits shall not possess you. These demons that serve the goddess of the deep seas, Mammy water, will be removed from you! That Mammy water and all her servant spirits do not want you to have a husband. She has sealed your fate with your lust for women because she has maintained you as a wife in the marine underworld. That evil spirit of lesbianism must get out of you. I shall break that chain of bondage she has placed on you! (Azuah 2020, 70–71)

Azuah's memoir ends when she relocates to the United States, but she has told me that when she goes back to Asaba in Nigeria for visits, her neighbors still view her as a spouse of Mami Wata. That she lives "overseas" and has no male spouse or biological children, she says, only validates this belief, and despite the fact that her pastor called Mami Wata a demon, Azuah says that neighbors line up to ask her for money, assuming that Mami Wata has made her a wealthy woman in the United States.[14] Though these two examples both come from Eastern Nigeria and not Ghana, they demonstrate what Newell refers to as the "slipperiness" of Mami Wata, a slipperiness that resurfaces in *Women in Love* and in *Jezebel* in ways that are quite similar to what Azuah and Newell describe, ways that also overlap with what M'Baye says of the Kumba Kastel/

Mami Wata water spirit who provides Karmen with "ambiguous identities and a dual capacity to do good and evil at once." What Newell and Azuah's writings also demonstrate is a form of rarely (and just barely) articulated queerness that is rooted in West African spirituality, for even though Mami Wata is associated with otherness, she is nevertheless understood to be an African water deity.[15] In this way, Mami Wata films register a form of indigenous queerness that is normally just hinted at, that is beneath the surface or threshold.

In Ramaka's portrayal of Kumba Kastel—a Mami Wata spirit not part of a Christian imaginary—the queerness invoked seems to be like that of Stuart-Young: a sign of eccentricity and spiritual affiliation that is ambiguous and generally accepted. But in Safo's very Christian-inspired films, Mami Wata is clearly associated with what Azuah's pastor called the "evil spirit of lesbianism." The anthropologist Serena Dankwa, in fact, notes that Safo's *Women in Love* was a film that, because of the way it linked lesbianism to dangerous spiritual forces and because of its wide availability throughout Ghana at the time of its release, proved to be damaging and harmful to the communities of women who sleep with women in southern Ghana, who took the film to be a spiritual warning. In the course of her fieldwork, Dankwa found many women referring to Safo's film as a cautionary tale about what might happen when working-class girls become involved with wealthy women (Dankwa 2009, 197). Dankwa explains that though it is difficult to tell to what extent stories about greed-driven lesbians "circulated prior to the film's production and to what extent they were triggered by it, derogatory stories about their Mami Wata bonds are particularly salient in the Ga areas of Accra" where the film takes place (197). Furthermore, such stories "reproduce Akan stereotypes of the coastal Ga people as lacking discretion and being inclined to blunt and 'shameless' behaviours, including same-sex practices—allegedly due to their early exposure to European colonialists," and they present same-sex desire not "as a force external to contemporary Ghanaian society, but as a spirit that possesses urban middle-class women who are obsessed with wealth, power, and modern consumerism" (197). It is important, then, not to forget that though the film focuses on the occult and spirits, many people, queer and straight alike, took it to be a film about actual queer-identified women and the actual "dangers" they pose or encounter. In other words, for many audiences the film did not, in fact, register as resistant or transgressive but actually warned against sexual transgression and the greed sometimes associated with it. In the next chapter, on Nollywood, I discuss in much more detail the ways in which West African video films reproduce pathologizing discourses around queerness, a discussion that, in some ways, is more suited to the Nigerian context because there is a much larger archive of gay-themed films that circulate there and because these films proliferated as Nigerians were debating and discussing laws that were aimed at imposing harsher prison sentences on same-sex practices. But for the moment, I want to discuss how Safo's *Jezebel*, perhaps unintentionally, uses the properties of video technology to showcase Mami Wata's eccentricity and inherent unknowability—which, in turn, sheds light on how indigenous queer spirits might open up new forms of queer possibilities and Afri-queer fugitivity. In other words, if one de-emphasizes the narrative of the film that positions lesbianism as demonic and focuses instead on the sensations that Jezebel, a sort of video femme-fatale, transmits, the story of her eccentricity and waywardness becomes, like Mami Wata, much more slippery and ambiguous, much more queer.

The Occult Worlds of Video Film

While Ghana's video film industry operates on a smaller scale than Nigeria's colossal industry, it actually came into being slightly before Nollywood and is now, because it often shares actors and producers with Nollywood, often discussed in conjunction with Nollywood. Both industries, in fact, began in the late 1980s and early 1990s, and both were made possible only because of the availability of inexpensive video technology. Though the widespread use of digital cameras is now eliminating the disparities between celluloid and video, when the Nigerian and Ghanaian industries began, they distinguished themselves from the Francophone African celluloid films—films, like *Karmen Geï*, that most often screened at international art theaters—because they were extensions of African popular culture and therefore appeared in mostly African spaces like video parlors, barbershops, street corners, and private homes. As was the case in the United States, "home video," as it was originally called, was first introduced into West Africa as a bootleg technology, as a blank format for recording. In the United States, consumers first used VHS primarily for recording television programs for later playback, or what is called "timeshifting." In West Africa, cassettes were originally used in piracy networks to dub and distribute foreign films.[16] But by the late 1980s and early 1990s worsening economic conditions in both Nigeria and Ghana led to the collapse of state film and television production, creating an opening that entrepreneurs and media practitioners who were being squeezed out of the formal economy were able to take advantage of. Using cheap video technology that had become widely available, Ghanaians and Nigerians began making their own movies, leading to what became known as the video boom.

Like the Hollywood melodramas, Indian love stories, and Latin American *telenovelas* that influenced them, these early West African videos focus on stories in which individuals struggle to maintain or obtain status, wealth, sexual security, and generational continuity against the overwhelming forces of a morally corrupt society. Following other media forms produced within the melodramatic mode, video films continue to be stories in which social conflicts are expressed through personal feelings, private dilemmas, and bodily sensations rather than through direct ideological contestations with the state. In both Ghana and Nigeria, the films that were credited with initiating the success of the industry were films that "typify the deep ambivalences generated by global capitalism" (Garritano 2013, 63) and that then tie this ambivalence to occult forces.[17] In this way, these earlier video films are linked to the notion of the occult economy theorized in the work of Jean and John Comaroff. For the Comaroffs, "occult economies" designate economies in which wealth, because it has been separated from formal, discernible labor practices, appears through seemingly supernatural or mysterious networks (Comaroff and Comaroff 2000). In other words, because money is increasingly acquired through fraud, speculation, pyramid schemes, and scams, and because its sources are inscrutable, wealth appears *as if* by magic, even when magic per se is not involved. But I want to emphasize that in occult videos, rumors about witchcraft, vampires, or water spirits are not just tied to economic anxieties; they are expressed through the conventional focal points of cinematic melodrama: love triangles; the instability of the middle-class, heterosexual family; scopophilic pleasure; and women's virtue, or lack thereof. I use the term "occult melodrama" to highlight how the occult and melodramatic aspects of these films should be taken together in order to focus on the centrality of gender and women's sexuality in these types of stories.

Although melodrama is a protean form, most scholars have followed Peter Brooks's argument in *The Melodramatic Imagination* that suggests that melodrama emerges from a secular society where sacred certainties can no longer provide assurance and ready-made meaning to individuals. Melodrama, Brooks (1985, 15) claims, is born in the wake of the "shattering of the myth of Christendom" when a "hierarchically cohesive society" can no longer validate social life; thus, melodrama exists in order to locate the "moral occult," the hidden forces of virtue in a desacralized society. But West African video film emerges at a moment when religion and Christianity in particular are expanding, not shattering, when a weakened nation gave rise to a dramatic expansion of Pentecostalism as churches stepped in to assuage and explain economic woes. Between the years of 1987 and 1992—the very years the video industry began to take off—the number of Pentecostal churches in Ghana grew by about 43 percent (van Dijk 2001, 219). Thus, many of the Ghanaian occult stories reflect a period of general economic uncertainty as much as they embody, both directly and indirectly, a Pentecostal ethos.[18] As Birgit Meyer (2004) suggests, this requires a rethinking of Brooks's foundational claims about melodrama. Meyer writes that the Ghanaian videos, which circulate in a context that is certainly not desacralized, act as a form of revelation: "The camera appears to trade upon Pentecostal claims of 'throwing light' into the 'powers of darkness'" (Meyer 2006b, 432). Meyer's work highlights Pentecostalism's emphasis on light, public presence, revelation, and visual witnessing, all of which, according to Meyer, characterize many of the West African video films produced in what she calls a "Pentecostalite" style (2004, 92).

What I find particularly interesting, especially when thinking about the way that Jezebel's queer eccentricity opens new and decolonized ways of knowing and seeing, is that the Pentecostalite films Meyer describes, of which *Jezebel* is certainly an example, highlight "a dialectics of revelation and concealment" that is also inherent to video technology itself (Meyer 2006b, 435). Laura Marks (2002, 13), in her discussion of "video haptics," argues that because video's electronic images are always impermanent and incomplete, video requires "giving up visual control"—it necessitates a willingness to involve the body's entire sensory apparatus in filling in the gaps left on the surface of the image. The significantly lower levels of pixel density, the variabilities and decay of the image, and the lower contrast ratios mean that video provides less detail than film and gives viewers an incomplete amount of visual information.[19] For Marks, the inherent "unknowability" of video lends an eroticism to the medium.[20]

Though I find Marks's theories much less applicable to Ghanaian and Nigerian videos made in the realist mode, I do agree that there is something sensuous in the partial visibility exhibited in the occult melodrama genre and in the ephemeral and unstable quality of images of the spiritual world just beyond one's control. For Marks (2002, xvi), "What is erotic is the ability to move between control and relinquishing, between being giver and receiver. It's the ability to have your sense of self, your self-control, taken away and restored." In occult melodrama, this type of dynamic is precisely what occurs: the viewer's sense of power and visual mastery is diminished; then, several hours later, everything is restored through a "happy" and expectedly Christian ending. In *Jezebel*, the "happy" ending restores the possibility of heterosexual reproduction and futurity, but what I argue is that the lingering unknowability—inherent

FIGURE 1.5. Still from *Jezebel* (2007–8). Susu (*left*) kisses a reluctant Nana Ekua (*right*).

both in video technology and in the waywardness of Mami Wata herself—also leaves open the possibility of a more slippery queer future, a future related to pasts where "impossible Africans" might find kindred spirits.

Jezebel Rises

Jezebel begins when a young working-class woman, Nana Ekua, confides in her friend Susu that she is having financial difficulties because her husband, Mark, needs one million cedis (the Ghanaian currency) to finish his studies. Susu laughs at the small sum of money her friend needs and pulls out a bulging envelope from the glove compartment of her shiny new SUV. Susu then explains that Nana Ekua can have her own car, and all the wealth she wants, if she agrees to sleep with Susu. Nana Ekua is initially shocked and disgusted by the idea but consents after minimal persuasion (figure 1.5). The next day Susu begins to initiate Nana Ekua into her privileged lifestyle. She dresses Nana Ekua in more fashionable clothes—short shorts, a low-cut tank top, and sunglasses—and takes her friend to the local car dealership. But once Nana Ekua has selected her car, Susu reminds her that she will need to fuel the car, and that to do so she will need to be able to get men to give her money. Susu says that she can arrange things so that when a man tries to sleep with her, he will become flaccid. That way, Susu explains, Nana Ekua can get money without having to give. In essence, Susu is describing a situation in which Nana Ekua will be a prostitute, albeit one without what the Comaroffs refer to as "ordinary labor costs." Nana Ekua is still hesitant, but she agrees.

Nana Ekua is then taken to the coast in order to join the cult of the spirit Jezebel. Jezebel's face appears superimposed against the backdrop of the ocean (figure 1.6). The water spirit is then summoned by a priestess dressed in a white robe and a silver cross. Jezebel emerges from the water and begins to initiate a frightened Nana Ekua by kissing her on the lips. As the two women kiss, the soundtrack turns to ominous studio music while the film rapidly cuts back and forth between the priestess's cross and Nana Ekua's initiation kiss. The music and movement create a sense of moral panic and anxiety as Nana Ekua's gaze focuses on the cross, reminding her of the un-Christian nature of her acts. The attention given to the cross in this scene situates the cult of Jezebel within a Christian tradition that is filled with false prophets, with agents of the devil impersonating the faithful. In the Bible, Jezebel—the evil wife of King Ahab—is not only someone who is sexually promiscuous and manipulative but also one who adorns herself and masquerades as a servant to God.

Here Jezebel is not simply a Biblical harlot: she is also, as noted above, a Mami Wata spirit who aids her followers—both men and women—in finding power, riches, and success. However, in many Mami Wata stories, the spirit demands sacrifices: pledging oneself to Mami Wata often entails choosing material success over a family life, a choice that can be traced to colonial-era

FIGURE 1.6. Still from *Jezebel* (2007–8). Jezebel's transparent image appears superimposed over the ocean.

interpretations of European lifestyles based on colonial officers, traders, and missionaries who, much like Stuart-Young, came to West Africa with an abundance of goods but no families (Frank 2008, 116). In *Jezebel*, Nana Ekua essentially gives up the ability to have children since men will no longer be able to attain an erection around her. However, her husband, Mark, is able to overcome the power of Jezebel through prayer. By invoking Jesus Christ before sex, he is able to penetrate and impregnate his wife. This angers Jezebel, who vows to destroy their marriage and to take the blood of their baby. As part of her revenge plan, Jezebel emerges from the sea, takes on a human form, and shoots fireballs that materialize into luxury automobiles and Jezebel's yellow Hummer (figures 1.7 and 1.8).

FIGURES 1.7 AND 1.8. Stills from *Jezebel* (2007–8). Jezebel shoots a fireball that transforms into a yellow Hummer.

This scene is quite likely based upon actual Mami Wata rumors that were circulating in Ghana in the 1990s when Safo first made *Women in Love*. In her discussion of *Women in Love*, Meyer (2008) describes a rumor about a policeman who reportedly witnessed a large jeep drive out of the sea. The jeep was full of perfumes and cosmetics and was driven by a light-skinned woman. Once the jeep reached Makola, Accra's main market, it disappeared from sight. A similar story circulated about a woman who saw a ball of light emerge from the sea and transform into a flashy car filled with luxury goods. After witnessing the event, the woman went mad and lost her senses. Meyer reads these stories as expressing the ambivalent views held by urban Ghanaian audiences at the time toward modern life and toward the goods they consumed. However, I would like to suggest that when such stories are placed on screen, they cannot simply be understood as responses to moral and economic anxieties. When the invisible world is made manifest in visual media, it is done in order to elicit an affective response. Therefore, the portrayal of Jezebel strolling along the beach and shooting fireballs that turn into luxury automobiles is more than just an explanation or metaphor for the hieroglyphic nature of capitalist consumption and more than just a visualization of invisible forces in a globalized world.

The special effects, the whizzing fireballs, and the morphing cars create a sensational scene of intensities that place the multisensory anxieties of contemporary urban Ghanaian life on vivid display. As Jezebel performs her magic, her headband and yellow tank top (which conveniently match the Hummer) sparkle in the strong sunlight and complement the shining flashes that emerge from her hand. The glittering light bounces off of her attire and turns the previously invisible spirit into a hypervisible body that literally reflects the visual effects of conspicuous consumption and that saturates the screen with an excess of light amplifying Jezebel's occult power. But as Jezebel conjures her cars, the soundtrack loops the chorus of the *Jezebel* theme song, a hypnotic chant that repeats the phrase "agents in the kingdom of Jezebel" layered over the sound of pigs snorting. Here, the rhythmic music—the *melos* of melodrama—transmits disgust by associating Jezebel's material excess and sexuality with the dirt and shamelessness of a pig. Thus, the scene captures the erotic pleasure-anxiety inherent in occult video film by synchronizing the glistening and glamorous with the morally abhorrent and socially destructive. Jezebel is "willful, reckless, troublesome, riotous," and, of course, "inimical to those deemed proper and respectable" (Hartman 2019, 227). And though Jezebel is nearly captured by the scopophilic gaze—as the camera is focused on a scantily clad Jezebel and her scantily clad female lovers—Jezebel is also a slippery, fugitive, constantly shifting figure who is perhaps sensed just as much as she is seen. Layered over the scopophilic pleasure, then, is what I call a *spectraphilic pleasure*: a pleasure derived from feeling and sensing the occult's presence, from experiencing the wonder and anxiety of a visible invisibility that, in Safo's film, can also be read as a queer pleasure.

In her work on video and digital media, Laura Mulvey (2006) suggests ways that new media open up different ways of seeing that help to explain the type of gaze I see at work in *Jezebel*. She argues that when Hollywood films are watched on video and on small screens, the process of identification is weakened. She argues that the spectator who can pause, skip, and repeat moments in the film becomes more fascinated with images and small gestures than with a plot or a character that otherwise holds the spectator in place. Mulvey (2006, 166) asserts that films watched on new media formats become "feminized": "In this reconfiguration of 'fetishistic spectatorship,' the male figure is extracted from dominating the action and merges into the image. So doing, he, too, stops rather than drives the narrative, inevitably becoming an overt object of the spectator's look, against which he had hitherto been defended." Thus, the cinematic viewing arrangement that Mulvey had in mind when she wrote "Visual Pleasure" (1975)—in which seated audiences (taking on a masculine subject position) gaze at a large screen as a celluloid filmstrip is projected from an apparatus behind them—no longer applies. In *Jezebel's* case, small screens allow the audience, which often consists of friends, family, or community members, to collectively experience the sensuality, imagery, and gestures of occult figures that they typically only get to hear about through rumors.

Moreover, in *Jezebel*, Safo plays with these new configurations of spectatorship and gender by delinking the male gaze from the power of visual technology. For instance, as her first act in destroying the marriage between Mark and Nana Ekua, the now-human Jezebel approaches Mark as a potential business partner. She then invites Mark to her mansion where he encounters an entire swimming pool of Jezebel devotees. He is clearly aroused by the sight and asks Jezebel if he can film them on his cell phone. Jezebel consents, but when she needs one of her followers to conjure up a drink from the bottom of the pool, she tells Mark that he must turn away. Jezebel hands Mark the bottle of wine and tells him it is a gift for his wife. He snaps a photo of himself with the spirit-woman and leaves for home. However, when Mark tries to show Nana Ekua a photo of Jezebel, Jezebel, the wayward woman who has eluded capture, has disappeared from the image. Mark appears standing by himself. In this scene, Jezebel forces Mark to turn away; then she disappears. Her ability to shape-shift and take flight therefore vitiates the power of Mark's gaze, just as she impedes, albeit only temporarily, his sexual abilities. It is Jezebel and not Mark who holds the power of the gaze and who can in fact deny or grant her own to-be-looked-at-ness. Thus, the spectraphilic gaze, unlike a scopophilic gaze, allows its object to slip away and flee, "to wander, to be unmoored, adrift" (Hartman 2019, 227). In *Jezebel* eroticism resides not in the ability to master women but in Jezebel's erotic autonomy, in her ability to confound the boundaries between the visible and invisible, to be both attainable and unattainable, near and far. Like Karmen, she is an Afri-queer fugitive who attempts to elude capture, and, like the video signals that generate her image, Jezebel is never fixed and never fully visible. Her affective presence is spectral: she is a mysterious but nevertheless constantly felt force.

"In the Nick of Time"

At the end of part 2 of *Jezebel*, Nana Ekua has fallen into a coma after drinking the bottle of wine given to Mark by Jezebel. As Nana Ekua sleeps, Jezebel appears as an apparition and tells Nana Ekua that she will go mad until her baby is born. Nana Ekua wakes up on a strange beach and begins wandering the streets of Accra. Her punishment, the literal loss of her senses, ejects her from the affective human community around her and further removes her from the realm of respectable citizenship. Parts 3 and 4 are occupied with finding a cure for Nana Ekua's madness and with her family's gradual discovery of the cult of Jezebel. Under hypnosis Nana Ekua reveals the cult's secrets. She tells her hypnotist almost exactly what Safo told me about cabals of lesbians occupying positions of power in Ghana: "There are many people who have joined the sisterhood. They are in corporations. They are the movers and the shakers in this country. . . . You barely know and you can't imagine." But, of course, the audience already knows. They have already spent parts 1 and 2 imagining. The point of the film's denouement, then, is not to reveal any secrets but to restore the order that Jezebel has overturned.

One of the common features of melodrama is that its endings always provide moral closure to the events that have unfolded throughout the story. As Linda Williams (2002, 30) writes, "Melodrama's recognition of virtue involves a dialectic of pathos and action—a give and take of 'too late' and 'in the nick of time.'" In the final installment of *Jezebel* this dialectic is neatly resolved, as pathos turns into action and the water spirit is killed just in time to restore the heteronormative and reproductive family. Thus, a "happy" ending requires releasing Nana Ekua from her punishment and reestablishing her virtue as a victim of the social forces around her. In essence, the ending depends on distinguishing the child-bearing Nana Ekua from the Jezebel devotees who are associated with lesbianism, prostitution, and witchcraft, all of which are figured as hypersexualized, animalistic, greedy, and nonreproductive threats to the survival of Christian virtue and "honest" capitalism. The rescue "in the nick of time," therefore, literally preserves time by saving both Nana Ekua and the social order itself from a nonprocreative time of "no future."[21]

But *Jezebel*'s final battle scene also goes beyond the tidy moral resolution that saves future generations from the "too late" scenario, in part because, as Bliss Cua Lim (2009, 25) argues, fantastic cinema always "exceeds the confines of secular, homogeneous time." And indeed, in *Jezebel*'s final scene, video technology turns the hidden occult world into a magical visual force field that suggests a "too late," an excess of spectraphilic imagery at odds with the "in the nick of time" narrative. As Nana Ekua lies on a table in what looks like a modern office building, she is surrounded by Jezebel's priestess and a group of followers. Just as the priestess is about to stab Nana Ekua, a pastor and his followers break into the building. A spiritual battle ensues in which Jezebel hurls fire clouds and radiating neon discs at the Christians, who volley them back with the Bible (figure 1.9). Red lightning bolts then strike the building and turn into flames that surround and destroy the Jezebel devotees so that Nana Ekua and her child both have a chance to be born (again). But though the narrative suggests that Jezebel has been contained, audiences attuned to her occult prowess might sense that Jezebel, defined by her unknowability, is uncontainable and uncapturable, that she might be able to reemerge once the flames have disappeared.

It is also worth pointing out that, just as Karmen's resistance and waywardness might be read within the context of a Sufi ethos, Jezebel's can be situated

FIGURE 1.9. Still from *Jezebel* (2007–8). In the final battle, Jezebel and her followers shoot fire at the pastor, who battles it back with his Bible as Nana Ekua remains comatose on a table between them.

within "the aesthetic possibilities" of what Ashon Crawley calls Blackpentecostalism. Recognizing that the Pentecostal Church has "proclivities for classism, sexism, homophobia, and transphobia," Crawley insists that there is nevertheless something in the aesthetic practices of Blackpentecostalism, in the sensual and affective experiences of shouting, dancing, whooping, speaking in tongues, and so on, "that serve as antagonistic to the very doctrines of sin and flesh that so proliferate within the world" (2017, 24). What Crawley finds in his own experience in Black Pentecostal churches is that the resources for critiquing and analyzing sexism, homophobia, transphobia, and classism exist within the otherwise possibilities and the "plurality and plentitude already within the world" of Blackpentecostalism (24). By including Crawley's understanding of Blackpentecostalism here, I suggest that, inasmuch as the ending of *Jezebel* might seem to save a heteronormative future, its affective excesses of fireballs and lightning bolts and flames flashing across the screen also open it up to a number of queer, spectral, and fugitive possibilities, possibilities that are enabled by Blackpentecostalism's disruptions and breaks with the known (5) and that seem to be key to the aesthetics of Pentecostalite video film. In this sense, one can see *Jezebel*'s Pentecostalite style as enabling rather than foreclosing queerness, despite the narrative closure that kills off the queer water spirit. And indeed, at the end of the day, Jezebel, a slippery and shifting water spirit who has existed for centuries in West African indigenous thought—who, in other words, is as much a figure of the past as she is of the future—might not be easily deterred by a bit of fire, and she might not be interested in submitting herself to a heteronormative future that she has continually defied. It seems likely, in fact, that her nimble practices of disruption might continue to quietly reverberate at an unearthly frequency. Though Jezebel's unmoored practices of resistance clearly do not align with legible strategies of queer opposition, as in the case of Karmen, this Mami Wata spirit makes waves that unsettle and disturb and that spread waywardly toward a horizon.

The Present Future

Though both *Karmen Geï* and *Jezebel* do open themselves up to multiple queer "tomorrows" or "horizons," it is important to note that each film was released just before, or just as, a regional homophobia erupted and spread to both Senegal and Ghana. In 2008, for instance, photos of a gay wedding in Senegal (that had occurred in 2006) were published in a journal and used to whip up moral panic just ahead of local elections in which the religious leader Imam Mbaye Niang was running on promises to rid Senegal of corrupting forces that were supposedly destabilizing Senegalese society (Coly 2019, 37). As Coly argues, this event shifted public discourse around homosexuality, leading to antigay vigilantism—most famously, the exhumation of a gay man's body by a mob in 2009—that had been absent from Senegal before 2008 (33). While Senegal was, as Coly notes, at one point considered the "gay capital of Francophone Africa," the events of 2008 and the political opportunism and zealousness exhibited by leaders unleashed a violent wave of homophobia. The tomorrow that the 2001 *Karmen Geï* imagines, then, might be the today that Coly describes, and the controversy surrounding the film, and around Angelique's burial, a harbinger of more violence yet to come. Or, to put it differently, the waves that Karmen made might since have been washed out by the more recent wave of homophobia.

Ghana, like Senegal, had experienced relatively little public homophobia before this period. But it too was swept up in the multiple surges of "unprecedented homophobic violence and criminal crackdowns on gender nonconforming individuals" that occurred in several high-profile incidents in countries like Kenya, Malawi, Nigeria, and Uganda as African leaders began to compete with each other for moral superiority (Coly 2019, 27). Kathleen O'Mara (2013, 188) discusses an early instance of gay moral panic in Ghana in 2006, when rumors of a supposed planned gay conference, or "homoconference" as it was called in the media, incited weeks of condemnation. Though the conference turned out to be a media hoax, Dankwa (2021, 51) notes that it marked a shift from the more discreet and indirect ways Ghanaians spoke about sexuality and became the catalyst for "noisy public debates" and "an ongoing outcry against the sexualization of the public sphere and the perceived threat of immoral practices attributed to the West." Wisdom John Tettey (2016, 91) points out that, beginning in 2010—when Ghana's first antigay protests were organized—the Ghanaian media began to more regularly and systematically paint homosexuality "as a creeping menace . . . corrupting the youth and undermining the heteronormative foundations of society." More recently, in the first half of 2021, the first LGBT+ center in Accra was forced to close its doors following police raids and threats of violence only months after opening, while twenty-one queer activists in the Ghanaian town of Ho were arrested for holding a human rights training session. In many ways, then, *Jezebel* might be read as anticipating these types of reactions to queer contestations.

But at the same time that I think it is important to acknowledge this context and to temper overly exuberant readings of waywardness and Afri-queer fugitivity, I am also wary of slotting either *Karmen Geï* or *Jezebel* into any sort of linear timeline or reading them only in relation to homophobia. In other words, the films are just as likely to foreshadow the future (the now-present) homophobia discussed in the above paragraphs as they are to point to an even more future future that opens to new queer freedoms and possibilities. (Indeed, it might also be difficult to separate the current wave of homophobic violence from the recent expansion of queer activism—and even explicitly queer feminist activism—in Senegal and Ghana.) What I am suggesting, then, is that these two films, both remakes or remixes of prior stories, both with new and remade emphases on fugitivity and flight, might produce a kind of time that, as Nyong'o (2018) suggests, opens space for something beyond, a space that is neither progressive nor regressive but that allows for a particular emergence to occur. In this sense, both *Karmen Geï* and *Jezebel* are films that can be read as cuts, breaks, or flashes of intensity that make waves in ways that do not register as part of any linear or legible social movement. In their eccentricity, they open up new ways of knowing and being that disturb the heteropatriarchal status quo in errant and fugitive ways, ways that are also very much tied to past knowledge systems and resistance figures. But I also want to underscore that I am reading these films in this way—as particular forms of disruption—because of the structures of the films themselves, because these two films, within their national contexts, do seem to flash up and break away from expectations and constraining structures. In their very particular cinematic languages, both films depict "impossible Africans" in a way that suggests the multiple possibilities that attach to queer women's eroticism; at the same time, however, the films also continue to register the various impossibilities of queer Africans at this particular moment.

Touching Nollywood

From Negation to Negotiation
in Queer Nigerian Cinema

Seven years after Safo's *Women in Love* and two years after Ramaka's *Karmen Geï*, the filmmaker Emem Isong wrote and produced *Emotional Crack* (2003; directed by Lancelot Imasuen), which became the first Nigerian film to make homosexuality central to its plot and to feature an actual relationship between a same-sex couple.[1] When I interviewed Isong in Lagos in 2010, she told me that she was originally inspired to write the film because she herself was being courted by a young woman who was sending loving text messages.[2] Although Isong did not return the girl's affection, she was intrigued that same-sex love existed in Nigeria, despite the fact that there were no public representations or discussions of it. In the film, Crystal, played by the leading Nollywood actress Stephanie Okereke, is an educated woman married to a patriarchal and abusive husband, Chudi, played by Nollywood front man Ramsey Nouah. Chudi forbids Crystal from leaving the house without permission, beats her mercilessly when he finds out she has taken an accounting job, and regularly returns late into the night from evenings with his mistress Camilla, played by another Nollywood powerhouse, Dakore Egbuson-Akande. When Chudi, Crystal, and

Camilla all attend the same party and Camilla witnesses Chudi slapping Crystal, the mistress's sympathies and affections turn toward her boyfriend's wife. Camilla begins to court Crystal by inviting her over for dinner and presenting her with gifts. Although Crystal is shocked at first, eventually the two begin an affair that leaves Crystal feeling more confident and free. She even stops cooking dinner every night for her husband.

But while Camilla falls head over heels for Crystal, Crystal seems torn as to whether this is a lifestyle she can continue, given the societal repercussions involved. Eventually, she ends the relationship and tells Camilla, "This is not me." The film—perhaps intentionally—leaves it vague as to whether Crystal is rejecting Camilla or is reacting to social pressures to end their affair. Camilla does not take the breakup lightly and, as revenge, she lures Crystal into bed one last time and arranges to have Chudi walk in on them (figure 2.1). Chudi reacts harshly and kicks Crystal out of their home, despite the fact that he too has cheated on her with Camilla. But, at the end of the film, when a rejected and now deranged Camilla invades Crystal's mother's home and attacks Crystal with a knife (figure 2.2), Chudi saves the day. He protects his wife and, in the film's final moment, Camilla turns the knife on herself. Though the ending seems abrupt, Isong told me that in order for *Emotional Crack* to be acceptable in Nigeria, there had to be a way to salvage the marriage of Crystal and Chudi, and this was the only way she knew how.[3]

FIGURE 2.1. Still from *Emotional Crack* (2003). Crystal (*left*) and Camilla (*right*) are caught in the act by Crystal's husband.

FIGURE 2.2. Still from *Emotional Crack* (2003). Camilla attempts to kill Crystal.

While *Emotional Crack* does perpetuate several stereotypes about queer women, branding Camilla as violent and unstable and suggesting that Crystal was led into a lesbian affair only after being mistreated by a man, the film was incredibly progressive for its time and place. Both Crystal and Camilla are complex characters who are treated with care and sympathy. They seem to fall genuinely in love and find comfort and safety in each other. In fact, the theme song of the film—a tune about the trials and tribulations of love—plays at moments when Crystal is distressed about both Chudi and Camilla, indicating that both are indeed legitimate and difficult relationships. Because of the film's nuances and complexities, it was, for many years, Isong's most famous film, and at a time when almost no Nollywood movies played internationally, Isong was invited to show *Emotional Crack* at the African Film Festival in New York City. The film can also be credited with launching the careers of its lead actresses. In fact, at a Women in Nollywood conference I attended in Lagos in 2010, seven years after *Emotional Crack* was made, the film was still being praised and singled out for its ability to address taboo topics and portray strong, independent women. Though the success of *Emotional Crack* inspired producers and directors to churn out films that depicted lesbianism, those that followed did so in a much more sensationalized manner and without the nuances of Isong's film. In the dozens of queer-themed Nollywood movies that followed *Emotional Crack*, women became lesbians only because they were interested in money, because they were possessed by the devil or were the objects of juju (witchcraft), or because they were raised by overbearing parents. When gay men began being the focal point of films in 2010 they were also treated as dangerous and sexually predatory.

Whereas chapter 1 of *Queer African Cinemas* provided a formal analysis of two films that demonstrated practices of waywardness and Afri-queer fugitivity, this chapter has a different aim and scope. Here my intention is to provide a history of queer cinema in Nigeria—the African country that has produced by far the largest number of feature films depicting same-sex desire—and to discuss the changing ways that Nollywood films perform resistance and address audiences, or touch them, at an emotional level. The first half of this chapter examines the treatment of homosexuality in Nollywood films before the 2014 signing of the Same Sex Marriage Prohibition Act (SSMPA), which further criminalized consensual same-sex relationships in Nigeria and added prison sentences for same-sex couples who cohabitate or show affection in public, as well as for those who register or support a gay organization, or even attend a gay wedding. What I argue is that, despite the fact that many of the pre-2014 gay-themed Nollywood films do have ambivalent and occasionally even affirming moments, these popular and widely distributed films as a whole often contributed to a public discourse that dehumanized sexual minorities in Nigeria by positioning homosexuality as something to fear. In this way, the pre-2014 films, even as they boldly registered queer existence at a time when it was rarely represented in Nigerian culture, also expressed a collective resistance, in the conservative sense of the word, to homosexuality as something that could exist within the moral codes of Nigerian social life.

As Karin Barber (1997, 2) has famously suggested, African popular culture ought to be understood as "the work of local cultural producers speaking to local audiences about pressing concerns, experiences and struggles that they share." Many scholars of African popular culture and Nollywood, myself included, have used Barber's work to explore the rich and complex ways African popular culture can critique corruption, address neoliberal economic anxieties, and condemn behavior that is harmful to a community's well-being. But in a society where homophobia is pervasive—around 90 percent of Nigerians support the criminalization of same-sex relationships and believe that the country would be a better place with no LGBT people (Nwaubani 2017)—it is often homosexuality that is framed as local audiences' pressing concern and that is condemned accordingly. When focusing specifically on the collective subset of Nollywood films that depict same-sex desire before 2014 and that so many members of the LGBTQ community find problematic and offensive, it is therefore difficult to celebrate Nollywood's ability to immerse itself in the moral dilemmas of African modernity or to praise the regional and pan-African popularity of this local industry in the same way that Nollywood scholars often do (again, myself included) when looking at the success of the industry more broadly. Therefore, what I attempt to do in the first half of this chapter is both to acknowledge the complex cultural work performed by individual early gay-themed Nollywood films as popular African texts—texts that are by no means monolithic—and to read these films as a cumulative body of work that negates and resists narratives that show queer Nigerian lives to be habitable.

The second half of the chapter examines the way in which the Lagos-based sexual and reproductive rights organization The Initiative for Equal Rights (TIERS) has, in the wake of the SSMPA, used the tools and conventions of Nollywood storytelling to create films to counter and resist the dehumanization that queer activists and members of the queer community have found to be so demoralizing. In the words of their former executive director Olumide Makanjuola, the aim of the TIERS-produced films and series is to "fire an alternative narrative into the imagination of the people," and their strategy is to capitalize on Nollywood's ability to speak to collective feelings and to reach audiences emotionally—to touch them.[4] In other words, rather than resisting Nollywood's paradigms, the TIERS films simply try to resist its homophobia by operating within its framework and under its umbrella: they use Nollywood directors, writers, and celebrities; they hold star-studded red-carpet premieres at upscale movie theaters; and they advertise and circulate in the same venues as other films considered to be part of a "New Nollywood" movement that makes films on bigger budgets, with independent producers and directors, and that debut in theaters rather than going straight to DVD or VCD (Haynes 2016, 285). In this sense, I argue that the TIERS-produced films deploy a strategy that is meant not only to touch and move audiences, to make them feel *for* rather than fear queer characters, but also to touch and move the Nollywood industry and to shift what is both possible and profitable.[5] Here, I underscore how TIERS mobilizes strategies of negotiation that, much like Obioma Nnaemeka's concept of nego-feminism, takes into consideration "principles of negotiation, give and take, compromise, and balance" that are part of "the foundation of shared values in many African cultures" (Nnaemeka 2004, 377). Therefore, unlike Karmen and Jezebel, who attempt to disrupt the status quo through waywardness, eccentricity, and errantry—who are, in other words, very much *not* negotiators—the queer characters in the TIERS films are often presented as everyday people living quiet lives in their communities and wanting to be loved and accepted. Rather than focusing on rebellious acts or grand gestures of refusal, the TIERS films perform their resistance by simply refusing to make homosexuality salacious and refusing to position it outside of social respectability. My intention in this chapter, then, is to provide a model for queering Nollywood studies that calls attention to the industry's historical denial of queer livability (a denial that certainly does not foreclose subversive readings) and shows how activists and artists carefully negotiate space for new types of stories within the industry itself.

Lesbians on the Loose

As I discussed in chapter 1, the West African industry of what were originally called "home videos" took off in the early 1990s because of already existing informal networks of distribution and what Brian Larkin (2008) calls the "infrastructures of piracy," and it continues to be the case that Nollywood has been so robust—some cite it as the second-largest film industry in the world—because it constantly adapts to the particular conditions of the Nigerian market.[6] For instance, one of Nollywood's main business strategies has been to produce mass amounts of films cheaply and quickly. Though formats have changed from VHS to VCD to DVD, Nollywood films—at least when they are material objects and not primarily digital ones—have, until recently, skipped cinematic release and gone straight to market stalls or street vendors. In order to mitigate the loss of profit that occurs when films are pirated, which typically happens after a few weeks, Nollywood marketers intentionally turn over films quickly, replacing films that have been pirated with new ones as soon as possible.

As Jonathan Haynes argues in *Nollywood: The Creation of Nigerian Film Genres*, one of the most definitive studies of the industry, this rapid turnover in the market also has an effect on the films' narrative content. Haynes writes,

> The resulting movies are inherently and essentially generic: individualizing a film costs time and money, and a film that does not give off strong generic signals will get lost in the market. Even beyond such necessities, Nollywood's culture is conservative, working and reworking a durable set of themes and plot types. . . . Individual films almost all disappear from the market to make room for others after only a very few weeks, so if a story hits a nerve with the audience, it needs to be retold to stay in public consciousness. The stories that are repeated, that don't wear out or that do so only after almost infinite repetition, have a special power: they are the most motivated and essential, the most deeply embedded in the tensions of contemporary Nigerian life. (Haynes 2016, xxv)

In other words, Nollywood is what it is today not simply because of the marketing strategies, but because these strategies created an industry that was able to consistently produce films that Nigerians want to watch. Over the past three decades, Nollywood has developed not only its own business model but its own themes and genres, as well as its own star system and awards shows, all of which depend on each other and work together to create films that appeal to audience's hopes, values, anxieties, and cultural and aesthetic tastes.

It is difficult to say whether films about homosexuality have a *special* staying power—with thousands of films produced every year, many topics and themes get repeated. And though Nollywood provides the largest archive of queer-themed African media to date, Nigerians themselves do not necessarily recognize it as a major plot in films.[7] But films with same-sex loving characters have clearly, to borrow Haynes's phrase, hit a nerve. They attract major Nollywood stars to play leading roles, and they overlap with several of what Haynes (2016, xxvi) identifies as Nollywood's enduring hallmark genres: "money ritual" films about occult ways of gaining wealth and success; "senior girls" films about independent women hungry for sex, money, and power; and "family films" about the threats to marriage. *Emotional Crack* opened the Nollywood market to the theme of homosexuality, but, for various reasons, films that positioned lesbianism as a social danger rather than those that evoked sympathy for queer characters are the ones that cracked audiences' emotions enough to be repeated again and again. Though many of these early gay-themed films have individual moments, scenes, or characters that might seem to affirm queerness, what I wish to demonstrate is how a "durable set of themes and plot types" (Haynes 2016, xxv) gets worked and reworked to produce a cumulative set of stereotypes that position queerness as threatening to the social order.

After *Emotional Crack* was released, two films, Kabat Esosa Egbon's *Beautiful Faces* (2004) and Andy Chukwu's *Women's Affair* (2003), became the blueprint for the popular cycle of lesbians films that followed.[8] Egbon, who wrote and directed *Beautiful Faces*, told me that he had not originally planned on making a film about lesbians. However, the film's producer, Chukwuka Emelionwu, popularly known as Kasvid, wanted to ride the coattails of *Emotional Crack* and asked Egbon to craft the script accordingly. Because of her role as Crystal in Isong's film, Kasvid cast Stephanie Okereke in the role of a campus cult leader and villainous lesbian. According to Egbon, Kasvid's "commercial instincts" led him to believe that this type of film would sell well and that it would stand out in the crowded market. Egbon confesses that he would have preferred more subtleties and nuances, and he also admits that *Emotional Crack*, which showed the possibility of love between two women, was a more daring and interesting film. However, as the producer and the one marketing the film, Kasvid had the final say on the direction that *Beautiful Faces* would take.[9]

Beautiful Faces opens when Vivida (Okereke), a young and stylish university student, enters a classroom where a lecturer is delivering a talk on the sins of hedonism. Upon seeing Vivida in her short jean skirt and revealing tank top, the lecturer refuses to allow her admission into his classroom. Humiliating her in front of her peers, he tells Vivida that he will not tolerate such "immoral" dress in his classroom. Vivida leaves quietly, but in the next scene she shows up uninvited to his home with several of her friends. They brandish a gun and force him to take his clothes off so that he may see what it is like to have his dressing habits dictated to him. After his clothes are removed the girls mock his penis and point out his large gut. They accuse the lecturer of "eating [their] money," referring to the common practice of lecturers forcing students to purchase handouts that have often been cribbed from textbooks or the internet. The film is therefore initially, like *Emotional Crack*, set up as a response to male hypocrisy. An audience familiar with the corruption of the university bureaucracy or the practices of lecturers who exchange handouts and grades for money or sexual favors will certainly understand why the girls feel that they are justified in seeking retribution: they are reacting to an educational system that has clearly failed them, and their response seems, at first, like a laudable feminist expression of agency.

However, any initial sympathy quickly disappears when the audience learns that Vivida is both a lesbian and the leader of the White Angels, a leading female cult on campus.[10] When she spots Natasha, the virtuous daughter of the president of the Senate, she wants Natasha both for the White Angels—who seek members who are "rich, beautiful, and well-connected"—and for her personal pleasure (figure 2.3). Vivida begins to court Natasha by sending her a gift basket with perfume, biscuits, and a G-string. As Natasha and her friends examine the contents of the basket, they are astonished and perplexed. However, on her next visit to Natasha's room, Vivida makes her intentions clearer by placing her hand on Natasha's leg and proclaiming her love. When Natasha still refuses to understand the advances, Vivida insists that Natasha must stop acting naive. Finally, Natasha snaps into awareness, quickly jumps up from her bed in a state of fright, and yells, "Don't you dare call my name, you bloody lesbian. Now you listen, I am not a lesbian and I should have nothing to do with a lesbian like you. So get up and get yourself out of my room this minute." Here, the shock of Vivida's lesbian advances is registered in Natasha's bodily fright.

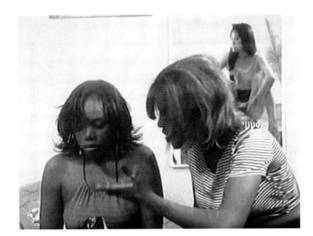

FIGURE 2.3. Still from *Beautiful Faces* (2004). Vivida seduces a young, confused first-year student.

At this point in the film, once lesbianism has been named, defined, and compulsively rejected by Natasha, the seduction takes a more violent and aggressive turn. After Natasha refuses to fill out forms to join the White Angels, the next "gift" that Vivida sends her is not lingerie but, rather, a miniature wooden coffin. Vivida's friends continually harass Natasha, and one night, while Natasha is in her room, she is accosted by two members of the Blood Brothers, a male cult that provides the White Angels with protection in return for sexual favors. The Blood Brothers accuse Natasha of being a lesbian who has severely beaten one of her lovers, and they demand she hand over money to pay the girl's hospital bills. Thus, same-sex desire in *Beautiful Faces* has nothing to do with love but rather is associated with physical violence, death, and the excesses of sexually autonomous women. The G-string that becomes a coffin comes to signify the interchangeability of female (homo)sexuality and destruction.

In the second part of *Beautiful Faces*, Natasha discovers that Vivida and her friends are also involved in an organized prostitution ring. Natasha is on a double date with her roommate and their respective boyfriends at the restaurant of an expensive hotel. As the group of four dines and jests, several of the White Angels walk into the lobby draped on the arms of older, wealthy men. The scene therefore juxtaposes two types of heterosexual coupling: one centered on dating, romance, and love; the other, registered as morally aberrant, based exclusively on the exchange of money. When the two groups notice one another, the camera, accompanied by intense drumbeats in the score, begins to cut rapidly back and forth between close-ups of Natasha and her friends, who look alternatingly bewildered and disgusted, and the Angels, who shoot back looks of delight and intimidation. The overall effect of the soundtrack and editing creates a sense of moral panic that is supposed to be shared between Natasha and the audience. Here, the White Angels' sexual desires for other women and their practice of prostitution are not only harmful to the heterosexual family but also self-aggrandizing and irrational. Because women who seek to join the White Angels must already be rich and well-connected, prostitution in this particular film is not positioned as a means of getting by or making do in tough economic circumstances. Rather, in *Beautiful Faces* it is there to alarm the audience and reveal the transgressions committed by the daughters of upper-class families.

In order to correct these transgressions, the film turns its focus to heterosexual love. Natasha, distraught over the continual tormenting by the White Angels, decides to seek the help and protection of Nick, the leader of the Blood Brothers. A good deal of the film's denouement revolves around resolving questions about Nick's moral character. When Nick is arrested along with all the campus cultists and Natasha goes on a hunger strike to convince her father to secure his release from prison, the audience is made to understand that Nick has renounced cultism and is deserving of rescue. The melodramatic mode of the story mobilizes the audience, as Linda Williams (2002, 13) suggests, "to feel for the virtue of some and against the villainy of others." Thus, despite his role in cult activities, all narrative codes point viewers to wish, along with Natasha, for Nick's release. And, of course, this is precisely what happens. In the final scene of the film, Natasha, whose father has decided to send her away to finish university in London, sits sullen-faced at her own farewell party. In the middle of the party, Nick appears, now sporting a fancy suit and shirt, and explains to Natasha that her father secured his release from prison and offered him a high-paying job that will keep him away from cults. Nick tells her that they will get married and that he will join her in London for his master's degree. In this way, he becomes a suitable upper-class husband and gentleman who, like Natasha's father, participates in restoring order to the disheveled world the film has presented. As Neville Hoad (2007, 57) suggests, the bourgeois nuclear family (or at least a nostalgic and anachronistic version of it) is seen as the pinnacle of modernity, and resisting and erasing—rather than accepting—homosexuality becomes key to achieving this desired family. The film ends with Vivida and the White Angels in jail and Natasha and Nick on the verge of marriage and safely out of reach from any other cultists who may attempt to harm them.

A similar fate befalls the main female aggressors in *Women's Affair* (2003), a film Chukwu made to call attention to the "social menace" of lesbianism, which he said was secretly infecting and destroying society.[11] In this film a young Genevieve Nnaji, perhaps now Nollywood's biggest female star, plays Brenda, a girl whose overprotective mother forbids her from interacting with boys and scares her with tales of rape and gruesome abortions. Convinced that women are "safer," Brenda begins an affair with her girlfriend Oluchi, then is lured by a wealthy older woman, Esther, and eventually becomes involved with several women on her university campus. The story ends badly when Esther hires thugs to murder Oluchi and, just before dying, Oluchi tells the police that both Esther and Brenda were out to get her. Brenda, who has been beaten by her fellow classmates, is arrested from her hospital bed, and Esther is carted off to jail.

Chukwu told me that in order to research the film he sought out a group of lesbians at a bar and began inviting them to hotel parties. He never told the women that he was researching a film, nor did he let on that he found what they were doing to be "disgusting." Not surprisingly, when my coresearcher Unoma Azuah and I screened *Women's Affair* for queer audiences in Lagos and Abuja, the women there said they saw nothing of their own lives reflected in the story line. In addition to being offended by the predatory acts and violent ending of the film, they were disturbed that neither the word *lesbian* nor the word *love* appeared once in the film; and they sensed that relationships between women were therefore somehow being erased at the same time they were being depicted and vilified. In fact, the only scene that the audiences applauded occurred when Esther visits Brenda at school. There, Esther is attacked by Oluchi, and a large, rowdy crowd surrounds the three women as Esther defends Brenda and tries to usher her into her suv. Here, an indignant Brenda calls attention to Oluchi's indirect insults, inciting her to declare in public why she has started a fight. From the car window, Brenda shouts, "Say it, just say what it is." When Oluchi remains silent, our audience members jeered and called Oluchi a coward for not naming lesbianism and having the same courage as Brenda (who, not unimportantly, is played by an actress many queer women admire and who has been rumored in tabloids to be attracted to women). Here, then, this scene, despite its intention, calls out the silencing of queerness in a way queer audiences find affirming. What our audiences found so harmful and even threatening to their own personal safety, however, is that in films like *Women's Affair*, as well as in the many lesbian-themed Nollywood films that followed, lesbianism becomes synonymous with debauchery and criminality.

It is also the case that *Beautiful Faces* and *Women's Affair*, like the earlier *Girls Hostel*, began a trend in which lesbianism and its dangers are located at the boarding school or college campus, and many of them are what Haynes would call "campus films." The campus film, a genre unique to Nollywood, often centers on young women whose "sexuality, freedom, and privilege are fascinating for the popular audience" (Haynes 2016, 259). Lesbianism is therefore just one of several ways that women assert their independence and their willingness to transgress—and are punished for it. "It is easy," Haynes says, "to read the representation of lesbian female cults as the projection of (predominantly male) fantasies or nightmares" (272)—or, I would argue, both. In *My School Mother* (2005), an older girl at a boarding school plies a younger girl with alcohol and then rapes her. In *Girls Cot* (2006), about a coterie of university girls involved in prostitution, two of the girls, Bella and Alicia, are sleeping together. But when Alicia confesses that she wants to marry Bella, Bella refuses Alicia and calls her mad. To get revenge, Alicia sleeps with Bella's fiancé and tells him about both the prostitution and the affair she has been having with Bella. The fiancé reacts harshly: he understands the prostitution—the money, after all, is intended to fund his and Bella's move to the United States—but the lesbianism is intolerable. He calls Bella a "dirty, rotten pig" and leaves her, dashing her hopes for an economically viable heterosexual marriage abroad. In *Rude Girls* (2007), university girls join a supernatural lesbian cult (or NGO, as they call it) involved in murder, robbery, and the destroying of "the family structure of Nigeria." Likewise, in *Before the War* (2007)—the cover warns, "Don't Fall the hands [sic] of Lesbians"—girls who receive a special powder from an apparitional spiritual mother wreak havoc on their campus and eventually become entangled with murderous sugar-mama lesbians. In *Sexy Girls* (2009), the actress Mercy Johnson (also in *Before the War*) plays the leader of a group of campus lesbians who inadvertently causes the death of a younger, "innocent" student whom she is chasing. In all of these films, lesbianism, though occasionally associated with forms of feminist agency that challenge patriarchy and corruption, is presented as something to fear because it directly threatens the ability of university women to receive an education and find a suitable male spouse.

Mr. Ibu and Keziah (2010) is a film that repeats many of these patterns but locates lesbianism in the hostels where the main character, Keziah, played again by Mercy Johnson, is serving in the National Youth Service Corps. It is interesting to note that, off campus, lesbianism seems less predatory, though still associated with excesses that threaten the social order. Like the 2008 film

Corporate Maid—a film in which Johnson is cast as Miss Rose, a hypersexual maid who sleeps with the husband, wife, and staff of the home where she works—*Mr. Ibu and Keziah* is, compared to the above-mentioned campus films, rather light. In this film Keziah is "jazzed" (made the victim of juju) when she lathers herself with soap that her roommate has infused with a potion. The soap turns Keziah into a lesbian; she has sex with her roommate; and then the roommate takes her to join a cult of lesbians devoted to women's empowerment where the women chant that "a woman can do anything a man can do" (figure 2.4). The plot thickens when one of the wealthy cult members tries to seduce Keziah by giving her a lotion also infused with magic. Keziah becomes "double infected" and sexually insatiable. In a slapstick manner she begins to literally chase any woman she sees, from her lover's house girl to the fruit vendor on the street. Still, at the very end of part 2, Keziah becomes a happily married, born-again Christian who achieves orgasm with her husband and becomes pregnant. Thus, like all the queer-themed Nollywood films discussed so far, *Mr. Ibu and Keziah* ends by restoring the heterosexual order. The common thread in all of these films is that each negates and resists queerness by ending with the death, arrest, or spiritual "salvation" of the criminalized and degenerate homosexual character.

FIGURE 2.4. Still from *Mr. Ibu and Keziah* (2010), showing the women's empowerment meeting where women assert that they can do anything a man can do.

Censorship and Punishment

While the recurrence of similar plots, settings, and themes in the above films might be attributed to market tastes and Nollywood's business model, which intentionally shies away from individualizing films, the repetition of these particular endings for queer characters can partly be explained by the National Film and Video Censors Board (NFVCB). The NFVCB, or Censors Board, is a body that is tasked with making sure that Nollywood films do not go against Nigerian culture, which means that any film that ended with a happy, well-adjusted queer character would never be given approval. But the precise mandate of the Censors Board is not straightforward. When I visited the NFVCB in Abuja with Azuah in 2010, the women there explained to us that there was not exactly a list of forbidden topics. Much of what films could show, they said, depended on "taste" and "degree," which is, of course, subjective. To elaborate, they mentioned the film they were watching before we arrived—it had a sex scene in a car that lasted just a little bit too long for them. We were also able to watch *Mr. Ibu and Keziah* with the censors before the film's release. Although they appreciated the acting and the comedy, they felt that the lesbians were enjoying themselves too much—"This is not a balanced representation," they said, and "These girls are having too much fun." It became clear that a "balanced" representation, a term the censors kept repeating, was one in which the consequences and immorality of homosexuality are made clear from the beginning. The censors therefore did not object to the depiction of two women sleeping together. What they found offensive—and insisted the director change, even to receive an "18-and-over" rating—was the level of enjoyment with impunity. However, despite the censors' strong objections, it seemed that very little changed between the original version and the one released to the public. We noticed that a few of the scenes that contained two women in bed were perhaps cut out or edited down, and that Keziah, at least at the beginning, was made to appear as more of a victim than an excited participant. But there were still many scenes in which Keziah is seen "enjoying" lesbianism quite a bit. What the example of *Mr. Ibu and Keziah* underscored, then, was that the Censors Board, as Paul Ugor (2007) notes, is not always effective in actually censoring Nollywood content and that enforcement might be lacking. The repeated negation of queer life that occurs in the films' endings cannot therefore be solely explained by the Censors Board's often arbitrary demands.

Even without official censorship, Nollywood movies thrive on the moral condemnation and punishment of acts outside of social norms and categories of respectability. As Moradewun Adejunmobi (2010, 111) writes in her discussion of Nollywood's appeal, "Nollywood's audiences are entranced by the spectacle of odious human behavior matched only by the certainty of commensurate judgment." Moreover, the fascination with female transgressions and its subsequent punishment has a history in Nigerian popular culture that predates Nollywood and the Censors Board by decades. For instance, Onitsha market literature published in the 1960s often expressed concern about the unmarried urban woman, or the "good-time girl," who chases money and men and, as Stephanie Newell (2002, 6) argues, is "the hoarder and private accumulator par excellence." In the 1960 pamphlet *Mabel the Sweet Honey That Poured Away* one can see many of the same associations between queerness and degeneracy that are seen in the Nollywood films of the early 2000s.[12] In the story Mabel, a fatherless and spoiled only child in Onitsha, witnesses her roommate Margie having sexual intercourse with a man behind the restaurant where they both work. Mabel becomes excited, and later that night, Margie seizes the opportunity to pounce on Mabel and grind into her. This initial act sets Mabel on a path of destruction—she begins to sleep around with men, and as those men lavish Mabel with gifts, she transitions from "good-time girl" to prostitute. When the story ends, Mabel has moved out of her room with Margie and has taken up residence at the Palace Hotel, where she eventually bleeds to death alone from a self-induced abortion. But, as is the case with the Nollywood films I have been discussing, the moral message in *Mabel the Sweet Honey That Poured Away* is clearly complicated by the narrative excesses and the pleasure that the reader or audience might take in encountering such women. While the story ends with the destruction of the female body who refuses to participate in marriage and heteronormative family life, it is also hard to forget that the pamphlet provides the reader with almost seventy pages of lurid and titillating descriptions about Mabel and Margie's sexual encounters. Mabel and Margie, like Keziah and many of the same-sex loving Nollywood characters, are clearly enjoying themselves. In other words, the "commensurate judgment" that takes place at the end of these stories is eagerly anticipated precisely because the narrative contains so much transgression. To a certain extent, this makes the task of the Censors Board impossible—the balanced representation the censors seek is often counter to the very formula that makes Nollywood films, like other forms of Nigerian popular culture, so appealing, and it is no wonder that filmmakers often make only minor adjustments to meet the censors' demands.

Moreover, the Censors Board is not wrong in assuming that the abundance of sexual transgressions displayed might work to make homosexuality itself look appealing, even if it is eventually condemned. As Schoonover and Galt (2016, 177) point out in their discussion of gay-themed Nollywood, there are many ways that *Mr. Ibu and Keziah* can be read "against-the-grain" for its queer, disruptive potential, and they point out how the film "could easily make a lesbian camp classic." Though the film, as far as I know, has not been interpreted in such a manner, Schoonover and Galt are right to read the lesbian cycle of Nollywood films as more than just a projection of homophobia. In fact, online reviews of Nollywood films that focus on lesbianism reveal that some viewers see them as elevating the importance of gay and feminist issues and, despite their punishing endings, as "promoting" the behavior by registering its existence.[13] In these cases, commentators feel that the films push an agenda that is too out of line with conservative social values and would prefer that Nollywood filmmakers act *more* conservatively. Of course, this also means that feminist readings are entirely possible, that audience members might see the representation of queer women and the exposure of patriarchal double standards as positive advancements, or that seeing some of Nollywood's biggest stars (some of whom are rumored to be queer) unafraid to take on these roles is affirming.

My argument, then, is not that the films should simply be read as creating villainous lesbians intent on destroying Nigerian society but that they should be read as layered works that repeat the same stereotypes and touch a nerve because they speak to the various tensions around such characters. In response to my earlier published essay on *Beautiful Faces*, in which I argue that the film reproduces the ideology of the heteropatriarchal state, Haynes writes the following:

> True, but the demonized transgressive figures share many characteristics with their virtuous adversaries. In spite of the fact that the screenwriters are almost all men, these female characters are powerful and empowering role models—tough, independent, willful, self-confident to the point of arrogance, sexually self-directed, capable, and stylish. Celebrity gossip in the press creates the impression that some of these women's behavior in real life bears a strong resemblance to that of their campus film's characters. (2016, 273)

And Haynes's point here is important. These are clearly rich texts which can be read and mobilized in multiple ways by audiences who are very capable of enjoying and valuing stories and admiring characters of whom they might also be critical. But what I am claiming here is that when the "demonized transgressive figures" are consistently queer women, and when there are no representations by or of queer Nigerian women to counter the pathologized lesbians that appear again and again in popular culture, the films participate in a much wider and problematic politics of erasure and negation. Therefore, though many of these films have feminist subtexts and have helped contribute to a Nollywood industry that increasingly centers women's voices and perspectives, it is still the case that cumulatively they have contributed to a public discourse that sees lesbianism as a threat to be feared and eliminated. As the editors of She Called Me Woman, Nigeria's first anthology of queer women's voices, write: "Queer people are both hyper-visible and invisible, talked about but missing from the centre of the conversation. The voices and realities of the millions of queer Nigerians (estimated to be more than the population of Lagos) are largely absent from the debate. . . . These erasures mean [public] conversations are divorced from the truth of our reality and lived experience" (Mohammed, Nagarajan, and Aliyu 2018, 1–2). Or as one queer-identified Nigerian woman told me during a screening of Women's Affair in Abuja: "These films are not about us; they are not made for us." In this way, Nollywood films, like other sensationalized accounts of same-sex relationships, tell us "much about the mechanisms through which lesbianism is imagined—secret cults, prostitution and promiscuity—but little about the day-to-day practices of women who love women" (Dankwa 2021, 3). And in the cycle of Nollywood films that depict stories about queer men, their lived experiences are no less distorted—even if, again, there are multiple opportunities to highlight subversive elements within the individual films and their online receptions.

Homophiles Fill the Homes and Streets

In 2010, three Nollywood films about male homosexuality were released— Hideous Affair (dir. Ikenna Ezeugwu), Men in Love (dir. Moses Ebere), and Dirty Secret (dir. Theodore Anyanji)—that associated homosexuality with criminality, violence, and greed.[14] Hideous Affair involves two wealthy chiefs who chase after young boys. One chief, distraught after his young lover leaves him for a boy his own age, kills himself. The other chief, unable to sexually satisfy his wife, pays a young man to break into his home and rape her. He then blackmails the boy into becoming his lover. Here, homosexuality is clearly associated with the abuse of power and is used to explore some of the anxieties about intergenerational romance. In the star-studded, much-talked-about film Men in Love (figure 2.5), Alex (Muna Obiekwe) drugs, jujus, and then rapes his friend Charles (John Dumelo). In Dirty Secret and its sequel, Little Secret, Obiekwe— who had already been strongly criticized for his role as Alex—plays a young gigolo who is involved in a three-way, incestuous relationship with a governor's daughter (Tonto Dike) and her father (Olu Jacobs). The film first centers on the sexual relationship between father and daughter and the outrage of

FIGURE 2.5. Still from *Men in Love* (2010). Alex rapes Charles.

the stepmother, who discovers the affair but remains married to the governor. Then the governor asks his daughter if she will share her boyfriend, and the three begin an affair together that leads to their demise. The film, which was one of the most sexually explicit Nollywood films at the time it was released, equates homosexuality with depravity, incest, and corrupt powerful men.

However, these Nollywood films—which were groundbreaking simply for the fact that they allowed for public dialogue on the topic of male homosexuality—do also have the potential to disrupt some of the logics of homophobia. Of these films, *Men in Love* stands out as being the most open to alternative readings. As Noah Tsika (2016) argues, *Men in Love* is unique both for its earnest depiction of a vibrant gay underground scene, in which gay men socialize at private house parties and fashion shows, and for its willingness to set forth a biological argument for homosexuality. Describing how the first part of the film positions homosexuality as something that is neither optional nor simply imported from the West, Tsika writes,

> Hoping to dissuade Charles from thinking that gayness represents a voluntary sexual orientation—a mere "lifestyle choice"—Alex suddenly announces that he's been in love with him "since school," that his overpowering love "still lives," and that it is as immune to "suppression as Charles's desire to cheat on his wife [Whitney] with a wide range of women." "I'm gay," Alex says. "I can't do anything about it. It's who I am." Having appropriated Charles's own self-justifying language—his own eagerness to excuse infidelity as biologically motivated, as "inherent"— Alex proceeds to suggest that both men are "sinners," and that neither can judge the other. Charles agrees, acknowledging that gay men "really

exist" in Nigeria and that Alex is helplessly in love with him, but finally and firmly concluding that he cannot return a gay man's affections. (2016, 207)

But this is Nollywood, and that is not the end of it. Contradicting his earlier stance on biological homosexuality—which, since it relied on the argument that both gayness and infidelity are not choices, was already riddled with contradiction—Alex tells his friends that if Charles could "experience being gay" then Charles would change his mind. Alex's friends, who are also gay, find this stance to be highly problematic and try to convince Alex that "converting" Charles is a bad idea. Alex does not take his friends' advice and spikes Charles's drink with juju, carries him unconscious to his bedroom, and rapes him. Though Charles, who wakens with a pain that alerts him to what has happened the previous night, is originally furious with Alex, the juju slowly takes effect, and Charles begins to return Alex's love. Alex then moves into Charles and Whitney's home under the pretext of needing a place to stay while his home is being renovated. Though Alex is the aggressor in his relationship with Charles, *Men in Love* interestingly subverts stereotypes by portraying Alex as someone who will fulfill the role of husband and caretaker—he buys Charles a car just as Charles had bought Whitney a car—as well as someone who will take care of Charles like a wife does. In fact, in the somewhat comedic domestic scenes, Alex and Whitney cook Charles competing breakfasts and try to outdo each other tending to his needs when he is tired. But when Charles and Alex are introduced as a couple at a fashion show where Whitney and her friends are present, Whitney's friend Flora finally explains to her what should have been obvious: that her husband is now gay. Horrified, Whitney frantically reads up on the (pre-2014) Nigerian laws that criminalize sexuality. Armed with the knowledge that homosexuality is illegal, she calls the police on Alex (who is promptly arrested and imprisoned) and calls a pastor to exorcize the "gay demon" from her husband so that they may continue their marriage, though, notably, no similar attempt is made to cure Charles of his previous (heterosexual) infidelities.

Tsika (2016, 209, 211) argues that the film's final "righting of wrongs" should not overshadow the competing narratives that *Men in Love* offers, especially given that the film has many online lives. In fact, he argues, the ambivalent arguments about homosexuality, the twisting of gendered stereotypes, and the detailed depictions of gay friendships between Alex and his friends provide the types of "gay representations on which digital paratexts thrive" (208). For instance, though the film does endorse homophobic legislation, some fans use digital clips to argue that homosexuality does indeed exist in Nigeria, while others focus on the film's erotic scenes (208). And, as Schoonover and Galt (2016, 179) argue, *Men in Love's* studio-released previews anticipate and even seem to invite queer readings by constructing "mini-narratives organized as gay romance stories, in which the homophobic discourse of the film is largely repressed." Furthermore, the clips and screenshots of the film that circulate online help to create complex discussions about the film that move beyond the mere denunciation of homosexuality. Tsika cites an entry on a site called The Zone in which the blogger uses screenshots to engage in a thoughtful discussion of the film's sexual politics and to criticize the film's "persistent conflation of masculinity and sexual aggression" (2016, 212). In this instance, gay-themed Nollywood films generate debates and discussions that "construct online monuments to gay subjectivities" that are often publicly denied (213).

Studying the online lives of gay-themed Nollywood films is therefore important not only because it focuses on the agency of the viewer but also because it pays attention to the specific ways that Nigerian films circulate. But I again want to emphasize that gay-themed Nollywood films—as a cumulative body of work, at least before the TIERs-made movies I discuss below—do indeed direct viewers to fear homosexuality. As Sara Ahmed (2015, 63) argues, "Fear involves relationships of proximity"—it is an emotion that establishes distance and apartness but depends upon the object of fear approaching or somehow being in contact with the fearful person. Moreover, Ahmed argues that this proximity, this interplay between closeness and distance, "involves the repetition of stereotypes" (Ahmed 2015, 63) and is "dependent on past histories" that shape how bodies become conditioned to react and to be moved by the proximate objects of fears (Ahmed 2006, 2). My argument about the Nollywood films discussed here, featuring both lesbians and gay men, is that they touch and move audiences by bringing them in contact with homosexual characters who are repetitively shown to be approaching and encroaching upon Nigerian social institutions and who, in the logic of the films, therefore need to be resisted and eliminated. Therefore, though it is important to acknowledge that there are moments and instances that can be recuperated for alternative readings or that highlight queer eroticism or queer existence, this does not undo the fact that the films continually repeat stereotypes that distance homosexuality from normal, functional social life and present no model for healthy and socially acceptable same-sex relationships. In other words, I would like to both affirm what Tsika (2016, 213) argues about online responses to "Gay Nollywood"—"that resistance may appear in the least likely of places"—and, without dismissing the complex cultural work the films perform, to maintain that they also resist discourse that would destigmatize queer love.

Moreover, though there are films like *Men in Love* that open themselves up to ambivalent readings, there are also films like Dickson Iroegbu's *Law 58* (2012) that work very hard to foreclose them. When I met Iroegbu in 2010 to interview him about *Last Wedding* (2004), a film in which a man walks in on his fiancée and her girlfriend, he told me he was currently making *Law 58*, which, he said, shows that "there is no freedom in allowing someone to be homosexual." He said that allowing homosexuality to exist is "like allowing someone to cut his own flesh, to inflict harm on himself . . . and it's an abuse of human rights."[15] Ironically, it was *Law 58*—and not *Men in Love* or *Dirty Secret*—that was held back by the Censors Board for nearly two years, indicating that, as the censors themselves admitted, much depends on taste and degree. According to Iroegbu, the Censors Board refused to "certify the movie on the ground that it dwells on an issue that is not allowed in Nigeria" (Njoku 2012). The filmmaker went back and reedited *Law 58* and also added the following clarifying opening text: "This is a true life story. The Nigerian society by its law frowns against the act of homosexuality, hence the need to tell this story. . . . The aim is to help present the . . . natural laws guiding true Africans' perception of the inordinate act, and not highlight or promote it." In other words, Iroegbu makes clear that anyone who reads scenes in the film as humanizing or as validating homosexuality is not a true African because true Africans will understand that homosexuality is unnatural or inordinate. Iroegbu implicitly takes the fight back to the Censors Board, implying that if they still read it as trying to promote homosexuality, it could only be because they are not truly African.

And indeed, when one watches *Law 58* it becomes immediately obvious why Iroegbu's opening crawl would be needed to situate the film's politics. *Law 58* begins with a very erotic four-minute scene in which a younger man, Charles, slowly and carefully grooms an older man, Chief Douglas, played by veteran actor Kanayo O. Kanayo (figure 2.6). Both men are wrapped in towels, and Charles, coyly smiling the whole time, delicately applies shaving cream to the Chief, shaves his face, dabs it dry, cleans his nails, and applies aftershave as slow elevator music plays in the background. Charles then wraps his arms around Chief Douglas as they gaze in the mirror and declare their love for each other. Isolated, this sequence, with its depiction of tender touching, could certainly be read as romantic and affirmative. However, somewhat suddenly, the screen turns white and the music changes to ominous electronic music. We see a close-up of Charles looking distraught, then another white screen

FIGURE 2.6. Still from *Law 58* (2012). Charles grooms and shaves the Chief.

that shifts us to the interior of a Catholic church as Charles approaches a priest muttering that he has sinned. Though he does not name his sin, another white screen takes us to a scene in Charles's living room, where his uncle says "It's a taboo" and tells Charles that his mother has told him everything. Another white screen takes the viewer back to the church, and the film continues like this for several minutes, cutting rapidly back and forth between twenty- to thirty-second scenes that each recur later in the film (i.e., Charles's mother rejecting him, Charles being beaten up and blackmailed by criminals, etc.) and the scene of Charles in the church trying to tell the pastor what his sin is. In the penultimate clip of the sequence, Chief Douglas explains to Charles, "The homophiles put enormous wealth in everyone's palms for a specific price: Law 58." This line is followed by the priest prompting Charles to tell his story, and the rest of the film is framed as Charles's confession (though it remains unclear where in the timeline of the film the opening grooming sequence occurs).

Setting up the film like this allows Iroegbu to show from the very beginning of the film that Charles will face consequences for his homosexuality and will seek to make amends. Unlike nearly every other Nollywood movie in which the punishment or redemption is reserved for the very end, in *Law 58* it is known from the beginning. This framing likely not only appeased the censors but was also, no doubt, welcomed by Christ the King Catholic Church, which participated in the film's production. However, it is also possible that this thwarting of Nollywood convention and the rather cumbersome opening contributed to the film's "cold" reception in the market and to it being called an "eyesore" in a local newspaper ("Gay Movie" 2012).

The main arc of the film—the point at which the confession begins—reveals how Charles had been lured into Chief Douglas's circle. The audience learns that Charles has been unable to pass his university entrance exams and that his recently widowed mother is extremely upset with him. Charles's gardener, James, overhears their argument and approaches Charles with a solution (figure 2.7). James, who walks and gesticulates in an exaggerated manner, is constantly drenched in sweat, and juts out his hip and bulges his eyes like Jim Crow, does not exactly fit or speak to any recognizable gay stereotypes (unlike the Burberry-clad, rainbow bracelet–wearing gay friends in Men in Love), but it does seem as if he is Iroegbu's version of what a slightly effeminate, slightly crazy deviant might look like. James convinces Charles that Chief Douglas will solve all his problems, and indeed, only months after beginning an affair with

FIGURE 2.7. Still from Law 58 (2012). James, the gay gardener, explains to Charles that the Chief will be able to help him with his test scores.

the Chief, Charles has not only passed his exams but is at the top of his class in the university. It is never explained how sleeping with the Chief enables this success (it does not appear that bribery is involved, and clearly James the gardener has not benefited from it in the same way), but later it is revealed that Chief Douglas is involved in a larger international network, and it is implied that occult forces are at work. At one point, a white man named Mr. Smith arrives and tells a group of men dining with the Chief that he will pay them each $1,000 if they bring him a "virgin fag." Later, the Chief reveals that the recruiting is part of a larger plan: "The plan is to have our homes and streets filled with homophiles! On that day a fag can conveniently marry another." Because the word "homophile" is used in the film to mean homosexual, this comment explains the actions of Mr. Smith, who seems to be part of the larger plan to turn Lagos (and perhaps other cities) gay. It is worth pointing out here that the characters in *Law 58* share the same logic as Alex in *Men in Love*—they too believe that, once someone has gay sex, he will become gay. However, unlike Alex, who uses this logic to win the man of his dreams, Chief Douglas and Mr. Smith seem to be interested in maintaining and further obtaining global networks of control. The vagueness with which this is all explained in the film is indeed part of the point—it captures rumors and fears that gay men at once already control the world and are recruiting others in an attempt to further their reach.

But *Law 58*, even more than other gay-themed Nollywood films (though not unlike *Jezebel*, discussed in the previous chapter), explicitly makes the argument that homosexuals want to abolish heterosexual procreation and literally stop the continuation of the human race. In *Law 58*, the price one has to pay for joining the "homophiles" and benefiting from their enormous wealth—the law of *Law 58*—is refraining from sleeping with women, who in the film are referred to as "infidels." Therefore, the plan to fill homes and streets with homophiles is also a plan to make men stop sleeping with women. The strictness with which this is enforced—two of Charles's friends are shot and killed for having girlfriends—causes Charles to doubt his affiliation with the Chief. When he is told by a pastor on television that Jesus has seen him and is saving him, he takes this as a sign and seeks refuge in the church. James informs the Chief that Charles is planning a secret church wedding, and the Chief shows up and shoots Charles during his ceremony. When he tries to shoot the priest as well, the gun freezes and he is struck by a flash of light. The priest gives him one last chance to give his life to Christ, but the Chief refuses and dies in the aisle. The ending of the film not only punishes the sinners but also enables the continuation of the human race. When, after the SSMPA was signed in January of 2014, Iroegbu took to Facebook to voice his enthusiastic support for the law, calling gay Nigerians "crazy" and pointing out their inability to procreate (Tsika 2106, 182), he echoed the message of his film—that homosexuality, left unchecked by higher authorities, will destroy society. Though Iroegbu certainly stands out for his vocal and public homophobia (which other directors do not necessarily share), *Law 58* only makes more explicit the fear of homosexuality that is implicit in nearly every single gay-themed Nollywood movie made before the SSMPA was signed into law. And in a society in which "queer people are seen as the absolute and dangerous Other: predators set on converting others, corrupted by outside influences, or focused only on marriage" (Mohammed, Nagarajan, and Aliyu 2018, 2), such representations validate those who argue that heterosexual marriage and reproduction need additional legal protection.

After the Law

On January 7, 2014, President Goodluck Jonathan signed into law the Same Sex Marriage Prohibition Act, which dramatically shifted public discourse around LGBTQ issues in Nigeria. The law had originally been introduced to the National Assembly in January 2006 but was not passed by the Senate until 2011. In 2013 the House of Representatives of Nigeria passed the law, but Jonathan, under pressure from foreign governments and human rights organizations, was slow to sign the bill. Many suggest that his willingness to sign in 2014 was an effort to gain public support and assert sovereignty before his reelection in a country that believes homosexuality to be a harmful Western import. The bill, then, served to distract the public, given the criticisms Jonathan faced, in part, for failing to stop the killings and kidnappings by Boko Haram in the north (Taylor 2014). The supposed purpose of the law was to prohibit same-sex marriage, which was not in fact legal in Nigeria, and to extend the antisodomy laws to legislate not only against sexual acts but also expressions of queer identities and public support for them. As a 2016 Human Rights Watch report states:

> The law forbids any cohabitation between same-sex sexual partners and bans any "public show of same sex amorous relationship." The SSMPA imposes a 10-year prison sentence on anyone who "registers, operates or participates in gay clubs, societies and organization" or "supports" the activities of such organizations. Punishments are severe, ranging from 10 to 14 years in prison. Such provisions build on existing legislation in Nigeria, but go much further: while the colonial-era criminal and penal

codes outlawed sexual acts between members of the same sex, the SSMPA effectively criminalizes lesbian, gay, bisexual, and transgender (LGBT) persons based on sexual orientation and gender identity. . . . [The] SSMPA, in many ways, officially authorizes abuses against LGBT people, effectively making a bad situation worse. (Human Rights Watch 2016a)

Although—at least as of early 2021—there have been no actual convictions under the SSMPA, the law emboldened police officers and members of the general public to ramp up violence against queer Nigerians and legitimized human rights violations that include "torture, sexual violence, arbitrary detention, violations of due process rights, and extortion" (Human Rights Watch 2016a). As Kehinde Okanlawon (2018, 641) writes, "The SSMPA was a blow to the hopes and objectives of Nigerian LGBTQ groups; it transformed the political and social landscape by fomenting heated public anti-LGBTQ vitriol and creating an atmosphere in which otherwise 'normal' citizens felt that they were working for the national good in acting upon homophobic sentiments." Shortly after the law was passed, there were several instances of people being dragged from their homes and beaten upon suspicion of homosexuality.[16]

After its signing, it was unclear how the SSMPA would affect Nollywood films, which were growing increasingly bold in their depictions of same-sex intimacy and, as noted above, already registered to some as promoting homosexuality. At first, if one were to go by the example of the film *Pregnant Hawkers*, a film produced on the cusp of the passage of the act, the answer might have been that the law would simply eradicate what some were calling "Gay Nollywood." *Pregnant Hawkers*, which was initially released in 2013, opens with a two-minute sex scene in which the chiseled Nollywood actor Khing Bassey is on top of a man bent over a sofa who is moaning in delight and whose full frontal nudity becomes visible just as the men are caught mid-act. Whether Bassey was actually penetrating the other actor became a hot topic for debate as a pirated YouTube clip of the scene went viral (Tsika 2016, 188). Though the two men fade into the background of the plot of *Pregnant Hawkers*, after the SSMPA was signed the film was swiftly removed from streaming sites, only to be rereleased under the title *Desperate Hawkers*—with the sex scene as well as all other references to homosexuality deleted (171). Given this literal erasure of queer sex in Nollywood, it is not surprising that it is difficult to find evidence of gay-themed Nollywood films in 2014 and 2015. It is notable that one of the only films that does touch on the subject of homosexuality in those years—independent director Kunle Afolayan's *October 1st* (2014), a dark, 1960s period piece in which a pedophilic priest is revealed to be behind the main character's psychological trauma—was a big-budget film that did not follow the typical Nollywood market distribution format, or, for that matter, a typical "gay Nollywood" generic formula. Most filmmakers simply avoided the topic immediately after the SSMPA was signed: in a profit-driven industry, making a film that would be censored or rejected by streaming sites would be a waste of limited resources.

But by 2016, when TIERs released their first fictional film, *Hell or High Water*, and gay plots began to resurface in a handful of mainstream Nollywood films, several things had changed. To begin with, much of the initial fear about the implications over the SSMPA had subsided given the lack of actual legal convictions. Though LGBTQ people and organizations were in a heightened state of anxiety given the increasing levels of violence and harassment mentioned above, there were likely no convictions for simply voicing support of gay rights or criticisms of the law. In fact, Okanlawon (2018, 648) recounts how Reuben Abati, who was spokesperson for and adviser to Jonathan when the law was signed, delivered a keynote at an annual LGBTQ rights symposium in 2016, in which he spoke against the legislation and acknowledged the vulnerability of the Nigerian LGBTQ community. One of the unexpected outcomes of the act was that, rather than stamping out discussions about gay rights, it actually increased these discussions and made it much less possible to deny the existence of queer Nigerians and the violence they faced.

The second thing that had changed by 2016 was the way certain higher-quality Nollywood films were circulating. When the bulk of the films mentioned in the first half of this chapter were being produced, Nollywood films all competed in the market in more or less the same way: they were either released directly on disc, shown on satellite television channels like Africa Magic, or both. Only rarely did a Nollywood film make it into the handful of Nigerian cinemas that existed, and online streaming, which was initially largely for diaspora audiences with broadband connections, did not begin to take off until around 2011. Films with bigger budgets or ambitious artistic visions did not necessarily have any leg up and could not easily recoup their production costs. But by 2016, the CEO of Film House Cinemas, Nigeria's largest chain of theaters, told CNN that there were about thirty-five cinemas in the country, with more in the works (Adejunmobi 2019, 221). While this number is still relatively low, it did begin to create spaces for director-driven films to make a profit without having to go through Nollywood marketers who wanted to continue to churn out low-budget movies (221). The year 2016 also marks the year that Netflix first launched service in Africa, but, even before that, a few select Nollywood films had been made available on the service—notably, in late 2015, both *October 1st* and the feminist drama *Fifty* debuted on the site.

That a Nollywood film would go straight to a globally accessible streaming service, or even from cinemas to a streaming site, was not new. In fact, several popular streaming sites for Nollywood films pre-dated Netflix, and some, like iRokotv, even turned to producing their own content long before Netflix announced that it would also produce Nollywood content. But what was new about Netflix was that it gave Nollywood a type of global visibility that it did not previously have, and it provided another platform, like Amazon and Google Play, for high-quality Nigerian independent art films that are almost completely absent from streaming platforms that specialize only in Nigerian content (236). Therefore, though Netflix's arrival in Africa in 2016 was largely symbolic at the time, it offered yet another concrete sign that filmmakers and directors could take the time and money to individualize films rather than repeat the types of generic plots that, as Haynes suggests, gave off the signals needed to sell in a glutted market. By 2016 there was a growing, vibrant sector of the Nollywood industry—often referred to as New Nollywood—that might, as TIERS's executive director at the time, Olumide Makanjuola, hoped, have space for films that could tell new types of queer stories and touch audiences in different ways than the previous era of Nollywood films.

Even before the SSMPA was signed, Makanjuola, a longtime LGBTQ rights activist, believed that activists should not just engage policy makers but should work to change the "cognition of the people." After the law's passage, the need became that much more urgent. In 2013 Makanjuola produced *Veil of Silence*, a documentary about what it meant to be queer on the eve of the SSMPA's passage and signing. It was the first time that queer Nigerians spoke out on camera about their experiences, not to a Western audience or filmmaker but to their own community. Unfortunately, the film did not have the kind of impact and circulation Makanjuola wanted. But *Hell or High Water* was a different kind of project: it is a thirty-minute Nollywood short about Pastor Gbolahan, a highly respected and adored leader in his community, who tries to deny his homosexuality, much to the detriment of his own mental health and marriage. The film contains no gay stereotypes or caricatures—no one is trying to convert anyone or find the cause of his homosexuality. *Hell or High Water* is quite simply a small window into the life of an exemplary community member who happens to be attracted to other men. The story was written by Noni Salma, a Nigerian trans woman who made the film under a previous name and who had also written and directed *Veil of Silence* and had been involved in the Nollywood industry for several years. The director of the film was Asurf Oluseyi. Though the idea to make a film like *Hell or High*

Water was Makanjuola's, Oluseyi's artistic vision—he was director, editor, and cinematographer—strongly shaped the look and feel of the film, which was promoted as a partnership between TIERS and Asurf Films, the production company Oluseyi started in 2011.

When I met with Oluseyi in the spring of 2019, he confessed that the film was both more challenging and more rewarding than he had expected. When he first received the offer to make the film, which came from his lawyer (who also represents TIERS), he said he did not think twice. He was interested in the project because he believes that, in his words, "LGBT people are people" and that the film would offer him a way to distinguish himself as a filmmaker, since the world would not expect to see such a story coming from Nigeria.[17] He was also drawn to Salma's script and to the character of Pastor Gbolahan because Gbolahan was a successful man who would likely resonate with audience members. Oluseyi reasoned that it would be easy to find others like himself, who were not a part of the queer community but who were open-minded, eager to begin a conversation that needed to be started, and excited about tackling something different despite the potential risks. But he struggled at first to cast the film. He had three actors in mind to play Pastor Gbolahan, each of whom turned down the role. The first actor said he would have taken the part if Pastor Gbolahan were a joke, but he could tell from the script that the character was meant to be serious and was not there for comic relief. The second actor refused on religious grounds, and the third never even returned the phone call. Oluseyi began to rethink the type of actor he wanted and realized too that he should begin by talking to gay Nigerians and thinking about who they are as people, beyond the images that circulate in the media. He realized that none of the gay men he'd met and spoken with fit his stereotypes (i.e., skinny, effeminate) and that he should broaden the range of actors who might take the role. He finally asked Enyinna Nwigwe, famous for his role in the Nollywood blockbuster *The Wedding Party*, and who, more importantly for Oluseyi, had spent time abroad and therefore, Oluseyi reasoned, might be more open to gay issues. Oluseyi's instincts were right, and Nwigwe agreed to take the part. However, it was not until the day before the shooting was to begin that he cast Daniel K. Daniel to play K.C., Pastor Gbolahan's ex-lover. Again, it was important to Oluseyi that K.C. defy the stereotypes that Oluseyi himself had had to overcome. Oluseyi also confessed that he had some trouble with the cast and crew, the majority of whom expressed homophobic views on set. He decided to stage a workshop (one that TIERS was, strategically, not involved with) to help the crew understand that the film they were making was about humanity and love, and he said that this approach—coming from a straight man who was not an activist and could therefore not be accused of having a particular agenda—was highly effective.

One of things that was most important to Oluseyi was making a film that, in his words, could "play with Nigerian sentiment." He said he wanted to make a film like Barry Jenkins's Oscar-winning *Moonlight* (2016), one that touches audiences and connects them emotionally to the characters whose sexuality is only one small part of who they are. But since the film was aimed at Nigerians, he wanted it to have the look and feel of a Nollywood film, a film that audiences would immediately connect with. *Hell or High Water* begins with the testimonial of a young boy whom Pastor Gbolahan mentored, rescued from gang life, and brought into the church when the boy's own father abandoned him. The testimonial transitions into Gbolahan preaching to a group of young men in his mentorship program. The camera cuts back and forth between Gbolahan and the youth, who are clearly connecting to him. The music begins to crescendo as Gbolahan concludes his sermon by saying, "Always know that no matter what it is that confronts you, you have Christ by your side to help you." Because of his innate ability to connect with church members as well as nonbelievers, Gbolahan is soon tapped to be the head pastor for a new branch of the church. But as he drives home after receiving the good news, Gbolahan looks worried, and the film cuts to flashbacks of him being beaten on the beach as part of an exorcism ceremony. The haunting music cues audiences to understand that something is not right. Later, a high-angle shot of Gbolahan and his wife, played by Ashionyne Raccah, captures the coldness and distance between the two of them: she is asleep in bed, with one hand resting on his shoulder, while he stares blankly at the ceiling (figure 2.8).

Finally, when Gbolahan shows up at K.C.'s home, begging to pick up where they left off, the source of the pastor's distress becomes clear. It is revealed that, eight years earlier, K.C.'s wife had planted cameras around her house to catch the two men in bed together and had sent a video to Gbolahan's parents, who subsequently forced him into marriage. K.C. and Gbolahan rekindle their relationship—though they are only shown cuddled up in bed together after the act, dreaming of running away together (figure 2.9). Gbolahan seems transformed. He is clearly lighter and happier; meanwhile, his wife is on the phone fighting back tears as she explains to her psychologist how Gbolahan is uninterested in her sexually. Unfortunately, K.C.'s now ex-wife makes an unannounced visit to drop off their child. In a highly dramatic scene, she finds Gbolahan hiding in the closet, calls K.C. a "cock sucker," and storms out with the child, of whom she now plans to seek full custody. By the time Gbolahan

FIGURE 2.8. Still from *Hell or High Water* (2016). Pastor Gbolahan lies in bed with his wife, who is sexually unsatisfied.

FIGURE 2.9. Still from *Hell or High Water* (2016). Pastor Gbolahan rekindles his affair with K.C.

returns to his house, she has posted the old videos on the internet. Gbolahan's wife has learned the truth and says, "I never knew you had such amazing blow job skills . . . that you never used on your wife!" But beyond the zinger, Raccah's emotionally charged performance conveys the buildup of pain his wife has experienced after enduring years of lies and feeling undesired. She tells him that she is leaving him, which she should have done years ago, and hopes that God forgives him. In the final scene of the film Gbolahan is accosted by paparazzi who ask him about the allegations against him and whether he is aware of the fourteen-year prison sentence he might face. He gets in his car to drive away from them, as Oluseyi uses a drone-mounted camera to pan out farther and farther on the car. The film ends there, not with an anticipatory or hopeful, fugitive flight or with gestures toward a queer horizon, but with a good man and community role model who has lost everything and is forced to abandon his home, his church, and the life he has built for himself.

That *Hell or High Water* might be considered a "gay rights film" or even a progay film, and one produced by an NGO at that, might be surprising to a Western viewer.[18] Not a single character expresses any criticism of the SSMPA or even any belief that homosexuality should be accepted in Nigeria, and no one, not even Gbolahan's own parents, advocates for better or more fair treatment of Gbolahan—who loses his wife, job, and reputation. And yet in a Nigerian context the film represents a radical shift from previous representations (perhaps with the exception of *Emotional Crack*) because it directs audience members to feel sympathy for Gbolahan, a character they like and are drawn to before finding out that he is gay. The decision to end the film inconclusively, and not to restore Gbolahan's marriage, is also a clear subversion of Nollywood's heteronormativity. The narrative does not neatly put things back together; it just leaves the audience with the many lives that have been shattered and it allows them to ask questions and negotiate their feelings about what should or should not happen to Gbolahan. In this way, the film was exactly the type of conversation starter that Oluseyi and Makanjuola had hoped it would be (Izuzu 2017a). Moreover, Makanjuola and TIERS worked hard to assure that the film would be highly visible. They hired one of Nigeria's largest public relations firms to help with the publicity and work with the press; they put up billboards, had Oluseyi on talk shows, made sure the film appeared on widely read blogs, and held a red-carpet premiere filled with Nollywood A-listers. Then, in a move most other New Nollywood filmmakers avoid, they put the film up for free on YouTube. And the strategy worked. Though people expressed different opinions about the film, many, according to both Oluseyi and Makanjuola, were touched by the film and said that it forced them to change the way that they thought about gay people. Makanjuola informed me that one woman who attended the premiere with her husband—but who had not previously known what it was about—was so moved by the film that she has become a key donor and ally of TIERS. And Oluseyi says that the film has, as he had hoped, only strengthened his reputation as a serious, high-quality filmmaker.

Whereas the pre–Same Sex Marriage Prohibition Act gay-themed Nollywood films I discuss above play to emotion by bringing audiences into contact with what they fear, *Hell or High Water* touches audiences in a different way. It operates with a soft touch, carefully negotiating the texture of the Nigerian social and political landscape.[19] In this way, the tactics TIERS utilizes are very much in line with African feminist strategies of negotiation—and in particular, Nnaemeka's work on nego-feminism, which values compromise and give-and-take and working with and through cultural norms in order to achieve social gains. Nnaemeka (2004, 378) writes, "The language of feminist engagement in Africa (collaborate, negotiate, compromise) runs counter to the language of Western feminist scholarship and engagement (challenge, disrupt, deconstruct, blow apart, etc.)." And she suggests that rather than subverting or overturning existing structures, the African feminism she sees practiced "challenges through negotiations and compromise. It knows when, where, and how to detonate patriarchal land mines; it also knows when, where, and how to go around patriarchal land mines. In other words, it knows when, where, and how to negotiate with or negotiate around patriarchy in different contexts" (378). And, indeed, TIERS follows many of these strategies as it navigates the land mines of homophobia (which, of course, are not separate from the patriarchal land mines). The organization's practices of negotiation and "speaking to Nigerian sentiments" are no doubt what contributed to the success of *Hell or High Water* and the lack of backlash that followed. It is a strategy on which they have continued to build.

Moving, Understanding

The second Nollywood film TIERS produced was *We Don't Live Here Anymore* (2018), directed by Tope Oshin, famous for, among other things, her role in producing two of Nollywood's most successful films to date: *Fifty*, one of the first Nollywood films on Netflix, and *The Wedding Party 2*, one of the highest grossing Nollywood films at its time. Oshin herself was named as one of OkayAfrica's 100 Women of 2018, and having Oshin's clout and her production company, Sunbow Productions, behind a queer-friendly Nollywood film was a strong statement. Once again, the script was written by Noni Salma and the film was highly publicized by TIERS. When I met Oshin at her Sunbow office in Lagos she told me that she was immediately drawn to the script because she felt it was a film that "could operate in our society," that it "represented humanity."[20] She said that one of the reasons that the film worked was because it was not a "gay agenda" film that would be read as overtly political. She said that after the SSMPA was signed, a lot of people in the gay community came out "with weapons drawn" and there was a lot of anger and shouting from the community. But, she adds, mainstream society was not responding well to that strategy, and no one's mind was being changed. This statement helped me to clarify a comment I had heard her make when she appeared in 2018 on *Untold Facts*, a TIERS-produced talk show available online. There she'd said, "Accepting is not the first goal. Understanding is. Before you can accept you must understand."[21] Some of the commentators online disagreed with Oshin, but her strategy was to make something that would not be immediately dismissed as subversive or political so that it might actually engage people. Like Oluseyi, Oshin says she wanted to make a film like *Moonlight*, which many Nigerians saw and loved and, because of its emotional gravitas, did not find offensive. She wanted a film that would bring out Nigerian audiences' emotions in a similar way in order to help Nigerians understand that no one chooses to be persecuted.

After the accolades that *Hell or High Water* received, *We Don't Live Here Anymore* was much easier to cast, and Oshin says she did not have the same problem as Oluseyi with a homophobic cast and crew. But *We Don't Live Here Anymore* did have its own hurdles. The first was the Censors Board. *Hell or High Water* did not need the board's approval because it was not attempting a theatrical run. The premiere was, as all premieres are, considered a private event, and so far the Censors Board has not tried to limit what can play at private events—or even at film festivals, which are also considered private. (This is why *Rafiki*, which was banned in Kenya on the basis that it promoted homosexuality, could screen at a festival in Lagos without a problem.) But since Oshin and Makanjuola wanted *We Don't Live Here Anymore* to have a Nigerian theatrical run and to stream on Nigerian platforms, it had to pass through the Censors Board. Makanjuola also emphasized that, while *Hell or High Water* was a testing ground (which is why it was made available for free on YouTube), he wanted *We Don't Live Here Anymore* to make money so that they could demonstrate that films treating homosexuality sympathetically could do well in the market. When the Censors Board gave the film a 15-and-over rating, Oshin and Makanjuola were pleasantly surprised; they expected that the film would be rated 18-and-over.

But they were also surprised when, even after this rating, theaters did not want to risk showing the film because they thought people would not buy tickets. Theaters wanted TIERS to pay them to have it screened, and then said they would pay them back if they sold tickets. This was not a model Makanjuola was interested in pursuing. A compromise was reached when Film One, the sister company to the cinema chain Filmhouse Cinemas, agreed to stream it on their platform. However, two weeks after debuting *We Don't Live Here Anymore*, Film One pulled it from their Nigerian site (though it remained available for viewers in other countries) because of complaints from viewers. According to Makanjuola, Film One was nervous that the government would come after them, and though he tried to convince them that there was nothing in the SSMPA that prohibited depictions of homosexuality, he eventually lost the battle. Oshin insists that the complaints came from people who did not watch the film and says that responses from both gay and straight people who have actually seen it—even those who were initially skeptical—have been unilaterally positive. When the distribution contract with Film One ended, Makanjuola was able to secure a contract to have *We Don't Live Here Anymore* available on Amazon Prime, which helps with international visibility as well as revenue but not with reaching a wider Nigerian audience, since most Nigerians do not have Amazon Prime. Still, the success of the film was clearly visible in Nigeria. The red-carpet premiere of the film, with its highly fashionable Nollywood stars in attendance, was discussed on Nigerian social media sites, and then the film went on to receive ten nominations and four wins, including Movie of the Year and Best Director, at the 2018 Best of Nollywood Awards.

Though *We Don't Live Here Anymore* has gained visibility as an LGBTQ film, the two gay characters, high school–age boys Chidi and Tolu, are arguably not the main characters or even the main focus of the movie. Rather, the film focuses more on the reactions of the two boys' mothers (and then the fallout from these reactions) after Chidi and Tolu are caught having sex in a classroom after school hours. The film, in fact, opens with a series of reactions: first, one of the teachers at the boys' school, Ms. Wilson, runs down the hall and vomits into the toilet. The camera, positioned as if it were in the toilet, is then covered in a white substance which dissolves into the title screen. Next, the audience meets each of the boys' mothers in her workplace. Chidi's mother, Nkem, works at a day-care center where she is clearly adored by the children. She receives a phone call at work that shocks her: "I'm sorry," she says to the caller, "can you repeat that?" Then, Nike, Tolu's mother, receives a similar call while holding a celebration at the philanthropic organization she runs, and her response is the same: "I'm sorry, can you repeat that?" The content of the call remains a mystery, but in the next scene the high school kids in the schoolyard begin to gossip: Ms. Wilson caught Chidi and Tolu with their pants down! Both mothers who are called in to speak with the headmaster deny that their studious Christian sons would ever do this and beg that their children not be expelled just before exams (figure 2.10). Tolu's mother attempts to bribe the headmaster and points out how much money her family has given the school over the years, but the headmaster says that the school board is "bent on making scapegoats" of Chidi and Tolu so that they can show that they take a strong stance against homosexuality. Interestingly, the SSMPA is not mentioned directly, but it is clear that it is the law that has created this type of atmosphere, and as the plot unfolds, it becomes clear just how detrimental this atmosphere is.

When the boys return home, the difference between their parents' reactions is put into stark relief. Nkem, a single, working-class mother, seems more upset that Chidi had never confided in her that he had "these feelings" than she is about him getting caught. The wealthy and well-connected Nike, however, immediately jumps into fixer mode and calls in a public relations expert that is a friend of the family (figure 2.11). The PR woman and Nike decide that the best way to spin the situation is to say that Chidi lured Tolu with alcohol and then raped him. Tolu is certain that this is a bad plan. Even Tolu's father,

FIGURE 2.10. Still from *We Don't Live Here Anymore* (2018). Chidi's mother, Nkem (*left*), and Tolu's mother, Nike (*right*), learn from the principal that their sons will be expelled for being intimate with each other on school grounds.

FIGURE 2.11. Still from *We Don't Live Here Anymore* (2018). Tolu's father comes home furious after learning about Tolu's sexuality. Nike has already brought in a public relations expert to help them spin the story.

who has just tried to beat Tolu, thinks it is a bad idea and asks, "You are willing to ruin someone else's life? This is ridiculous." But Nike replies, "Oh, we are so doing this." Tolu and his father are not given much choice. Nike returns to the headmaster to tell him that Tolu was raped; she then forces Tolu to see a therapist so that the rape will look real; and she makes him get a girlfriend to deflect rumors that he is gay. Tolu protests every step of the way, but Nike reminds him that if he does not play along, he will be expelled, his father will hate him, and his life will be over.

Meanwhile, Nkem has neither the resources nor the connections Nike has, and she struggles with how best to help and support Chidi. She tries to seek the help of Chidi's estranged father, but news that his son is gay only makes him distance himself further. Nkem tells Chidi that he should fight back, that they should sue the school for expelling him and not giving him a fair chance to defend himself against the allegations. But Chidi wants to lie low and says that if they sue, more people will hear about it. Nkem, like Nike, does not listen to the sound wisdom of her child. She calls a friend who is a journalist and asks the journalist to look into the story. But once again she is outmaneuvered by Nike, who catches wind of the investigation and calls the journalist to her office. Nike delivers a stunning sob story about how Tolu was raped and begs the journalist not to let Chidi get away with it. The journalist agrees and publishes a story in the local paper with Chidi's face on the cover. Chidi is subsequently beat up in the street, Nkem is fired from her job, and their front door is vandalized with graffiti that reads "God Hates Fags" and "Leave This Town" (figure 2.12). Chidi begs his mom to do just that. He wants to escape, to flee, to begin a new life away from his small town. His mother says that they can go live with his grandmother but that she needs to find a job first so that she is not a burden. In what is perhaps the film's most poignant scene, Nkem, tending to her son's wounds, says that she wishes he had told her sooner that he was gay. She thinks that she could have helped him fight it, that she would have prayed or fasted for him. But Chidi sits up and turns to her, "You think I chose this? Do you know how many nights I stayed awake praying to God to make me like other boys?" She embraces him and keeps him close, trying to help in the only way she knows how (figure 2.13). But she has missed the mark. Before she can get him to safety, Chidi drowns himself in the ocean. He leaves a suicide note saying that he could not change himself no matter how hard he tried and that he did not want to be a burden or source of shame for his family anymore. His mother is devastated.

When Tolu, who had already been having regular panic attacks, finds out about Chidi's death, he runs home to lay the blame on his parents. He storms into his house screaming, "The poor boy you framed is dead. You pushed him to suicide. You are evil." They deny culpability and maintain that they did what was best for Tolu. No longer able to look his parents in the eyes, Tolu runs

FIGURE 2.12. Still from *We Don't Live Here Anymore* (2018). Chidi's mother discovers their front door has been vandalized.

FIGURE 2.13. Still from *We Don't Live Here Anymore* (2018). Chidi and his mother are distraught over the rape allegations against Chidi and the homophobic violence that has been unleashed.

away from home and becomes a fugitive. Weeks turn into months, and Tolu's parents, who have not heard a word from their son, slowly deteriorate. His dad begins drinking, while the once-glamorous Nike appears disheveled and despondent, shouting out apologies to a Tolu who is not there. She confesses everything to the journalist who exposed Chidi, but the confession neither brings solace nor brings Tolu back. Meanwhile, Nkem is not faring much better. She has nightmares in which Chidi is drowning and calling out her name and she is unable to save him, nightmares which are fairly close to the reality of what happened. In the final scene of the film, Nkem walks out into the water, presumably to follow Chidi. As she wades in farther, a boy in a fisherman's hat is standing nearby watching. The camera zooms in to reveal that it is Tolu, his face completely vacated of expression. The film ends there, without revealing whether or not he will save her.

When I asked Oshin about what she wanted audiences to take away from the ending, she admitted that it is not the kind of comfortable resolution that Nollywood films usually deliver, and that this was intentional. She did not want the film to have a happy ending because she wanted to show the type of destruction that occurs not because the boys are gay but because of the way that their parents and community react to it. Indeed, one of the last things Nike says in the film is "I hope that this darkness does not consume me, the darkness of the peoples' lives I have destroyed." Though the film does not voice any overt support of homosexuality, it is clear not only that Tolu and Chidi are considered the victims but that they are the characters who have the strongest moral compasses. In this way, *We Don't Live Here Anymore* does indeed uphold "the bedrock values" of Nigerian audiences: "moral purpose and the sense of community" (Haynes 2016, xxvii). It simply redirects who is perceived as a threat to those values.

What *We Don't Live Here Anymore* does not do, though, is ask audiences to support the love between Tolu and Chidi, who never even appear on screen together except in a scene in which they deliberately try to avoid each other at a supermarket. (This lack of explicit on-screen intimacy is perhaps what led the censors to give the film a 15—rather than an 18-and-older—rating.) There is indeed a quietness around the two boys that does not erase their love story but that sets it gently in the background so that, as the writer Noni Salma told me, straight audience members could reflect upon and reconsider homophobic presumptions and focus on the boys as human beings rather than simply as sexual beings.[22] In fact, both Salma and Oshin emphasized to me that the film intentionally begins with Ms. Wilson's reaction rather than a shot of the two boys together in the classroom before they are caught. Unlike Mohamed Camara's 1997 *Dakan*, which does actually begin with two teenage West African boys from different class backgrounds making out—and which ends with them pushing past homophobia and attempting to create a life together—*We Don't Live Here Anymore* is not interested in creating openings and spaces for queer love. Oshin delicately avoids lingering on the boys' feelings for each other and says that she was making the film as a mother, for mothers, posing the question to them: "What would you do if you found out your child was gay?" Or, referring to post-SSMPA incidents of gay Nigerians being dragged out of their homes and beaten: "What would you do if that was your brother or son?" Salma, when she wrote the film, says she considered all the characters, even Nike, to be victims of Nigerian society. *We Don't Live Here Anymore* is, like older gay Nollywood films, a cautionary tale. But here the script is reversed: the film does not caution against being gay; it cautions against not supporting loved ones who are—and, as Salma emphasizes, it debunks the notion that homophobia is simply a question of personal opinion or taste with no real consequences. Oshin's soft touch and the touching performances of both mothers certainly moved audiences as well as jury members at the Best of Nollywood awards. Makanjuola said that the kind of emotion he witnessed at the *We Don't Live Here Anymore* premiere was something he had never seen before in all his years of activism.

Out of the Shadows

To date, TIERS's largest project is a coproduced adaptation of Jude Dibia's 2005 novel *Walking with Shadows*, which has the distinction of being the first West African novel to feature a gay protagonist. For this production Makanjuola teamed up with Funmi Iyanda, an award-winning journalist, media personality, and blogger, best known for her popular morning television talk show *New Dawn*, which ran for eight years. In Nigeria's queer community, *New Dawn* is perhaps best remembered as the show on which Bisi Alimi, a well-known Nigerian actor, in 2004 became the first Nigerian to publicly come out on television, an act that forced him to flee the country for his safety and resulted in cancellation of the live format of *New Dawn*. When Iyanda and Dibia met at an event in London, a few years after Alimi had come out and Dibia's novel had been published, she expressed interest in making an adaptation. Makanjuola and TIERS had also been in discussion with Dibia, and though it took several more years for the project to get on its feet, eventually Makanjuola and Iyanda came together, with Makanjuola in charge of resources and funding and Iyanda leading the artistic direction of the film. Iyanda worked hard to find a director who could strike the right chord and eventually approached the London-based Irish director Aoife O'Kelly, whose short film *Lula* had impressed Iyanda. Iyanda and O'Kelly cowrote the screenplay, and Dibia, who was asked to approve a few sample scenes, took a back seat, feeling that his novel was safe in the hands of Iyanda, O'Kelly, and Makanjuola.

Walking with Shadows tells the story of Adrian Ebele Njoko, a successful businessman with a wife and daughter, who is forced to face his past when a colleague maliciously outs him to his family. The novel follows Adrian on his path to self-discovery as he confronts his wife, his brothers, the gay friends he rejected after his marriage, and his coworkers. The more Adrian tries to explain why he deceived everyone, the more he realizes that he no longer wants to deceive people. By the end of the novel, Adrian decides to move to London where he can live as an openly gay man and feel secure that his career will not be jeopardized. Ironically, for the novel was published a year before the Same Sex Marriage Prohibition law was introduced, as Adrian leaves the country he hopes to return to it at a time when social attitudes around homosexuality have improved.

Though the narrative is focused on Adrian's self-transformation, Dibia's novel takes care to demonstrate that gay men and women in Nigeria choose many different lifestyles and find various ways to form community. For instance, after Adrian's wife, Ada, finds out that her husband is gay and kicks him out of the house, Adrian's first stop is the apartment of Femi and Abdul, a gay couple with whom Adrian had been friends before his marriage. As Adrian's life appears to be falling apart, Dibia reminds the reader that this is not the only path he could have taken. When Adrian asks how they handle the gossip and disapproving looks, Abdul responds, "I love myself and my life, and I love Femi. This is all that matters. Of course, I don't go about advertising the fact that I'm *queer* . . . [but] I don't need their validation or approval" (Dibia 2005, 27–28). Abdul and Femi seem to possess what Adrian thought impossible: respectability without heterosexual marriage and an ability to acknowledge the threat of violence without allowing it to determine the course of one's life. To Adrian, Abdul and Femi represent a form of resistance—one that resembles the very homonormativity dismissed in Western queer theory but that, in this context and to Adrian, requires a certain amount of bravery that deftly negotiates between risk and self-acceptance.

Furthermore, as both Adrian and Ada discover, many gay men and women have figured out how to negotiate Nigerian homophobia. When Ada is distraught about Adrian's sexuality, a friend takes her to the home of an acquaintance named Carole who regularly hosts a group for women who are happily married to gay men. Each woman has a different story—one woman is a lesbian and finds the situation to be quite convenient; the others are fine as long as their husbands provide them with money, luxuries, and the freedom to travel. Ada learns that there are many influential gay men and lesbians in business and politics, and though they do not live openly, their lives are clearly not ruined because of their sexual identities. Ada is surprised: "The society had indeed evolved and she had missed it all" (Dibia 2005, 146).

In many ways, the novel is just as much about Ada's evolution as it is about Adrian's. When Ada first receives the news about Adrian's sexuality, she is shocked and upset. She feels betrayed by Adrian and worries immediately about his HIV status (which is negative) and how his sexuality will affect her reputation. She also repeats many of the standard homophobic charges: homosexuality is unnatural, un-African, and against the Bible. But her encounter with the wives of the gay men begins to change her mind, and when a friend fears that her son, who likes to play with dolls, will turn out gay, Ada realizes that it would be absurd for a mother to love her son any less simply because he is gay. Eventually, the couple amicably part ways and decide to tell their daughter the truth about her father (figure 2.14). What Dibia seems to be doing with the character of Ada is giving the average Nigerian a character with whom to identify in order to alleviate some of the fears and concerns that Nigerians may have about an issue they know of mostly through stereotypes. And though one of Adrian's brothers sends him to a pastor to be beaten, Adrian's other brother rescues him, holds him tenderly, and tells him that, though he wishes Adrian weren't gay, he will

FIGURE 2.14. Still from *Walking with Shadows* (2019). Adrian and Ada discuss their future after Adrian has been outed by a coworker.

support Adrian's decisions. Just as Dibia demonstrates multiple ways of being gay in Nigeria, he also presents readers with multiple ways for Nigerians to accept and understand same-sex love and relationships.

Though he had trouble finding a local publisher (even before any talk of further criminalizing homosexuality), Dibia was determined to publish *Walking with Shadows* with a Nigerian press. When it was finally published, the novel took on a life of its own. When I interviewed Makanjuola and Dibia together about adapting the novel into a film, Makanjuola described the profound impact the novel had on him: "I remember when I read *Walking with Shadows* in 2006, literally I was just a fucking bloody young gay man in Lagos who just read a book and it changed me, and I remember everyone I met during this period had read *Walking with Shadows* and everyone could recognize how real that story was to them" (Green-Simms 2021, 107). But the intended readership of the novel was not just the gay community. In 2013, at the sixteenth Time of the Writer conference in South Africa, Dibia told his audience that he wanted his novel to change Nigerians' opinions about homosexuality and mentioned that his brother gave a copy of *Walking with Shadows* to his homophobic boss, who said that it did indeed make him rethink his attitude.[23] Dibia's wish for his own novel, then, is precisely what Makanjuola and those at TIERS want from their work in general: to help the Nigerian public negotiate their attitudes toward homosexuality through sympathetic characters.

The filmic adaptation of *Walking with Shadows* stays quite close to the original, though there are a few changes. For instance, the film ends before Adrian leaves for London, leaving the ending more open to interpretation and leaving open the possibility that, rather than taking flight, Adrian will stay in Nigeria to build his queer life. The biggest change, perhaps, revolves around the character of Antonio, Adrian's ex-boyfriend. In the book he is Spanish, and after he and Adrian break up, he contracts HIV. But in the movie he's no longer Antonio but Antoine, a French man, and he and Adrian are attacked after leaving a bar one night in Lagos. The attack leaves Antoine dead, and one of the attackers, it turns out, is a man named Tayo, the same man who becomes Adrian's coworker and who outs Adrian to his wife and family after Adrian verifies that Tayo had been involved in fraud. This has the effect of making the film feel more contemporary—by referencing the violent attacks that have increased since the SSMPA—and also, as Dibia notes, avoids perpetuating certain stereotypes about queer men as all having HIV (Green-Simms 2021, 105). But it also gives the story a more pronounced villain, making Tayo, and not any of the queer characters, the focus of the audience's moral condemnation.

Much of the novel seemed to hammer home the idea that homosexuality is not a choice. As Chantal Zabus (2013, 103) writes, "By propelling homosexuality into the realm of biological determinism, Dibia breaks with a long line of West African writers, who exclusively confined same-sex practices to Westernized behavioural imports." But in the film, unlike in the novel, these arguments are not made in long speeches; instead they come forth in the emotional interplay between the actors. For instance, in one scene that both Dibia and Makanjuola single out for its gravitas, Adrian's mother comes to him after he has been beaten by a pastor and asks her son if he is cured. The conversation is in Igbo, the only scene in the film not spoken in English, and—though it is subtitled—it is here through the performance of Ozzy Agu, the actor who plays Adrian, that, as Makanjuola says, one can tell that "Adrian had already accepted himself and was ready to begin a new journey" (Green-Simms 2021, 106). One of the things that *Walking with Shadows* seems most routinely to be praised for as it makes its rounds on the global festival circuit is the performances of the cast. (Some of this might be credited to Tope Oshin, who joined the team as casting director.) Dibia calls the film "a quiet film" and "an actor's film," and indeed many of the performances are filled with a deepness that gives the film its soft, gentle texture.

In this way, the film eschews typical Nollywood melodramatic flare, a flare that is most certainly present in *Hell or High Water* and *We Don't Live Here Anymore*. And yet, despite this tone and despite its Irish director, Makanjuola notes that Nollywood, the industry that cultivated all of the film's actors, is claiming the film. And of course, like most Nollywood films, *Walking with Shadows* features beautiful, well-dressed Lagosians who provide Nigerian audiences with the type of aspirational glimpses of the city's glamorous upper class that have made the industry so popular and successful.[24] The film *Walking with Shadows*, much like the novel and much like other TIERS films, is pitched in a way that challenges Nigerians' assumptions about queerness by drawing them into a story that is aesthetically engaging and familiar enough so as not to be alienating. And though the film faced similar obstacles as *We Don't Live Here Anymore* when it came to screening in Nigerian theaters, the intention is, by creating buzz about the film at international festivals, including the industry-focused Africa International Film Festival (AFRIFF) in Lagos—where it showed in five different packed screening rooms—that once it comes to a streaming platform such as Netflix or Amazon Prime, Nigerian audiences will eagerly seek it out. What *Walking with Shadows* does, both in its ending that gives Adrian and Ada space to create new beginnings unencumbered by homophobia and in its visible circulation as a story about queer self-love in Nigeria, is to open up different possibilities for being queer in the world and different spaces for resisting obligations to accept the status quo.

Busting Nollywood

In addition to producing Nollywood movies, TIERS is also trying to move the boundaries of what can be said in Nollywood by creating talk shows and a web series for their YouTube channel. The queer-focused talk show *Untold Facts*, hosted by media personality Arit Okpo (and originally hosted by Moses Omoghena when it began in 2016), interviews guests on topics such as sexuality and spirituality, mental health, digital security, and human rights. TIERS encourages audience engagement using the hashtag #UNTOLDFACTS on social media and also invites people to comment directly on YouTube. And the TIERS-produced web series *Everything In Between* opens the door for dramas that focus on queer characters navigating Nigerian society in increasingly more multidimensional ways. Created by Raccah (who played the pastor's wife in *Hell or High Water*), *Everything In Between*, in part because it is a free web series and does not have to pass through censors or cinema houses, allows for more of a focus on the love lives of queer characters. In the series, the three main characters, a successful lesbian talk show host, a gay male human rights attorney, and a straight woman who chooses to get pregnant via sperm donor, all battle with social and parental expectations in surprisingly similar ways. Though the web series takes on serious issues (such as blackmailing, domestic violence, parental estrangement, etc.), it is also decidedly more playful than *Hell or High Water*, *We Don't Live Here Anymore*, or *Walking with Shadows*, and one hopes it foreshadows future Nollywood stories in which queer characters might be treated the same as any other character with a complicated love life. Increasingly, queer people are also beginning to tell their own stories through cinema and video: Pamela Adie's coming-out documentary *Under the Rainbow* (2019); Harry Itie's documentary *Defiance* (2020), about young, queer activists and artists; video art by Tyna Adebowale; and Uyaiedu Ikpe-Etim's short film *Ifé* (2020) are all indications that queer screen media in Nigeria is further expanding to include different voices and aesthetic expressions.

In fact, *Ifé*, the 35-minute film produced in partnership with Adie and her organization The Equality Hub, points to the possibilities of new types of stories that focus on the complexities of same-sex intimacy and that, unlike the TIERS films, highlight relationships between women rather than men. *Ifé* begins with the titular character preparing for a date with Adaora, a woman she has not yet met in person. Adaora comes to Ifé's home, and although the two women are initially nervous, they quickly bond over their love of Warsan Shire's poetry, playfully bicker about audiobooks, and open up emotionally to each other about their pasts. The one-night date stretches into three intimate days. At one point Adaora asks, "Is it too soon to say I'm in love with you?" and Ifé, referring to the often joked-about speed with which queer women fall in love, replies, "We're lesbians, this is the perfect time." Unlike the TIERS films discussed above, *Ifé* is not about how these women's love might affect their larger community. Confined to just the three days of the date and to the four walls of Ifé's home, *Ifé*, a story that is written, produced, and directed by queer women, is an up-close and deliberately slow-paced study of queer women's intimacy in Nigeria when it gets to exist, for just a moment, in a protected space, walled off from the outside world. Ifé and Adaora cook, drink wine, make love, and cuddle, all in a room of their own. But one of the things that the film demonstrates is that declarations of sexual identity (i.e., "we are lesbians") do not always articulate the complexity of queer women's lived reality. At the end of the three days, Ifé learns that Adaora is engaged to be married to a man, an engagement that she plans to keep due to familial obligations made all the more pressing by the death of her sister. And yet, despite this surprising, heartbreaking ending, I would argue that *Ifé* is very much a cinema of *what could be*—not just because it creates space for Ifé and Adaora to share their pasts, imagine their futures, and explore their bodies on their own terms, but also because Adie, in looking for ways to screen *Ifé* during a global pandemic, has created her own website and media platform for queer Nigerian media content on *her* own terms. Adie's website—EhTvNetwork.com—allows viewers to subscribe and pay for content, thereby creating an income-generating way to showcase media that does not depend on Censors Board approval or require viewers to have a Netflix or Amazon Prime subscription. This model might very well be one that future creators of queer Nigerian content use.

But despite all of these new developments, it is certainly not the case that gay stereotypes and pathological representations have disappeared from Nollywood. In fact, in the same year that *Hell or High Water* was released, the films *My Gay Husband* and *Gay Pastors* also appeared online.[25] *My Gay Husband* is a film where, once again, the survival of a heterosexual marriage is contingent on the gay man's Christian salvation; and in *Gay Pastors*, the demonic gay pastor who "initiates" young men into homosexuality could not be any further from Pastor Gbolahan. Furthermore, a search for "lesbian Nollywood" on YouTube shows a list of full and partial Nollywood videos with titles like *Horny Nurses, The Lesbian Sisters, Ungrateful Lesbians, Hot Maids*, and, a slightly more perplexing title, *Finger Me Whisker*. To be clear, these are likely not the films' actual titles, and it is impossible to tell if the films, illegally uploaded, were made before or after the ssmpa. For instance, Safo's *Jezebel* comes up in this search as a video called *Spiritual Lesbians*, posted in 2015 and with no way to tell the original film title or release date. The name of Safo's production company is removed from the film and replaced by "Bold Face Productions," and the original title is likewise edited out and replaced with one that reads, *Crazy Fun*, a title that does not even match the new metadata on YouTube. While many of the other films that one can find online are clearly altered from older films, some are not, and in many cases only those who have seen and can identify the older films are able to tell them apart from the new ones. Most of the newer gay-themed films found on sites like YouTube are movies that would now be considered "Asaba films," films that are made cheaply and quickly— oftentimes but not always in the Eastern Nigerian city of Asaba. These movies are often not submitted to the Censors Board because filmmakers and marketers are not attempting any type of wide release. This informality makes it quite difficult to track the newer gay-themed films as a corpus, but the fact that it is impossible to tell the pre-ssmpa films from post-ssmpa films based on their content solidifies the point that, even as tiers is moving Nollywood in different directions, the same types of sensationalized and stereotypical stories persist.

But what *has* changed about mainstream Nollywood movies is that, when they do rely on homophobic tropes and wind up with a wider platform than the typical Asaba film (i.e., when they attract bigger stars or hit the theaters), they are being called out by the Nigerian press. For instance, in January 2017 *Pulse Nigeria* published an article titled "Nollywood Tackles Homosexuality in a Tacky Way" that includes the following:

> In less than a week, two indigenous gay-themed and transgender-themed movies made their debut online. With no graphic sex scenes between two same-sex individuals, these movies "Duada" and "Feyint'oluwa," still come with a certain kind of tackiness that evokes anger. The problem isn't that gay-themed movies are being made or that Nollywood shouldn't portray characters that are not in line with Nigeria's moral beliefs. The problem however is that no research is being carried out by Nollywood writers, directors or even the actors that interpret these characters. No attempt is made to capture believable moments. These movies simply fall back on crass stereotypes.
>
> A 2016 Nigerian movie "Roommates" which stars Amaka Iruobe and Charmaine Cyril as lesbian partners and some love scenes between Femi Adebayo and his "boyfriend" are examples of stereotypically flawed and exaggerated Nollywood LGBT movies.
>
> It's either you want to shoot a gay love scene or you don't. It's either they are cuddling or kissing or they are not. Stop creating flawed and unrealistic characters. (Izuzu 2017b)

An article like this indicates that there might be a shift in how these mainstream gay-themed Nollywood films are perceived. They no longer hit a nerve in the sense that they speak to deeply embedded tensions of Nigerian life; they hit a nerve because they seem out of step with realities of queer life in Nigeria, realities that are no longer as hidden as they were before the SSMPA created an explosion of discourse around homosexuality in Nigeria. And the *Pulse Nigeria* article also points to *Hell or High Water* as a counterexample, a film that tells a believable gay story. In this case *Hell or High Water* is praised not so much for its progressiveness but for its aesthetic achievement, for telling a story that feels real. And given the fact that Nigerian audiences are now more accustomed to representations of Black gay life in movies like *Moonlight* or shows like *Empire*, both popular in the country, it is no wonder that "tacky" gay caricatures are off-putting.[26]

It is perhaps not surprising, then, that a film like Lisa Onu's *Busted* (2018), which aspired to a long theater run and a Netflix deal, lasted only a week or so in cinemas and has yet to find any online streaming platform despite featuring stars like Liz Benson and Kate Henshaw-Nuttal.[27] The description of the film on the site Nlist reads as follows: "The gripping movie reveals the intrigues of a gay couple's love story. It tells the story of Queen Edwards, a girl born into a decent home where her father's strict nature as well as her mother's ignorance led her into the arms of a maid who lured her into lesbianism." According to online descriptions of the film, Queen's father sends her to an all-girls' boarding school because he sees her spending too much time with a boy, and this exposes her to lesbianism and leads her into the arms of the housemaid. Queen then falls in love with a woman named Blessing who "surrenders" to lesbianism because of economic hardship. Despite trying New Nollywood distribution tactics, the film repeats many of the old tropes of pre-SSMPA lesbian films—an overbearing parent, a deviant house servant, a girls' boarding school, economic incentives for homosexuality, and punishment for women who have transgressed. But the difference between *Busted* and the earlier cycle of lesbian films is that not many people have actually seen *Busted* outside of those who attended the private premiere and the small handful who were willing to pay to see it in the theater. It is not available online or in the market, and the filmmakers are unwilling even to release screeners (which is why I rely on online descriptions of the film). It seems that the film itself is what is now under erasure. Makanjuola assured me that a film like *Busted*, despite its aspirations, would never stream on Netflix or Amazon, or even iRokotv, none of which would want to be associated with this type of homophobic content. And when I asked Makanjuola if he'd had a chance to see the film himself, he told me that his PR team had actually helped ensure its flop. "I busted *Busted*," he told me happily, though without further detail. There are, indeed, many ways to touch Nollywood.

On Simple Touching

I have used the trope of touching in this chapter primarily in the emotional, affective sense, though, of course, what is at stake in queer Nollywood films is precisely the question of who is physically touching whom. As Sharon Holland (2012, 99–100) writes, drawing on a range of philosophical and feminist reflections on touch, "Though touching a person may seem simple, it is anything but. Both physical and psychic, touch is an act that can embody multiple, conflicting agendas. . . . It can be safely dangerous, or dangerously safe. It also carries a message about the immediate present, the possible future, and the problematic past." In all of the films discussed in this chapter, physical touch has the capacity to destroy, as the touch between two same-sex lovers in a homophobic society often leads to ruined families, wrecked careers, or communities torn apart. But, of course, touch—in both its physical and psychic senses—has the capacity to heal too. Touch can create empathy, break boxes, reach out to those who are alone or alienated: it can imagine new ways of being and belonging. What artists and producers like Makanjuola, Adie, Oshin, Oluseyi, Raccah, and Iyanda are doing with their soft-touch tactics and strategies of negotiation, then, is the imaginative work necessary to touch Nigerian audiences, to move them to new spaces of understanding, and to resist dehumanizing and salacious representations of homosexuality. Yet it is important to emphasize that none of these films is particularly unruly or oppositional in its presentation of queer life or queer sex. They do not resist by making grand political gestures or participating in a larger protest culture. They do not celebrate wayward subjects or eccentricity or artful evasion, nor do any of them (with the notable exception of *Ifé*) show much in the way of queer touch itself. Unlike the earlier Nollywood films that showed queer touch as both alluring and destructive, these films focus primarily on queer subjects' internal struggles, larger communities, and quiet moments. But what these new queer Nigerian films indeed do with their touching portrayals of the immediate present is work toward different possible futures, futures where queer touch can be simple and ordinary, where it need not be radical or illegal, dangerous or destructive, and where queer Nigerians do not have to seek escape routes.

3

Cutting Masculinities
Post-apartheid South African Cinema

"We made a provocative film and the intention of the film was always to transgress and challenge certain norms and ideas. Not just the norms and ideas of traditionalists but also the norms and ideas of so-called liberal, middle-class audiences who might engage with this film, particularly on an international platform" (Joffe 2018). This is John Trengove, in an interview with the British Film Institute, discussing his Oscar-nominated film *Inxeba* (2017), which sets a queer love story in the mountains of the Eastern Cape of South Africa against the backdrop of the three-week period of Xhosa male initiation rites and circumcision rituals known as *ulwaluko*. Trengove goes on to say, "To be an out and proud gay person is still regarded as a middle-class privilege in our society. . . . But as soon as you move into the vast majority of the rest of the country, particularly the rural areas and the more impoverished areas of South Africa, this is just not something that exists—this idea that you can be out and proud and fight for your rights at all costs" (Joffe 2018). Trengove, himself a white, middle-class, gay South African, is here commenting on how his film presents very different types of queer characters in order to challenge certain expectations of what a "gay" film might be. Though one of the film's key characters is the initiate Kwanda, a well-off, fashionable, and self-assured gay teen from Johannesburg, the film actually centers on the love affair between Vija, a hypermasculine man in a heterosexual marriage, and Xolani, a quiet storeroom worker from Queenstown, who come to the mountains to be care-givers for young initiates and to resume their annual love affair. *Inxeba* depicts how life for Xolani and Vija, who live in small towns, differs from that of the cosmopolitan Kwanda and how, in turn, the decisions and life choices these two men make are determined very much by their class position and cultural context. In other words, what it would mean for Xolani or Vija to be "out and proud and fight for [their] rights at all costs" is very different from what it would mean for Kwanda to do so, and it is not clear that this is something that either Xolani or Vija desires. Kwanda, in fact, becomes the film's antagonist by insisting on being "out and proud" and putting Vija and Xolani's relation-ship in peril. In this way, as Trengove suggests, the film is intended to resist the norms of both middle-class audiences who would identify with Kwanda and the "traditionalists" who would deny the existence of same-sex intimacy during initiation. But Trengove's comment above also points to the way that queer films are produced and consumed in South Africa, a country that has the continent's most progressive laws on sexual orientation but also grapples with a homophobia that is entrenched in the legacies of colonialism and apartheid and is often at odds with the image of the progressive rainbow nation that the country tries to present.

This chapter focuses on queer feature films produced in South Africa in the 2010s, a decade that saw several internationally recognized queer films ex-plore the complexity of apartheid and post-apartheid queerness as it intersects with and contests forms of hegemonic masculinity. Along with *Inxeba*, by far the best-known South African queer film, I analyze two Afrikaans-language films, Oliver Hermanus's *Skoonheid* (2011) and Christiaan Olwagen's *Kanarie* (2018), both of which explore the links between whiteness, Afrikaner identity, toxic masculinity, and homophobia in South Africa. In the final section I also briefly discuss Hermanus's newest film *Moffie*, which, like *Kanarie*, focuses on white soldiers during the South African Border War. What I argue is that these films highlight both the necessity and difficulty of resisting or undoing het-eropatriarchal systems of oppression, showing the multiple ways queerness can register as both subversive and complicit. As was the case in the previous chapter, this chapter continues to explore different modes and forms of queer resistance within a national cinema context. In this chapter, however, I focus on the specificities of South Africa's complex history and entanglements of race, class, sexuality, gender, and ethnicity and discuss the very different aesthetic practices of Trengove, Hermanus, and Olwagen, all of whom come from different racial and cultural positions. But the films I focus on demonstrate, each in their own particular way, that the opening up of queer possibilities in the past decade has also often been accompanied by resistance to the otherwise. These films, then, present forms of resistance that are muddy, muddled, or murky, and sometimes disorienting. What I see in this set of aesthetically rich and sometimes imperfect films, then, is a way to register and track the messy and contradictory resistant practices that unfold in a very imperfect post-apartheid South Africa.

A Brief, Queer Cinematic History

Before the end of apartheid, which criminalized homosexuality, representations of queerness were generally limited to white men who cross-dressed for comedic effect, and censors limited the representation of same-sex (as well as cross-racial) intimacy in both local and foreign films (Andrews 2018b; Peach 2005, 114). However, though censorship laws prevented films from being shown, several filmmakers still made films with queer content, mostly as a way to criticize or provoke the apartheid government. For instance, in 1985 Matthew Krouse and Jeremy Nathan wrote a short film called *De Voortrekkers* satirizing Afrikaner pioneers (or *voortrekkers*). Though the script was seized in a house raid by the police, *De Voortrekkers* was later filmed and inserted into an anti-apartheid film called *Shot Down*, directed by Andrew Worsdale and cowritten by Krouse and Nathan in 1986.[1] *Shot Down* was immediately banned, and as Tymon Smith (2021) writes, "Krouse and Nathan's short film contribution garnered its own banning order from the apartheid censors, who wrote in their official decision: 'In front of their wagon, a Voortrekker couple drop the Bible, shed their Voortrekker dress, and then they copulate while the man enters her from behind. They crawl over the ground. This lengthy scene intrudes on the privacy of the sex act. Walking naked the man finds his son and a friend in a homosexual sex-act. This is indecent and obscene. In a short film with 85 percent undesirable, there is no way to pass *De Voortrekkers*.'" But two years later, Krouse and Nathan went on to make *The Soldier*, a film that, like *De Voortrekkers*, was an intentionally scandalous attack on Afrikaner iconography and national identity. The filmmakers sneaked a camera into the Voortrekker Monument, a building in Pretoria commemorating Afrikaner pioneers who left the Cape Colony to find their own homeland independent of British colonial rule, and distracted the tour guide in order to film establishing shots. Because of the subversive content of the film—namely, a gay rape scene made to look as if it is occurring at the grave of the unknown soldier at the Voortrekker Monument—the negative was smuggled out of the country to be developed but was destroyed in a fire that broke out in the London lab and was never completed (Peach 2005, 139–42).[2] That same year Cedric Sundstrom's *The Shadowed Mind* depicted sexual encounters between male inmates in an asylum, but the film was also banned and available only on video after apartheid ended (Botha 2012, 242).

In 1988, however, Helen Nogueira's *Quest for Love* managed to slip through the notice of censors. *Quest for Love* depicts a lesbian couple (played by prominent Afrikaner actresses Sandra Prinsloo and Jana Cilliers) reunited in the fictional postliberation African country of Mozania after one woman is released from prison in South Africa, where she had been jailed for critiquing her country's military intervention in Mozania (Peach 2005, 135). According to Grant Andrews (2018b, 55), the film's "subject matter was so far outside the conservative milieu that it effectively passed under the radar," but given that there was a cross-racial affair depicted as well, it is hard to explain how this film existed and screened for two weeks in South African theaters (Peach 2005, 137). It is also, I argue, hard to believe that a film made in the 1980s would end with a lesbian couple alive and together, but the film does seem anomalous in all respects. Toward the end of apartheid, another film that did circulate was the documentary *Out in Africa* (1988), made by Melanie Chait, a white South African using overseas funding. *Out in Africa* is about the Black, gay anti-apartheid activist Simon Nkoli (who had also been the subject of a short 1987 Canadian documentary called *A Moffie Called Simon*) and Dr. Ivan Toms, a white, gay anti-apartheid and anticonscription activist.

When apartheid ended and South Africa's 1996 constitution became the first in the world to ban discrimination on the basis of sexual orientation—a move that paved the way for the country's legalization of same-sex marriage in 2006—representations of homosexuality on screen became much more common, with many moving beyond stereotypical, one-dimensional, or comedic depictions. And it was also the case, as Brenna Munro (2012, ix) argues, that "the gay, lesbian, or bisexual person then became a kind of stock minor character in the pageant of nationhood in the 1990s, embodying the arrival of a radically new social order and symbolically mediating conflicts over race and class." Therefore, unlike Nigeria's filmic representations of homosexuality in the 1990s and 2000s, South Africa's representations were often part of the new, modern image that the so-called rainbow nation was very keen to project.

Queer representations on screens in South Africa began to shift almost immediately after the country's first democratic elections in 1994. That same year the Out in Africa Film Festival became the first national and officially recognized queer film festival on the continent (though there had been several underground—and therefore undocumented—festivals across the country during the apartheid years). Out in Africa grew out of private fundraising screenings hosted in homes and organized in 1992 and 1993 by Jack Lewis, a white South African filmmaker, and ABIGALE (Association for Bisexuals, Gays and Lesbians), a mostly Black queer grassroots organization committed to fighting for sexual rights (Peach 2005, 146). As Ricardo Peach (2005, 145) documents, the 1994 festival—organized by Lewis, Nodi Murphy, and people such as Theresa Raizenberg of ABIGALE—was in fact part of the "lobbying process to have sexual orientation included in the equality clause of the new South African constitution." Though the festival also focused on catering to an LGBTQ and ally market (a market that Murphy had noticed during her work for the Cape Town International Film Festival), the Out in Africa Festival's manifesto included language that listed one of their main goals as "the retention of the sexual orientation clause on the Bill of Rights of the interim constitution" (148).[3] Therefore, film, and its concomitant project of promoting queer visibility and shifting consciousness around LGBTQ issues, was integral to imagining a South Africa whose future, as the introduction to the 1994 festival states, held "the hope of building a democratic, tolerant and free society" (quoted in Peach 2005, 149). The festival's success at packing theaters and foyers in Cape Town, Johannesburg, Durban, and Bloemfontein indicated both the social need and the political potential of film and cinematic spaces during this period.

Not surprisingly, then, the first post-apartheid decade saw the release of several South African queer films. These films included, though were certainly not limited to, Zackie Achmat and Jack Lewis's *Apostles of Civilised Vice* (1999), the activist Beverley Ditsie's own documentary on her friendship with Simon Nkoli, *Simon and I* (2001), John Greyson and Jack Lewis's historical drama *Proteus* (2003), and a number of short films that benefited from Out in Africa's film development initiative.[4] Ditsie herself was even the first out, queer cast member on the South African version of the reality show *Big Brother* in 1994–95, and *Simon and I* shows a clip of Ditsie's emotional response to a white homophobic male participant on the show. Likewise, as April Sizemore-Barber (2020, 11) notes in *Prismatic Performances: Queer South Africa and the Fragmentation of the Rainbow Nation*, the state-owned South African Broadcasting Corporation (SABC), from the early years of democracy, produced nightly soap operas that included multiracial gay and lesbian characters. Though they were certainly not without controversy, shows like *Yizo Yizo*, which showed two Black men kissing on South African national television for the first time in 2004, and *Isidingo*, which featured a wedding between two men just five days after same-sex marriage became legal in 2006, paved the way for queer representation on many other SABC shows that millions of South Africans watch.[5] In 2007 the soap opera *Society* became the first South African show to have lesbian characters, and the SABC even commissioned a feature film based solely on the lesbian plotline, though because of legal complications relating to the fact that the soap opera was still airing, the feature film screened only once or twice in the theaters before it was pulled.[6]

Of course, as has now been well documented, the implicit promises of what Pumla Gqola (2001) calls "Rainbowism" did not exactly come to fruition in the way many had hoped, especially in the face of continued economic inequality. As Gqola argues, not all citizens "have equal access to the mythic pot of gold" at the end of the rainbow. Some, in fact, are literally confined to the (gold) mines (Gqola 2001, 100). And, as Xavier Livermon (2012, 303) argues, efforts to fight homophobia were not always tied to efforts to fight racial inequality: "The equality clause as it relates to sexual orientation was part of a concerted effort to retain the white minority population in postapartheid South Africa by suggesting that even those most abjected under apartheid rule (white queers) would be safe in the postapartheid state." Livermon also notes that, in the same way that many gay whites held conservative views on race, many South African traditional leaders as well as members of the African National Congress did not support the Civil Union Act that paved the way for same-sex marriage (301). Therefore, though there was certainly much hope and improvement in the immediate post-apartheid years, it was never the case that homophobia and racism had simply disappeared with apartheid. Throughout the early twenty-first century, growing levels of poverty, high rates of crime and violence, and the AIDS epidemic all became irrefutable signs that the rainbow nation was perhaps not so rainbowy after all, and as homophobic rhetoric increased across the continent, South Africa proved no exception. Indeed, while there has been a considerable amount of queer representation on both big and small screens in South Africa, many of these films and shows have highlighted the continuation of homophobia, violence, and racial inequity.

Tellingly, the film *While You Weren't Looking* (2015), which was produced by the Out in Africa festival as a final farewell project for the long-standing festival, highlights many of the frustrations queer communities had with the rainbow nation. In the film, there is a scene in which economically privileged queer South Africans of various racial backgrounds discuss the sharp divide between what the constitution promised and the realities of everyday life for both straight and queer Blacks without economic privilege. In this way, the film registers the gap between what the festival organizers like Nodi Murphy (who is one of the writers for *While You Weren't Looking*) imagined in 1994 as the festival was first being organized and the experiences of the present day. The film also underscores the very different lives led by Asanda, a queer Black woman in Cape Town who is raised by a wealthy same-sex interracial couple, and Shado, a Black masculine-presenting lesbian who grows up in the township. While Asanda roams the city's elite spaces in a carefree manner, Shado is threatened with rape and violence in her township and is read as "trouble" by a Black housekeeper who works for—and presumably accepts—Asanda's two mothers. The film underscores how, as Livermon argues, "visibility for black queers in specifically black cultural spaces continues to be policed" and how a specific type of "black queer body remains the threat to African culture and tradition" (Livermon 2012, 300, 302).

It is this very type of racial and economic split that Trengove refers to in the quote with which I began this chapter, a split he wants *Inxeba* to challenge by privileging the story of Xolani and Vija—who exist in specifically Black cultural spaces—over that of Kwanda, who lives an elite, urban life. And *Inxeba* does not only seek to challenge the image of South Africa as a liberal and open society. The film also probes the connections between the continuation of heteropatriarchal institutions and the country's continued homophobia. In an interview with Aramide Tinubu (2017) in *Shadow and Act*, Trengove explains that, when he began making the film with coproducer Batana Vundla, the media "was quite saturated with statements of people like Robert Mugabe saying that homosexuality was un-African—a Western decadence, that it was against traditional African culture" and that to make a film about same-sex desire in a traditional African context seemed to be politically important. He adds, "It allowed us to kind of speak about bigger things like patriarchy and fractured masculinity and all these ideas I was interested in unpacking."

Like *Inxeba*, the films *Skoonheid* and *Kanarie* also speak to these larger issues; however, the point of these two films is not to disprove that homosexuality is un-African but rather to show how its denial and suppression are a part of an oppressive and violent form of Afrikaner masculinity. Hermanus's *Skoonheid*, a film that Trengove said in a tweet made him realize that different types of queer stories were possible, is a psychological portrayal of François van Heerden, a conservative Afrikaner man in Bloemfontein with a wife and two grown daughters who secretly likes to have sex with other white men and who sexually assaults his friend's son. *Kanarie* is a coming-of-age and coming-out musical drama about a queer Afrikaner boy, conscripted into the South African Defense Force in 1984, who joins the force's church choir. Examining these three films together—one by a mixed-race filmmaker (Hermanus) who examines white masculinity, another by a white filmmaker (Trengove) who looks at Xhosa masculinity, and the third by a straight, white, Afrikaner filmmaker (Olwagen) who dramatizes the army experience of his queer Afrikaner collaborator and co-writer Charl-Johan Lingenfelder—allows me to discuss both the possibilities and limitations of queer masculinity at this particular moment in South Africa.

It should be noted that queer feature filmmaking in South Africa has been largely a male endeavor and that racial and gendered structures have made it difficult for directors of color and, more specifically, Black women and trans people to break into directing feature films.[7] Cinemas themselves are still primarily located in white and more elite areas, which means that funders tend to back films that they think those audiences will prefer.[8] Moreover, with the exceptions of *While You Weren't Looking* (which was directed by a white woman, though some of its producers were women of color) and the British filmmaker Shamim Sarif's *The World Unseen* (2007), which was inspired by her family's Indian South African heritage, the queer South African feature films that have had national and international theater runs have exclusively centered on male relationships. By contrast, documentaries by Beverley Ditsie, Zanele Muholi, Zethu Matebeni and Busi Kheswa, Musa Ngubane, and Luvinsa Kavuma, to name just a few, have documented the struggles and joys of Black lesbians and trans people in post-apartheid South Africa. These powerful documentary films by Black women, nonbinary people, and trans men have participated in what Zanele Muholi (2013, 169) calls a "journey of visual activism to ensure that there is black LGBTI visibility." As Muholi says of their own work, the point of these documentary projects is to present images of queer Black women and trans people beyond the sensationalized media headlines, to show the many different identities, stages, and forms of "resistance and existence" faced (169–70). Feature filmmaking, which is the focus of this book, has not, however, seemed to be engaged with the same type of visibility project in South Africa. Rather, South African feature films have often focused on the difficulty of resistance and existence, and what I focus on here is not so much how these feature films make visible the complexity of queer lived experience but more so how they make visible the complexity of the hegemonic institutions and ideologies that order that experience.

Of course, I do not want to dismiss the South African Black feminist documentary tradition, and though there is an abundance of academic and popular writing on Muholi's archive, there is certainly much more that could be said about the visual activism of these impressive documentarians. But fictional narratives perform a certain type of work that I want to focus on here. As Caroline Levine (2015, 19) argues, fictional narratives can often be "productive thought experiments that allow us to imagine the subtle unfolding activity of multiple social forms." In this chapter, the films I examine are precisely such thought experiments, experiments that register the unfolding—what I call the *cutting*—of hegemonic masculinities in post-apartheid South Africa. Hegemonic masculinity, a concept defined and refined by R. W. Connell, has been described as "a set of values, established by men in power that functions to include and exclude, and to organize society in gender unequal ways" (Jewkes et al. 2015, S113). Neither fixed nor essentialized, hegemonic masculinity has different iterations in different cultures but consistently "combines several features: a hierarchy of masculinities, differential access among men to power (over women and other men), and the interplay between men's identity, men's ideals, interactions, power, and patriarchy" (113). In this chapter I argue that, although the feature films discussed here do often cut out female voices and perspectives—none, in fact, contains a speaking role by a woman of color— they also cut through, or rearrange and take apart, the sets of values and social forms that order gender inequalities and idealized forms of heterosexual masculinity. Moreover, they do so in a way that highlights narrative art's ability to "set in motion multiple social forms and track them as they cooperate, come into conflict, and overlap" (Levine 2015, 19) in ways that often productively highlight imperfections, inconsistencies, and unresolvable tensions.

In chapter 1 I discussed the way that the formal cinematic and musical cuts in Ramaka's *Karmen Geï* create a queer structure that demonstrates the multiple and overlapping ways that Karmen breaks away from the status quo. But I also discussed how these cuts were, to paraphrase Alexander Weheliye (2005, 63), in dialogue with dominant forces and structures. Karmen, in other words, at once departs from the normative heteropatriarchal world and is contained within that world. Though the structures of the films examined in this chapter are far less eccentric and improvisational than that of *Karmen Geï*, I want to return to the concept of the cut and to the way it can incorporate both an unexpected flight from a structure and a return to it. Throughout this chapter I pay attention to many different overlapping and contradictory forms of cutting. A cut, to list just a few meanings, may mean an incision; a physical or emotional wound; a transition from one situation or moment to another (as in cinema and music); a cut away to something different; an omission (something that is cut out); a way through something (a shortcut or cutting across); something that divides, stops short, or signifies an end (as when the director says "cut" at the end of a scene); and, in fact, even the product of a film itself (i.e., a director's cut, a rough cut, a final cut). When Fred Moten talks about the cut in *In the Break*, he plays with some of these complex meanings. At times he uses it to describe something jolting or rupturing, a shocking departure from the ordinary or the "shock of the shock" (Moten 2003, 200). But he also utilizes it to indicate the "insistent beat" of that which has been cut off, the "otherwise occluded sensuality, otherwise occluded sound, otherwise occluded *content*" (180). In this chapter I highlight the complex and sometimes contradictory ways that *Skoonheid*, *Inxeba*, and *Kanarie*—all of which also contain important scenes of literal cutting—break from (i.e., cut away and cut through) hegemonic and racialized forms of homophobia and hypermasculinity. But my main argument is that, at the same time that these films allow for breaks and openings, they also cut off the "the kind of fugitive time that allows for access to something beyond" (Nyong'o 2018, 10) and, in the process, return to the heteropatriarchal and racial structures that continue to constrain the present.

Irritating Beauty: Hermanus's *Skoonheid*

Though Oliver Hermanus knew that he wanted to make a film about the sometimes destructive nature of beauty and desire, the inspiration for the Afrikaans-language film *Skoonheid*'s disturbingly desirous main character came to him after he encountered a classified ad in a Cape Town newspaper. The author of the ad was looking for other white, married (to women) Afrikaner men to join a twice-weekly orgy. A marriage certificate was even required to join (Steele 2011). "They didn't want anybody who was unmarried, gay, or not white to attend," Hermanus says, adding, "Because I'm not white, it just seemed so strange to me to find that kind of rhetoric in a post-apartheid South Africa" (Wilson 2012). From this ad, Hermanus, who also has writing credits for the film, created the character of François van Heerden, played by well-known Afrikaner actor Deon Lutz. François owns a modestly successful sawmill and lives in a white suburb of Bloemfontein, a city that is not only, according to Hermanus, a segregated "bastion of Afrikanerdom" (Phillips 2012) but also a city with one of the highest rates of homosexuality in South Africa and a long tradition of secret gay meeting places and cruising grounds.[9] François, like the men in the classified ad, attends regular meetups where white men drink beer and have sex with each other. On one level, this seems to be working quite well for him. François has his family, his business, the life he is expected to have, and a sex life on the side that does not appear to be a source of shame or conflict for him. On another level, though, François barely conceals his increasing annoyance and irritation with the world around him, and it is implied that he has had anger management and alcohol abuse issues in the past. The film opens at his daughter's wedding, where François reconnects with an old army friend from Cape Town and sees his friend's son, Christian, grown up and exceedingly handsome (figure 3.1). Hermanus spends much time on this scene, slowly panning the crowd at the wedding from François's point of view before methodically zooming in on Christian, the character who seems to threaten the careful balance François has thus far been able to maintain.

But *Skoonheid* is decidedly not a rosy coming-out narrative for François, and from the very beginning of the film Hermanus establishes a tone that is disarming, intentionally Hitchcockian, and brooding. What Hermanus creates, then, is not any sort of political manifesto or celebration of queerness but rather a piercing psychological portrait of an Afrikaner man who has no desire for change—he is unhappy with the rebalance of power in post-apartheid South Africa, uninterested in claiming any sort of gay identity, and incapable of expressing feelings that might move him in any alternative direction. Moreover, the film is completely devoid of pleasure, with Lutz performing nearly every scene in a flat, unfeeling manner and the other characters responding to his deadpan with equally indifferent comments and expressions.

Though the film is inspired by an ad for an orgy, the scene in the movie that depicts François's regular sex meetup is not some sort of hedonistic bacchanal but rather a bland and unsettling, almost lifeless, gathering of middle-aged white men. Hermanus films François driving to a farmhouse in his pickup

FIGURE 3.1. Still from *Skoonheid* (2011). Christian (*left*) and François (*right*) at the wedding of François's daughter.

truck, or *bakkie*, which, as Nicky Falkof (2016, 20) suggests, has long served as a symbol of Afrikaner manhood. François enters the kitchen as several white men, dressed much like him, are standing around drinking beer. At first it is unclear what the gathering is about. François is introduced to the new member of the group, Brian, while the men make stilted small talk about the weather and email and agree with François, who cuts his finger on a can of beer, that the cans are too sharp and that there should be a better way of opening them. When Gideon, another member of the group, walks in with an effeminate-presenting and darker-skinned companion, the men stare at him blankly. Gideon tries to assure the group that his friend can be trusted and would not expose anyone, but one member of the group speaks up, saying, "You can't bring him here." Though Gideon tries to make his case, François turns to him and says: "Look at him! We're not faggots, Gideon!" (figure 3.2). Finally, Henry, the group leader, escorts Gideon out saying, "No faggots, no coloureds. You know that." When Henry returns he explains that this is Gideon's second offense and that he will no longer be welcomed. The men shrug off the incident and continue to drink until the camera abruptly cuts to the outside of the farmhouse for several seconds, then cuts back to a somewhat unexpected scene: the men have all moved to a small, dark bedroom and have paired off to have sex while watching a vhs tape of a white man masturbating. But the sex the men have with each other is silent, mechanical, and as unanimated as their kitchen conversation. François is receiving oral sex from Brian, but, as Andrews (2018a, 35) points out, "The camera is positioned above François's head . . . a regularly

FIGURE 3.2. Still from *Skoonheid* (2011). François (*left*) and Brian (*right*) at the farmhouse drinking beers when Gideon arrives with a young, effeminate Black man.

employed angle in the film which demonstrates a feeling of abstraction even in seemingly 'intimate' settings. The suggestion is that François is never fully present in the scene, detached from the sexual activities and observing his life from a remove." When he tires of the oral sex, François turns Brian over and begins dispassionately grunting and thrusting himself into his backside. Throughout, Hermanus keeps cutting away to still shots of the farmhouse and the pickup trucks outside, using the repetition of these quiet establishing shots and the flat landscape outside to highlight the flatness and even ordinariness of the Afrikaner farmhouse "orgy" within.

As Falkof (2016) argues, *Skoonheid*, a film in which characters speak to each other almost exclusively in Afrikaans rather than English, is deeply embedded in Afrikaner culture. And she underscores the importance of understanding that though the English translation of the film's title is *Beauty*, the word *skoonheid* in Afrikaans is also associated with cleanliness and purity (21). Falkof therefore reads the farmhouse as "a space for the exclusive expression of white—and specifically Afrikaans—desire, where any relation to a gay male culture or community is explicitly repudiated and the boundaries of whiteness, even in transgression, are policed" (21). She understands the rejection, or what I would call the cutting out, of Gideon's companion as "the aggressive expulsion of the non-white, openly gay interloper" that "suggests a purification of the body politic, a sanitisation of the closed community of ethnic whiteness" (21). And this is not the only type of sanitizing that occurs in the film. When he is done having sex with Brian, François returns to his pickup truck, splashes water on his face, and returns home. Throughout the film, in fact, there are many shots of François washing himself, swishing with water, or showering. It seems that he just cannot quite get things clean. On top of that, when he returns home from the farmhouse, his wife tells him, "We have to do something about the pool. It's been green for weeks." Moments later he expresses his annoyance that the cut on his finger from the beer can has not stopped bleeding. To a certain extent this quest for cleanliness, albeit constantly thwarted, might be a way of tying François's Afrikaner identity to the Puritan ideals that "developed concurrently with the Dutch Reformed Church and Afrikaner nationalism" (Sonnekus 2013, 30). Theo Sonnekus, in fact, argues that François's performances of hegemonic Afrikaner masculinity can "be viewed as manifestations of Christian Nationalist ideology, buttressed mainly by the Dutch Reformed Church, which placed great emphases on morality, asceticism, industriousness and heteronormativity" (24). In this way, François's pursuit of a man named Christian, alongside his desire for purity and cleanliness, can be seen as extensions of rather than departures from his claim to Afrikaner identity.

Furthermore, though it is tempting to read François's desire for other men as one that "leads to self-loathing and shame" (Sonnekus 2013, 36), Hermanus does not give us any clues that François thinks of himself as departing from the "morality, asceticism, industriousness and heteronormativity" of Afrikaner cultural identity. There are no moments of self-reflection for François—other than when he brags to Christian that he can show him how to "keep it all together"—no signs that he is suffering internally, afraid of being discovered, or conflicted about his sexual desires. His expression is in fact highly unreadable for almost the entire film. He does, however, describe himself as feeling "irritated." At one point in the film François visits a doctor, confessing, "I feel irritated all the time. I just don't feel well." The doctor asks if he has pain or nausea and he says no, "I've just had bad moments lately." When asked if he might lose control again, François responds in a surprisingly honest matter, admitting, "I don't know." It seems that François sees himself not as an outlier or transgressor but as someone who simply finds himself perpetually irritated at the world he cannot make perfect or clean enough.

For Sianne Ngai (2005, 6), irritation is one of the negative affects that, unlike shame (or other "morally beatific" states like melancholia or sympathy), "are explicitly amoral and noncathartic, offering no satisfaction of virtue, however oblique, nor any therapeutic or purifying release." Ngai writes that these amoral (by which she means outside the scope of moral debates) and noncathartic affects can be understood as "ugly feelings" that respond to "the general state of obstructed agency" (3), regardless of whether that obstruction is actual or merely fantasized. Ngai argues that moods like irritation or anxiety are "defined by a flatness or ongoingness" (7); unlike anger and fear, they are not sudden or explosive but tend, rather, to linger without "an explicit occasion or object" (179). And indeed François is irritated, it seems, at nearly everything. He is irritated with his wife, who nags him about cleaning the pool and his drinking and his business decisions, and he is irritated at his younger daughter, who flirts with Christian and later takes François's car without permission to see him. He is irritated that he keeps cutting himself on beer cans and that his cut keeps bleeding. He also seems to be irritated that the world is changing, that masculine, white men are losing power. He bemoans the fact that "moffies," the powerfully derogatory Afrikaans word for "faggots," seem to be able to "get away with a lot these days," and he commiserates with his friend Wilhelm, Christian's father, who says, "I know things were bad in the old days, but at least we felt safe. Now they're forcing us to become racist." What appears to bother François is therefore less his sexual desires—which in the film do not seem to condense into any sexual identity—and more so "the general state of obstructed agency" that men like François and Wilhelm feel in a world in which they are no longer in charge of making and enforcing the social and political rules.

Moreover, toward the end of the film when François's irritation does indeed transform into explosiveness, it is a surprisingly noncathartic and emotionally unintelligible moment. In the second half of the film François decides to pursue his obsession with Christian by visiting Cape Town, ostensibly on a business trip. He visits Wilhelm's house for dinner, where he sees Christian again and learns more about his comings and goings. François then stalks Christian around the city. First, he spies on him from a distance at the University of Cape Town, where Christian is studying law. He sees Christian greeting his friends and then embracing a man of color, happily chatting with him, and giving him a peck on the cheek—notably, however, the conversation between Christian and the man is muted. The audience can see their lips moving and their smiles but cannot hear the words—the sound is cut out. Here, then, it becomes clear that, despite his power as the stalker, François is limited in his access to Christian—he cannot hear Christian's conversation, cannot read the nature of the relationship between him and his friend, and is cut off from whatever new world this group of friends has created. When he continues to stalk Christian and sees him at the beach with his daughter, he therefore uses what little patriarchal power he has and calls the police to report stolen the car that his daughter took.

Later that night, François takes himself to a gay nightclub in Green Point, Cape Town's queer-friendly district, where he checks out white men that do not pay attention to him, has too much to drink, physically pushes away a Black man who flirts with him, and finds himself vomiting outside. He then calls Christian to come pick him up. The two grab a bite to eat at a nearby diner, where François expresses his frustration at the current government, tells Christian that it's important to "know yourself and not become like that scum" (though it's unclear who the scum is that François is referring to), and tries to figure out if Christian is interested in men by asking him if he ever goes out in Green Point. Though Christian responds that he occasionally does, it is still unclear whether Christian is gay or simply not homophobic—nor does it really matter to the plot. As they return to François's hotel, Christian has been pitching a business proposal to François, whom he has always viewed as an uncle, in the hopes of some financial assistance. François offers Christian a drink and as the two sit down on the bed, François initiates a kiss but is pushed away by Christian. Suddenly, François begins beating and choking Christian until Christian is pinned facedown on the bed with his pants down. At one point, a bloody and shocked Christian ceases to fight back and François attempts to penetrate him. However, François is unable to get an erection and resorts to masturbating on top of and then next to Christian. When he is still unable to climax, he goes to the bathroom to rinse off while Christian quivers on the bed (figure 3.3). The film then abruptly cuts to François, expressionless, in the car with his wife back in Bloemfontein. His assault on Christian—his failed rape—offers him no release, physical or emotional, and rather than becoming some moment of expressive suffering or guilt on François's part, it is never again mentioned in the film. Instead, the audience sees François back in his daily life, cut off from Christian and the events in Cape Town and as emotionally deadpan as ever, though finally cleaning out his dirt- and debris-infested pool.

Similarly, the final sequences of the film offer little in the way of reconciliation, redemption, or punishment. François receives a call at work that the audience cannot hear but that seems to leave him feeling vaguely perturbed. He goes home, asks his daughter if she has heard from Christian, and then goes to the bank to withdraw a large sum of money. Though it is never explicitly said, the implication is that the call was from Christian or someone Christian knows demanding money from François. François takes the envelope of money and sits down at the Bloemfontein Spur, a popular Native American–themed family restaurant chain. François orders food and then sees a young, white man sitting at another table. He watches the man from a distance until the man's boyfriend sits down across from him and the two young white men exchange kisses and happily chat. As was the case when he was watching Chris-

FIGURE 3.3. Still from *Skoonheid* (2011). François stands up to go to the bathroom after assaulting Christian in the hotel room. Christian remains in bed motionless.

tian converse with his friend at school, François sees the boys' lips moving but again the sound is muted or cut out. François is audibly excluded from whatever exchange or form of relationship they have. Here, for the first time, François seems visibly sad, albeit still in an underperformed way. When the boyfriends glance over at him, he averts his gaze, and melancholy piano music begins to play on the soundtrack. In the final shot of the film François is again in his *bakkie* driving down the spirals of a parking lot. He presumably sees in the two boyfriends, who can publicly express affection in an ordinary and everyday public location, a life not lived or a path not taken—or perhaps just a reminder of Christian's youth and unattainable beauty—but it does not seem likely that François will do anything different. *Skoonheid* is not a cinema of otherwise possibility, at least not for François, who continues to resist change on both the personal and political levels.

In an essay on "structures of unfeeling," Lauren Berlant (2015) contrasts the type of "performative subtraction" that I have been identifying in *Skoonheid* to what Raymond Williams describes in his famous essay on "structures of feeling." Williams, Berlant writes, "places the historical present in the affective presence of an atmosphere that is sensed rather than known and enacted, a space of affective residue that constitutes what is shared among strangers" (194). Structures of feeling therefore indicate a collective, emotional experience. By contrast, underperformativity "sneaks around the codes of sincerity and intelligibility that make possible normative social trust and trust in the social," disturbing any presumptions of emotional universality or collective belonging (195). These types of performances of unfeeling "stage a crisis in the register of making any claim on the world—political or intimate—as such" (197). In this sense, the underperformativity of François makes it difficult to attach any clear ethical reading to *Skoonheid*, and Hermanus very clearly leaves his audience with a film that remains devoid of forms of catharsis, virtue, or communal feeling that might register any discernible claims about the transformative possibilities of queerness.

The film ends by suspending itself in mid-air, with François literally in the middle of driving down a spiral ramp, perpetually irritated and left out of any type of shared collective intimacy. François's irritation at the world around him, his racism, abusive masculinity, and homophobia are, even in the film's final moments, characterized by their ongoingness. And that, of course, is the point. Hermanus presents this disturbing psychological portrait of a man who remains ensconced in his stagnant bastion of Afrikanerdom, a man whose violence is enacted from, not in contrast to, his position as an Afrikaner patriarch (Falkof 2016, 20) and who, despite or perhaps because of his queer desires, deliberately cuts out and cuts off any alternatives to his irritating life. *Skoon-heid*'s brief cuts to an otherwise are always followed by a cut back to a François who seems more bothered by a beer can cutting his finger than by his sexual assault on a friend's son and whose cuts keep him constantly on edge.

Wounded Manhood: Trengove's *Inxeba*

While the epidermal cuts in *Skoonheid* are irritating and relatively minor, in *Inxeba* the cutting of flesh plays a much more central and controversial role, and the film itself is clearly much more interested in cutting to the types of otherwise occluded sensualities that might challenge the status quo. *Inxeba* begins with a series of cinematic cuts—first, a shaky camera films a few seconds of a waterfall, then there is a cut to the title sequence, then briefly back to the waterfall, then a cut to Xolani operating a forklift in the storage facility where he works for a white man. Then there is a cut to Xolani, shot from behind, putting on his black cap and leaving the storage facility, and then in the back of a Datsun pickup truck catching a ride, it turns out, to the scene of the main cutting: the mountain where the circumcision takes place. Xolani meets with Kwanda's father, and we learn that Xolani will be the boy's caregiver during his initiation and transition to manhood. Kwanda's father, a wealthy businessman in Johannesburg, hands Xolani a roll of money and says, "I want you to be firm with my son. The boy's too soft. If you ask me, it's his mother who spoiled him. She didn't want him to come here. She wanted him to go to a hospital." He also adds that lately Kwanda has been bringing home friends, "rich boys from Joburg" who "lock themselves in their room." He be-lieves that "something is not right" with his son and that the initiation will fix that. Then, after the discussion of the physical cut that should make Kwanda right, there is a cinematic cut to an older man speaking to the initiates, who are wrapped in traditional white blankets with two bold red stripes and are splashed with water to be cleansed (figure 3.4). Still less than six minutes into the film, there is yet another cut: the traditional surgeon enters the scene, approaches each boy, tells him to spread his legs, not to look, and to repeat, "I am a man!" The cutting of the foreskin itself is never shown on film, and in fact, bodies and blankets always stand between the handheld camera and the initiate being circumcised. In the next scene, Xolani is washing and caring for Kwanda's wound in a very dimly lit hut. As he applies white paint to Kwanda's face he explains that Kwanda will stay in his hut for eight days without sleeping or drinking water and that any questions should be directed to him. He gives Kwanda a smoke, his "medicine," and says, "When you go home, don't speak of

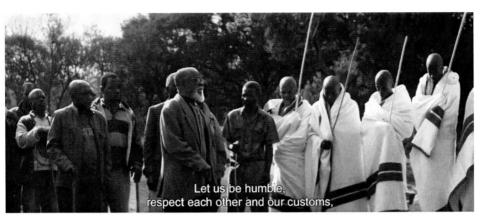

Let us be humble,
respect each other and our customs,

FIGURE 3.4. Still from *Inxeba* (2018). The young initiates gather before they
are each circumcised.

what happened here." Xolani is referring here to the secrecy that is supposed
to surround *ulwaluko*, which, as Gqola (2007, 151) explains, "is an elaborate
religious/social ceremonial process composed of weeks of rituals and stages"
and not simply about the circumcision or cutting itself.

While Hermanus received minor criticism—as someone from outside the
culture—for making a story about Afrikaner men, it was nowhere near the level
of criticism Trengove received, as a white man, for making *Inxeba* and, as some
accused, exposing Xhosa secrets.[10] Before the film was even screened in theaters, it was met with resistance, primarily from the Xhosa community. After
the online trailer was released, social media opposition to the film coalesced
around the hashtag #InxebaMustFall, which took its cue from the #FeesMust-
Fall and #RhodesMustFall student movements that had been campaigning for
a decolonized educational system in South Africa. In this way, #InxebaMust-
Fall positioned *Inxeba* as part of a larger colonial project that undermined
South African traditional cultural practices with values from the West. The
filmmakers and cast responded with several defenses. First, they argued that
the film did not divulge anything about ulwaluko that was not already general
public knowledge. And indeed, though the film mentions that Kwanda must
stay in seclusion, nothing about what he goes through during this period of
seclusion is actually depicted on screen. Most of the film takes place in the two
weeks after the seclusion, as the wound heals. The focus is therefore almost
solely on the way that the characters interact with each other rather than on
portraying anything specific about the ritual. In fact, nothing about the ritual

is ever explained to the audience besides Xolani's few sentences to Kwanda, and the cinematic cuts and blocking seem to deliberately obscure the ritual as well as the sense of time so that it is difficult to tell where the boys are in the process. Perhaps the one moment when we do see what happens during ulwaluko is at the end of the film when the initiates' huts are burned to symbolize the leaving behind of boyhood. But this aspect of the initiation is again public knowledge.[11] Moreover, since the protests against *Inxeba* mobilized before anyone had a chance to see the film, it is difficult to tell whether people truly felt specific secrets or scenes should not have been shown, whether there was just general uneasiness with the dramatization of secret rites, or whether the anger had to do with the depiction of same-sex intimacy during the initiation.

Second, in response to those who felt the film was not Trengove's to make, the director, in nearly every interview about the film, is quick to point out that the film was a collaborative process and that it accurately reflects the different experiences Xhosa men have during initiation. The idea for the film began, Trengove says, with conversations between himself and the coproducer Batana Vundla, a queer Xhosa man, and was based on months of research and conversations with Xhosa men who had been through the ritual. Trengove also notes that both of his cowriters were Xhosa men who experienced ulwaluko. The first to join the project was Thando Mgqolozana, who had written about botched circumcision in his novel *A Man Who Is Not a Man* and who was interested in further interrogating the ideas of masculinity that are attached to ulwaluko. The second was Malusi Bengu, who joined many of the research trips. The filmmakers also cast Xhosa speakers and those who had been through the initiation and encouraged them to improvise and use their own experiences while acting. Nakhane Touré, the out gay musician who plays Xolani, was also vocal in interviews, insisting that queer love and desire do indeed exist during ulwaluko. In one interview, he talks about seeing gay boys on Twitter talk about their experience on the mountain and confirms that he too was propositioned during ulwaluko (Collison 2017).

Nevertheless, despite these defenses and the deeply collaborative nature of the filmmaking process, *Inxeba* was subject to a tremendous amount of backlash. When the film did finally open in theaters, two cinemas in the Eastern Cape, where the film takes place, suspended screenings of the film after protests and pressure from the community. A theater in Cape Town and a few in the Western Cape also decided to stop screenings. A subsequent attempt by traditional leaders to reclassify the film led to the film being pulled out of all South African theaters for almost five months. When the film was originally released in July 2017, it was given a 16SNL classification by the Film and

Publication Board, indicating that the film was not suitable for children under sixteen because of sex (S), nudity (N), and language (L). However, an organization called CONTRALESA (Congress of Traditional Leaders of South Africa) lodged a complaint with the board saying that it was culturally insensitive and misrepresented ulwaluko. Next, CONTRALESA and the Man and Boy Foundation filed an appeal asking that *Inxeba* be reclassified as 18-and-over. Unexpectedly, the Board's appeals tribunal went one step further and, in February 2018, reclassified the film as X18, essentially labeling it hard-core pornography that could be shown and distributed only in adult premises like sex shops, despite the fact that the film shows no full frontal nudity. The new rating also forced the immediate removal of the film from the cinemas where it was showing. As in the case of those who protested *Karmen Geï*, the protesters initially focused much more on the film's cultural inappropriateness than on its representation of homosexuality. But the classification battle and discussions of pornography put questions of sexuality at the forefront and, for many South Africans, harked back to the days of apartheid censorship. The producers challenged this reclassification and in June 2018 the Gauteng High Court in Pretoria reissued the "16" classification and allowed the film back in theaters.

But, interestingly, the controversy around the film seemed to overshadow the fact that the filmmakers actually refrained from putting ulwaluko in a negative light. For instance, there are no mentions of botched circumcisions or unclean instruments, despite the fact that the cowriter Mgqolozana's novel dealt with the subject and there has been growing public opposition to ulwaluko as more and more boys have been hospitalized or have died from the process. Both Xolani—who calls city boys who do not get circumcised "cowards"—and Vija speak of the process with respect, and many of the initiates offer heartfelt monologues about what being a man and taking responsibility mean to them. Meanwhile, Kwanda, the one character who shows consistent disrespect for the process and the caregivers—he asks, "Why do we have to sit around and watch our dicks heal for two weeks?"—is arguably the most transformed by it. For most of the movie he stands off to the side, unwilling to engage with the other initiates who constantly tease him, and remains aloof from the cultural practices that create meaning for the other initiates. But toward the end of the movie he responds to Vija's challenge to slaughter a goat stolen from a white farmer—a reminder that they are on Xhosa land that had been stolen by European colonists—and later is shown drinking and dancing around the fire with the initiates. Kwanda seems to be somewhat more willing to participate in the aspects of ulwaluko that address more than just the wound (or *inxeba*) of the circumcision cut. Kwanda also seems to have thought the most deeply about what being a man means. When, on the last day of initiation, Xolani says to him, "You are a man now," Kwanda responds, "Yes, I'm a man. I'm not taking anyone's shit anymore. Not my dad's. Not anybody's." For Kwanda, who scorns men "who follow their dicks around like it's the most important thing," the transition from boyhood to manhood does not mean taking a wife and building a home but insisting on being the type of man he wants to be and psychologically liberating himself from versions of manhood he finds to be violent and problematic.

What the film seems really to be challenging and rupturing, then, are not the rites of ulwaluko itself but the hypermasculinity that positions manhood as something fixed and part of an authentic cultural practice. As Siseko H. Kumalo and Lindokuhle Gama (2018, 4) write in their discussion of *Inxeba*, "In the process of attaining an *authentic* status of Manhood, cultural practices and tradition appeal to violences—such as the policed sexualities of feminised bodies, the exclusion of women in cultural practices—that create and recreate violent masculinities manifesting as Manhood." But they argue that, "in its ideal structure, the custom of *ulwaluko* teaches young men the values of discipline and integrity, while inculcating a laudable moral position" (4). In other words, ulwaluko, at its core, "is neither fixed nor factual, but changing and constantly negotiated and reimagined in line with the social conditions" (4). Neville Hoad (2016, 2) makes a similar point about the "flexibility and nimbleness" of South African customary practices more broadly, contrasting them to the rigid dichotomy of legalization/criminalization that obscures the gradations and ranges of sexual practices within the country. He writes that "one of the few generalizations that can be made about the customary is that it is constitutively not fundamentalist" and argues that traditional and customary practices "may provide intellectual and affective resources to reimagine forms of African sexual self-sovereignty" (2). Xolani and Vija's love affair, which exists not only within the space of ulwaluko but because of the bond that began when they themselves were initiates, is a perfect example of that reimagining. Moreover, ulwaluko is a ritual that has the potential to bring out men's ability to care for and nurture one another. As Nakhane Touré says in an interview, ulwaluko is a "space where men are allowed to be vulnerable. You put your life and your penis, literally, in the hands of other men" (Collison 2017).

Furthermore, as Lwando Scott (2021) argues, perhaps one of the most important aspects of the film is that it creates space for public reflection on African queerness and, more specifically, Xhosa queerness. For Scott, who discusses growing up Xhosa and queer, as well as for the queer Xhosa friends with whom he saw *Inxeba*, the film felt so transgressive precisely because it disrupted

the conventional assumptions that queerness and Xhosa culture were mutually exclusive: "The film specifically challenges dominant forms of Xhosa masculinities and does so by going to the foundation, the 'factory' of dominant
Xhosa masculinities—*ulwaluko*. . . . The film poses a challenge to Xhosa culture itself, by boldly asking what the position of Xhosa culture is on same-sex
intimacies, because not only do these intimacies exist, they exist deep in the
most sacred of Xhosa cultural spaces" (L. Scott 2021, 27). Scott emphasizes
the film's ability to start conversations and encourage deep, complex thought
about queer African masculinities because it asserts that "queer Xhosa boys
and men matter and that the complex terrain in which their intimacies operate
and find voice needs to be engaged with fully" (36). Scott's attentiveness to the
critical possibilities opened up by *Inxeba* is important to keep in mind, and not
only because there are so few queer Xhosa discussions of this much-discussed
film. Scott's discussion also makes space for a reading of the film as resistant,
and as resistant in a way that matters to some of the people it represents.
However, I want to add to Scott's reading by suggesting that as much as the
film breaks away from and cuts hegemonic masculinity, it also dramatizes
the challenges of breaking away and speaks precisely to the complex terrain
Scott references.

To be sure, if the film had focused solely on Xolani and Vija's affair, it would
have been a much simpler film to gauge; its politics and insistence on same-
sex desire in "the most sacred of Xhosa cultural spaces" would have sent a
clear message. But Trengove, Mgqolozana, and Bengu complicated the script
by adding the character of Kwanda. And while Kwanda might be the one character to call openly for more nuanced understandings of manhood, he is also,
in many ways, the film's antagonist, the one who makes Xolani and Vija's transgressive affair on the mountain unsustainable. Up until Kwanda's time on the
mountain, Xolani and Vija seem to have their routine—the places where they
slip away to be together, their own unspoken rituals and rhythms. In public
they are the best of friends, despite the fact that Xolani's softness stands in
stark contrast to Vija's aggressiveness. At one point Vija puts his arm around
Xolani and declares to everyone in earshot, "We go way back. We will always be
friends." In private, they maintain a sexual relationship that is passionate and
intense and has its moments of tenderness. For Vija, this seems to be enough.
He has a wife at home who has just given birth to their third child, and though
he should be working to support his family, he takes time off to come to the
mountain to be with Xolani and perhaps also to have a space where he can feel
like a man rather than a struggling father. But Xolani, when he is not on the
mountain with Vija, is alone. He lives alone. He eats alone. He is stuck at his job.

When Kwanda enters their lives, the initiate immediately picks up on this imbalance and says to Xolani, "Do you think [Vija] thinks about you? I see what you are, but you can't admit it. You want me to be a man and stand up for myself, but you can't do it yourself" (figure 3.5). It is unclear what motivates Kwanda here, whether he has feelings for Xolani, is simply unable to support same-sex relationships that do not fit his model, or is motivated by a hatred for Vija—who refers to Kwanda as a "faggot" and whose hypermasculinity and bellicose affect symbolize all that Kwanda finds repellent about ulwaluko. Xolani tries to dismiss Kwanda and certainly denies the nature of his relationship with Vija, but after a while it is evident that Kwanda has gotten into his head. At one point, Xolani confesses his loneliness to Vija and says that his only reason for coming back to the mountain is to be with Vija. Vija is not pleased to hear this and tells Xolani that they cannot keep going on as is. He returns the money Xolani had given him in the previous scene (the money presumably was to help out Vija's family but, ironically, was likely the same roll that Kwanda's father had given to Xolani). Xolani is upset and, echoing Kwanda, asks Vija when he will stop hiding. Vija responds by attacking Xolani and in a later scene embarrassing him by telling everyone that Xolani will not return to the mountain, speculating out loud that Xolani might be ready to take a wife. But as the initiation period comes to an end, the two cannot stay away from each other. In what is the film's most sensual sequence they find themselves swimming and kissing in a waterfall—the one we see in the cuts of the opening sequence—and making love beside it. Cradled in each other's bodies, the two naked men fall asleep only to awake to Kwanda peering over them (figure 3.6).

FIGURE 3.5. Still from *Inxeba* (2018). Kwanda (*left*) confronts Xolani (*right*).

FIGURE 3.6. Still from *Inxeba* (2018). Xolani (*left*) and Vija (*right*) are discovered by Kwanda.

While the lovemaking scene is shot with close-ups of body parts—a crook in the arm, a foot flexed, a hand draped over a torso—that emphasize the tightness and connection between Vija and Xolani, the shot of the two men from Kwanda's point of view reveals the full lengths of their bodies and shows them completely exposed. As they scramble to put on their clothes, Kwanda says to Vija, to whom he has been churlish the entire film, "Excuse me, brother, does your wife know the shit you get up to in the mountains?" Vija begins to chase Kwanda, but Kwanda slips away and Vija slumps down cradling his head between his knees. Later, Xolani finds Kwanda, who had gotten lost in the mountains, and as they walk back to the camp, Kwanda cannot contain his anger at the entire situation he has found himself in. At first he expresses anger about the homophobic culture of his country: "This is South Africa, not Uganda or Zimbabwe. We're not led by Mugabe. Like, Africa doesn't know gay love? I'm sure Shaka and his warriors all wanted each other. Probably Jesus and his disciples were the same. How can love destroy a nation?" But then he begins to dig into Vija, saying, "He's a little boy posing as a big Xhosa man like the rest of them. You need to free yourself from this bullshit." Xolani reminds Kwanda that Vija has a wife and family and that things are more complicated than he presumes. But Kwanda replies, "I don't give a shit. Someone should expose him as a liar and a hypocrite. You think he loves you? You think you're the only guy he fucks? Fuck! I'm so angry. Aren't you fucking angry? Doesn't he make you mad?" Xolani does not reply directly but leads Kwanda up a different path that he says will get them to the road. Off the edge of the mountain, the waterfall comes into view. Then, without warning—"shock of the shock" (Moten 2003, 200)—Xolani pushes Kwanda off the side of a cliff.

Because so many of the articles and reviews about *Inxeba* focus on the controversy it stirred up in parts of the Xhosa community, not much attention has been given to this controversial ending to a film that, after making space for alternative masculinities and same-sex practices within traditional Xhosa spaces, winds up killing one Black queer, turning another into a murderer, and protecting the honor of a man who is aggressive and homophobic. In an unaired episode of *AfroQueer*, a podcast put out by the Nairobi-based queer media organization None on Record, host Aida Holly-Nambi asks Trengove specifically about his decision to have Kwanda killed. (None on Record was kind enough to share with me the unedited transcript of the discussion between Holly-Nambi and Trengove, which includes what I find to be a very important exchange between the two and one that, ultimately, would have had to be cut out if the podcast had been aired so as to not contain spoilers.) What Holly-Nambi asks of Trengove, then, is an important supplement to Scott's argument that sees the film as the opening up of possibilities and a perspective that has largely been left out of public discussions of the film. Crucially, Holly-Nambi asks Trengove directly why it was necessary to kill Kwanda, stating, "We can't be killed. Why is that the cost of being? I felt like the killing of that initiate was like a cutting down of that tree, or that root. . . . We're fighting more and more to be young, Black, and free. Young, queer, Black, and free. And then that was impossible. It felt anachronistic in a sense."[12] Trengove responds by saying that he has heard that criticism of the film, especially from gay, progressive audiences, but to him the focus is not on Kwanda but on Xolani, who, he says, "is prepared to assert himself to that extent for what he has decided he wants." He elaborates:

Now that choice might not be the one that you would make or that I would make. But I do want to kind of create a space for somebody like [Xolani] to challenge us to say, "You don't know me. You are waving your flags for me, telling me to move to Johannesburg and come to the gay bar. Whatever it is, find your community. But I love this man, and I don't want to see his life destroyed. And also, I have a cultural identity, and you don't know what that means for me." And so that gesture in the end is about throwing it right back in our laps. And I get it, for a lot of people that's an unacceptable kind of moment. A sense of betrayal. And all I can say to it is that that is an intended disruption. That is a moment where I am asking the audience to kind of not trust everything that they think they know about the world, and to think more about the story that they've just seen.

A few minutes later, Trengove, who has already explained that Kwanda is the character with whom his own personal views most align, adds, "You know, it's a weird thing. But I am getting lambasted right now . . . and I think rightfully so . . . for my presumption to tell this story. But these things that I'm describing were my way of trying to reflect something of my own problematic relationships with this subject matter. And to own up to the limitations of my perspective." Kwanda's death, in other words, intentionally cuts off the perspective of the out, gay, urban liberal.

In this exchange, Holly-Nambi agrees that what Trengove says makes sense and points out that she was in the minority, that the other people working on the podcast were not upset with the ending. But buried in Trengove's explanation is what I read as an uncomfortable elision of race. Trengove says that killing off Kwanda, who most embodies his own perspective, was a way of highlighting the problems of that perspective. But Holly-Nambi's specific critique was not about Trengove directing the film but that he had killed yet another Black queer character, that *Inxeba*'s ending felt like a throwback to stories in which young Black queers had no future. In other words, though Trengove and Kwanda are alike because they are both economically privileged and urban and feel at ease in the gay bars in Johannesburg, Holly-Nambi's critique emphasizes the fact that Kwanda's race matters—and so too, I might add, does his Xhosa identity. While film and media provide many examples of queer white males having successful, fulfilling lives, those who watch the film and identify with Kwanda because of his Blackness (or Xhosaness) and his queerness are given yet another example of Black, queer death.

Furthermore, though the ending does indeed highlight Xolani's agency and his rejection of Kwanda's values, it is difficult to see how Xolani might be an example of the "young, Black, and free" queer subject that Holly-Nambi wants to see in African cinema. Or, to put this differently, it is not easy to see how an Afri-queer fugitivity, an artful fleeing of objectification and capture, can be sustained by the queer characters in this film, despite the initial indication that the mountain makes this type of fugitivity possible for Vijay and Xolani. Nor does it seem probable that Xolani will be able to, as Hoad suggests, use the flexibility and nimbleness of traditional space to "reimagine forms of African sexual self-sovereignty." In fact, after losing the initiate he is supposed to be caring for, it is unlikely that Xolani can ever return to the mountain, the one space of love and cultural identity that nourishes him and to which he can in fact flee to year after year. And though Xolani scoffs at Kwanda's suggestion that he move to Joburg, the final shot of the film is Xolani doing just that, traveling to the city, to the one place he specifically says he does not want to be. For different reasons, Holly-Nambi and Trengove both see this ending as a type of cut. Holly-Nambi says that the killing of Kwanda was like the cutting down of a tree, while Trengove calls it an "intended disruption" that breaks away from the expected. In other words, while Holly-Nambi wishes that the film did not cut off hope, Trengove argues that the ending was a cut intended to disturb. For Trengove, then, the ending of the film is one that should make audiences uncomfortable enough to think and question: like *Skoonheid*, which Trengove claims as an inspiration, it is not a film that attempts to offer perfect routes of freedom or reconciliation or healing, despite the fact that it takes place almost entirely during the healing period of ulwaluko.

Here, then, I read the disruptive killing of Kwanda at the end of the film as profoundly disorienting. As Sara Ahmed (2006, 1) writes, "If we know where we are when we turn this way or that way, then we are oriented. We have our bearing. We know what to do to get to this place or that." But the ending of *Inxeba* leaves the audience without bearing, not knowing where to turn—as Trengove himself says, he throws things back in the viewer's lap. And the final few minutes of the film after Kwanda's death amplify Xolani's disorientation. While the other initiates are being welcomed back to the community and are walking toward a crowd of singing women, men, and children, Xolani walks alone alongside a road as atonal organ music plays, highlighting his disconnection from the end of the ritual. As Xolani walks, Trengove crosscuts to shots of the welcoming crowd but turns the camera sideways or upside down, bringing bodies in and out of focus so that Xolani's relation to them is thrown into disarray. Then the atonal music cuts out and Xolani is on the back of a flatbed driving to Johannesburg. The film ends with the word *Inxeba* superimposed over his image. In this way, though there are many different types of wounds and wounding throughout the film, it is Xolani's wound (*inxeba*), the one that takes him away from the few people and places that anchor him, that becomes the film's final cut.

This disorientation does not mean, however, that *Inxeba* is without the queer and critical possibilities that Lwando Scott suggests. Ahmed, who uses the concepts of disorientation and orientation to think about what it means to have a sexual orientation, or to be oriented in a certain way, writes, "The emergence of the term 'sexual orientation' coincides with the production of 'the homosexual' as a type of person who 'deviates' from what is neutral" (2006, 69). Sexual orientation, in other words, emerges when certain sexual practices become linked to a type of person—a species, as Michel Foucault says. *Inxeba*, which tries to delink the practices from the person, is therefore also disorienting in the sense that it refuses the neatness of categories and expectations around sexual orientation as an identity: its disorientation therefore has a certain liberatory function. What I am suggesting is that *Inxeba* opens up space for queer resistance but does so in a way that disorients resistance itself, that shows resistance not to be following any well-trodden path. In describing disorientation, Ahmed writes, "The body in losing its support might then be lost, undone, thrown" (157). This is what happens physically to Kwanda as he is pushed off the mountain and then psychically to Xolani. That *Inxeba* leaves us with no sense of how to proceed after this disorientation is certainly queer in the sense that it is nonlinear and disorderly: it calls into question assumptions about identity; it breaks rules; it provides much-needed and sometimes deeply felt, messy but beautiful alternatives to dominant heteropatriarchal masculinity. But it is also disorienting in that it does not show us where the previously excluded bodies, the Xolanis of the world, can be at home. Like *Skoonheid*, which ends suspended in mid-air, *Inxeba* ends with a cut, an intended disruption that rearranges and disorients hegemonic, toxic, and injurious sets of values but that does not yet give us our bearings.

Borders of Denial: *Kanarie*

Where *Skoonheid* and *Inxeba* focus on the overlaps between hegemonic masculinity and homophobia in very different post-apartheid communities, Olwagen's *Kanarie* takes viewers back to South Africa circa 1984–85, at the height of the South African Border War (also referred to as the Namibian War of Independence and the Angolan Bush War). The Border War began in 1966 as South African forces clashed with South West Africa People's Organization (SWAPO) insurgents in Namibia, then known as South West Africa and an occupied "mandate" of South Africa after having been a German protectorate from 1884 until the end of World War I. The year after the war started, the South African Defense Force began military conscription for all white men over the age of sixteen, eventually requiring two years of service plus many years of periodic "camp duty" after that. In 1975, when South Africa invaded Angola after the Portuguese colonial government collapsed and granted independence to the colony, military combat became more frequent. The South African government at the time framed the war as a fight against a "total onslaught" of communists and terrorists who were part of neighboring countries' liberation movements, but by the mid-1980s soldiers were deployed to quell a growing insurgency inside South Africa and, more specifically, inside the townships. In 1985, the apartheid government, under President P. W. Botha, declared a state of emergency that led to even more draconian law enforcement and military operations against non-white

South Africans. And it is precisely at this moment that Johan Niemand, the small-town Boy George–loving protagonist of *Kanarie*, begins to tour with the Defense Force choir.

Kanarie joins a small but significant number of films that queer military life in South Africa. As Ricardo Peach (2005, 114–17) notes, the very few South African films from the 1970s that dealt with homoeroticism, though certainly not explicitly, were army movies such as *Seuns van die Wolke* (*Sons of the Clouds*, 1975, dir. Franz Marx) and *Mirage Eskader* (1975, dir. Bertrand Retief). These films were followed in the 1980s by films such as *Boetie Gaan Border Toe* (*Boetie Goes to the Border*), a 1984 satire that was part of a genre of Border War films that were full of homoerotic images (Peach 2005, 117). As the writer and film producer Mark Gevisser states in an interview with Peach, "All those films . . . about going off to war. They are so fucking queer. . . . Whether it was about male bonding in the army, or a response to that, there is a lot of homosexual imaging and positioning happening in the whole white boys and the army thing" (117). Krouse's 1988 film *The Soldier*, mentioned above, was the first film to focus very explicitly on same-sex sexuality and sexual violence in the army. Many of the participants in the film had been conscripted into the military and were keen to critique the institution along with the foundations of Afrikaner culture. A description of the film on Krouse's website explains that the film was made to depict an event that had actually occurred in the army barracks when a soft-porn pinup was placed on a soldier's back during a gang rape. But because *The Soldier* was never completed, it was not until after apartheid that the first film explicitly addressing homosexuality in the military was screened in South Africa: Gerald Kraak's documentary *Property of the State: Gay Men in the Apartheid Military* (2003), which aired on South African television and chronicles the homophobia and abuse to which gay men were subject, from bullying to shock therapy to labor camps.

Kanarie also fits into a larger tradition of the *grensverhaal* (border story) or *grensliteratuur* (border writing) that included several queer voices that critiqued the hegemonic forms of masculinity holding apartheid culture together. And though apartheid film censorship meant that the films of the 1980s could only hint at the homoeroticism of military culture, white gay writers like Johann de Lange, Koos Prinsloo, Mark Behr, and Damon Galgut—as well as André Carl van der Merwe, whose novel *Moffie* was recently made into a film by Hermanus— were able to be much more forthright in their representation of same-sex desire and intimacy in the military. The writing of these types of stories continued through the 1990s and early 2000s and provided an important contrast to the nostalgic and heteronormative border stories that were published in the post-apartheid era. However, as Brenna Munro (2012) argues, though queer border writing was clearly critical of white apartheid masculinity, it did not always advocate for active political resistance and was often overdetermined by conflicting visions of race and the nation. She writes,

> This is a body of writing, then, that helped make gay sexuality a part of antiapartheid culture and thus imaginable within the "rainbow nation"; but it is also an ambivalent genre that imagines masculinity, race, and sexuality in complex and contradictory ways. En masse, however, this archive's queering of the militarized fraternity of apartheid also (re)produces gayness as whiteness. (Munro 2012, 82)

In this sense, *Kanarie* is no different. It is at once a warm and comedic gay love story, an aching drama of self-acceptance, a harsh critique not only of toxic masculinity but of the role of religion in justifying oppression, and a story that very ambivalently links queer sexualities to anti-apartheid politics.

Kanarie's queerness is on full display from its very first image—a close-up of Johan dressed up in a wedding gown and veil—and the film's main narrative arc is about Johan coming to terms with this queerness in a space and time that make no place for it. In the film's opening sequence Johan has requested that his two female school friends dress him up as Boy George, but the result, he says, makes him look more like Lady Diana. Before Johan has the chance to take off the dress, his friends dare him to walk down the street in it. He agrees to do it if they give him enough money to buy the new Depeche Mode and Queen albums. As he walks down the street Johan morphs into Boy George and begins to lip-synch to Bronski Beat's "Smalltown Boy" (figure 3.7). As Johan and his friends strut down the streets of Villiersdorp, different versions of Johan's younger self leave what they are doing to join the parade: first a Black nanny and toddler-age Johan join in, then a young Johan at a ballet bar, then a slightly older Johan playing piano, and other Johans at a sewing machine, arranging flowers, getting spanked at school, and so on. The lyrics seem apt—"Mother will never understand why you had to leave / But the answers you seek will never be found at home / The love that you need will never be found at home"—and as the chorus of "Run away, turn away, run away, turn away, run away" kicks in, the various Johans run down the street and begin a choreographed dance until the fugitive fantasy sequence is interrupted by the sound of a honking horn and Johan is caught in the wedding dress by his reverend. When he returns home, his two friends have beat him there and give him the news that the postman has brought his call-up papers from the army.

FIGURE 3.7. Still from *Kanarie* (2018). Johan Niemand dances down the streets of Villiersdorp imagining himself as Boy George.

Though Johan joins the Kanaries (Canaries), the Defense Force's Church Choir, and not a combat unit, he is nevertheless subjected to the rigors of military life (figure 3.8). He is stripped of his identity, is given a uniform, a military haircut, and dog tags, and is subjected to a basic training that is degrading, humiliating, misogynistic, and homophobic. However, within this process he is able to make two close friends: Ludolf, an affable, overweight tenor and soloist who has a particularly difficult time in training, and Wolfgang, a sensitive trumpet player who shares Johan's taste in 1980s pop music. Over the course of their performance tour—the Kanaries tour the country and stay with sympathetic white families (figure 3.9)—Wolfgang and Johan develop feelings for each other, and Johan struggles to accept who he is. Rather than allowing himself to fall in love and open up, Johan, after sharing a kiss with Wolfgang, becomes more forlorn and unable to accept himself and begins to lash out at his friends. Though they share several more intimate moments, Johan keeps pushing Wolfgang away.

Throughout the film, Johan's emotions are often processed through cuts to campy musical fantasy sequences. For instance, when he visits his first nightclub on a weekend pass, he is at first shy and embarrassed when his friends start singing out loud. But, then, he is again transformed into Boy George regalia, commanding the dance floor as the camera tracks to other dancers in the club

FIGURE 3.8. Still from *Kanarie* (2018). Johan joins the army.

FIGURE 3.9. Still from *Kanarie* (2018). The Kanaries perform on tour in front of the apartheid-era South African flag.

dressed as David Bowie, Prince, Michael Jackson, Annie Lennox, and Grace Jones. When Johan realizes that this is just a fantasy, he is again uncomfortable and becomes even more so when he witnesses two men emerging from a bathroom stall together. In another fantasy cut, he follows Wolfgang outside during a choir performance and begins to kiss him. In this case, the cut is not a musical performance per se, but music provides the occasion for the cut. In an earlier scene, Johan confesses to Wolfgang that music was always his refuge, the one thing that enabled his survival in his small, Afrikaner town. He describes how kids would ride their bikes past his house and ring their bike bells just to taunt him because they knew he was inside and thought that he was "weird." But Johan worked for years to save up money to buy Sony headphones because "with the headphones on, the bike bells didn't matter—the music did." In this sense music and the cuts to musical sequences allow for a break to an otherwise, a temporary departure from the main beat, which for Johan is most often a steady rhythm of shame and discomfort. But ultimately, these breaks are not enough for Johan. When he explains to Wolfgang why he is so obsessed with Boy George, why he collects interviews and articles and carries a picture of him in his Bible, he says he is hoping that one day Boy George will admit that he is gay. Johan explains, "I just thought that if he admitted it, it will somehow make it okay. . . . But instead he's said, 'I prefer a nice cup of tea to sex.' And who can build a life on that?" Here, then, Johan articulates his deepest frustration: he has, at this point, nothing to build a life on.

Without this foundation Johan begins to spiral toward self-destruction. When the film cuts to a chapter titled "State of Emergency," this is just as much an indicator of Botha's 1985 declaration as it is of Johan's mental health. As Johan begins to hear political opinions about apartheid that contradict the message of the army, and as the choir travels to the border, the fantasy sequences become increasingly dark. Rather than opening up to otherwise possibilities, the cinematic musical cuts open up Johan's psychic and physical injuries. During a performance for border soldiers, the camera focuses in on Johan's face as he plays the piano and then cuts to a series of shots that are made to resemble photographic stills where characters pose for the movie camera as if they were having their picture taken. The audience is presented with homoerotic images of naked soldiers holding guns and images of the Kanaries smiling, a Black child holding a bomb, a white soldier standing with a gun over a prone SWAPO soldier, and another SWAPO soldier's bloody body draped over a Jeep. The camera then returns to Johan playing piano, but, unlike the other cutaways that are clearly fantasy, here it seems that all these things actually happen at the border. As his mental state deteriorates, the line between fantasy and reality becomes increasingly difficult to distinguish.

Then, later that night, Johan is faced with the impossibility of drowning out unpleasantries. As the Kanaries huddle in their tent before bed, they hear a gunshot and are informed that a cow has accidentally been shot and has fallen behind a ridge. Because soldiers are not allowed to leave the camp at night, they cannot kill the cow, and the entire camp must listen to the loud groans of the injured animal. Johan nearly loses his mind and runs to the latrine to try to find peace, telling Wolfgang, who has followed him, that their relationship has "fucked him up." The cow returns in the final fantasy sequence, when Johan finds himself alone in the barracks after a failed attempt to come out to his sister during a weekend pass. By himself on the eve of his nineteenth birthday, Johan is haunted by sounds of bike bells ringing, and when he follows the sound he finds not only the kids on bikes but also a cow next to an army rifle. He picks up the rifle as the film crosscuts to various close-ups of Johan throughout the film. He shoots the rifle and then puts on his headphones to dance to a techno remix of Boy George's "Do You Really Want to Hurt Me" (a song he would play for his friends who would then tease him by answering "yes"). Johan's dance repeats some of the movements of the "Smalltown Boy" sequence, but he also incorporates military salutes and marching. When the fantasy ends, he finds himself on the floor and discovers he has destroyed the barracks. Trunks and mattresses are overturned, and his hands and arms are all cut up and covered in blood. He makes his way to Reverend Engelbrecht's home to ask the reverend, who is also the choir leader, to pray to God to give him the will to change himself.

Throughout the film, then, the cuts to fantasy sequences have opposing effects. They point both to otherwise possibilities and to Johan's resistance to these otherwise possibilities. In fact, Johan resists the cuts to the otherwise so vehemently that he literally cuts his flesh, and in the fantasy sequence in the barracks Olwagen quite masterfully uses cinema and sound to make palpable and resonant Johan's deep psychic cuts or wounds. But cutting operates in yet another way in this film—namely, there is a great deal of political and racial tension that is either cut out of the film or offered up momentarily only to be cut away from. For instance, in what one might presume would be a pivotal scene during the Kanaries' tour, an English-speaking woman approaches Johan and several other soldiers after a performance. She asks the soldiers if they have been into the townships, and when they say they are not sure what she means, she says, "Well, Botha sends troops into the townships. I'm asking if you have been." Johan replies, "That's not really the purpose of the Kanaries. . . . We deliver a message of hope to those who have loved ones in the army." She then asks, "Do you really believe that the color of our skin makes us superior?" When they reply that they do not and that they did not have a choice about being in the war, she states emphatically, "You always have a choice. Do you understand that the purpose of this war, the sole purpose, is to keep whites in power? . . . I am very upset that all of you can stand on that stage and pretend that God supports this war." After Reverend Engelbrecht comes to disband the conversation, Johan finds himself unable to move and remains, looking shocked, holding his plate of food. This is the first moment that any character in the film points out the hypocrisy of the Kanaries or challenges the party line, but then almost immediately the camera cuts away to an unrelated scene. And though the glimpses of his subconscious suggest that Johan might feel guilty about participating in the army, he never contemplates other options or articulates his own critique. Even when he fears that one of the superiors might suspect his relationship with Wolfgang, and Wolfgang suggests that they go AWOL and move to England, the option is immediately dismissed as "crazy." Fugitivity or running away might be an option for Johan in his fantasies, but he seems unwilling to entertain the idea of actually fleeing.

Much of this, one might argue, is in line with how an eighteen-year-old Afrikaner boy, especially one who has been introverted and ostracized his whole life, would likely behave and see the world at the time. In an interview with Daniel Dercksen, Charl-Johan Lingenfelder, whose life story the film is based on, discusses the moment during the film when Johan tells the reverends that he wants to join the Kanaries in order to "live all that I believe, all that I love, and all that I am to the fullest." Lingenfelder states, "At every screening that I have attended thus far, people always laugh when the protagonist talks about his passion for his church and for his country. The script at that point is literally just taken from what I know I would've said. . . . In those days, we simply did not question everything the way we do today. We didn't know we had the right to question anything" (Dercksen 2018). And while that may be the case, the film's main events take place in 1985, at a time when the End the Conscription Campaign (ECC), which was only one of many war resistance organizations, had organized the "Troops out of the Townships" rally and hunger strike. The year 1985 was therefore a significant moment in the antiwar movement. As Gavin Evans (2009) writes,

> In 1985 it was announced in parliament that 7,589 conscripts had failed to report for the January national call-up, compared with 1,596 for the

whole of 1984. By 1986 around 7,000 war resisters were living in Europe (many of them supported by the ANC-aligned Committee of South African War Resisters), with emigration outstripping immigration for the first time. Many others dodged the call-up by prolonging studies indefinitely or evading the over-stretched military police. In 1986 a Witwatersrand commanding officer revealed that one in four conscripts was failing to report for army camps.

It would therefore not have been unheard-of for white men like Johan and Wolfgang to make choices other than staying in the army, even though such choices could have had severe consequences. Moreover, one of the founders of the ECC was Dr. Ivan Toms—an openly gay white conscientious objector who gained much attention for his three-week hunger strike during the "Troops out of the Townships" campaign and who reasonably could have been known to characters in the film. But rather than referencing or alluding to any of these otherwise possibilities, *Kanarie* stays focused on Johan's mental "state of emergency."

Likewise, none of the characters converse with a person of color, and the only people of color who appear in the film—in addition to the servers who set up a banquet hall during one of the performances—are those who have cameos in Johan's fantasy sequences. None of them have a speaking role. In this sense, as Chantelle Gray (2021, 10) argues, the structural absence of people of color on which the apartheid system was based, and on which it relied to keep functioning, is reproduced in the film. But Annel Pieterse, who discusses *Kanarie* in relation to Olwagen's earlier film *Johnny Is Nie Dood Nie* (*Johnny Is Not Dead*), in which one character is a white gay police informer, sees *Kanarie*, like Olwagen's earlier work, as deliberately problematizing the insulated world of his young Afrikaner characters. She argues that *Kanarie* "seems to signal its awareness of the marginality or limitation of black representation in white Afrikaans narratives" and that the cutaways to Black bodies "comment on how black South Africans were represented in the interests of Afrikaner Nationalist propaganda: as peripheral servile characters, or as dead terrorists" (Pieterse 2019, 380). Admittedly, it is hard to tell which is the case, whether *Kanarie* is itself silencing Black voices or whether the film is registering this silencing in order to critique it, and it is certainly possible that the film does both of these things at once. Likewise, though Johan certainly begins to open his eyes to the oppression around him, it is difficult to tell to what extent he becomes fully conscious of apartheid's injustices and aware of his own complicity in the system.

Indeed, throughout the film Johan's attempts to deny his identity and sexuality are juxtaposed with the Kanaries' denial that they are participating in an oppressive war. But rather than articulating any of the many paths of political resistance that might have been available to the men, the narrative focuses on Johan's path to self-acceptance and makes any concern with accepting responsibility for upholding the apartheid regime secondary. For instance, when Johan meets a woman on tour who encourages him to be a canary that flies away and follow his dreams, she places him in front of a mirror and tells him the biggest bully is himself. Of course, she means that he has been too hard on himself, but given the brutal violence inflicted by the actual bullies in the film, this line seems to reinforce political denial at the same moment that Johan is prodded to stop denying his identity and passions. A similar move occurs in the penultimate scene of the film, when Johan, Wolfgang, and Ludolf are tasked with creating the program for the Kanaries' second tour. Johan, who is still bandaged and raw from his breakdown, puts together an arrangement of Culture Club's "Victims" spliced with an Afrikaans translation of an eighteenth-century German folk song and a Psalm. For someone who has been so keen to play by the rules and not draw attention to his queerness, this is, for Johan, a bold move, one that signals he is willing to accept himself and that indicates an otherwise is perhaps possible. The choice of the song "Victims" is, no doubt, intended to gesture to the multiple forms of victimhood in apartheid South Africa that Johan and Wolfgang discuss when they are at the border. But since the film has only passingly referenced these other victims, it is difficult to say how much they really matter to the Kanaries and how much they really understand or even care about their own complicity in the war. As Gray (2021, 15) writes of the film, "Elided are the ways in which the South African Border War destabilised neighbouring states—especially Angola—in an increasingly aggressive manner to bolster Afrikaner, and thus white supremacist rule and legitimacy in an attempt to retain sovereignty over the then South West Africa region." And since "Victims" is a song about lead singer Boy George's (officially unacknowledged at the time) relationship with his drummer Jon Moss, a relationship Johan deeply wishes Boy George would acknowledge, it reads easily as a sort of veiled coming-out anthem for Johan, a statement that queerness does and can exist, but only obliquely as a political statement about the nonwhite victims of the Border War who remain in the background.[13] Again, it is unclear whether the film is intentionally reproducing these denials of complicity in order to show how difficult it was for white soldiers like Johan to accept their role in upholding apartheid or whether it also participates in that denial to a certain extent.

However, I do argue that by not explicitly engaging with any other forms of racial or geopolitical victimhood, the film cuts out anything that might speak to the lasting legacies of apartheid and the Border War. And in a film in which the Kanaries, who are told by commanding officers that they cannot sing their "Victims" arrangement, are asked by a sympathetic Reverend Engelbrecht to "remember this feeling, this anger, otherwise it'll just turn into nostalgia one day," legacies seem important. On the one hand, the film certainly avoids the nostalgia that Munro argues is present in much border writing by straight white ex-combatants who pine for the good old days (Munro 2012, 98), and the film very emphatically and explicitly cuts through and against any celebration of white hegemonic masculinity in the Defense Force. But, on the other hand, a film whose color palette is, as one reviewer puts it, "bleached as if faded like an old Kodak colour print of the time" (Thamm 2018) and that meticulously utilizes 1980s music and props (including the apartheid flag) is difficult to see as one that can fully cut against nostalgia and sustain anger. Perhaps this is because the same character who tells the Kanaries to remember their anger also says, "There are political agendas on both sides. We are simply here to minister to the conscripts caught in the middle." And though the audience is very much invited to be critical of this line, the film does, in many ways, seem to be aimed at a white audience, especially a gay white audience, who might see themselves caught in the middle and might be comforted by seeing Johan's beautifully rendered, and admittedly arduous, journey to self-acceptance. For instance, during the course of his interview with Lingenfelder, Daniel Dercksen (2018), a white playwright and well-established film and theater journalist says, "*Kanarie* is a film that is not only life-changing but an eye-opener to a past legacy tainted by divide and rule, inbred hatred and religious conservatism that destroyed many lives. In South Africa today we can celebrate our sexual preferences without shame." In contrast to *Skoonheid* and *Inxeba*, *Kanarie* creates an opening for this uncritical understanding of the present, an understanding that seems to completely gloss over the continued violence against certain types of queer bodies. Therefore, while the film does indeed encourage its characters to embrace rather than deny forms of difference, it also carves a space where (white) denialism can continue in comfort.

In many ways, part of what makes *Kanarie*'s politics more ambiguous than *Skoonheid*'s or *Inxeba*'s is its reliance on camp aesthetics. As Richard Dyer (2002, 49) writes, "Camp kept, and keeps, a lot of gay men going. And camp is not masculine. By definition, camping about is not butch. So camp is a way of being human, witty and vital, without conforming to the drabness and rigidity of the hetero male role." And indeed in *Kanarie* Johan's camping about provides an important alternative to the violent hegemonic masculinity he encounters in the army: it provides him space to be himself—to be human and witty—and it provides ways to resist conformity in a society where conformity is brutally enforced. But as Dyer also notes of camp, "The emphasis on surface and style can become obsessive—nothing can be taken seriously, anything deep or problematic or heavy is shimmied away from in a flurry of chic. Camp seems often unable to discriminate between those things that need to be treated for laughs and style, and those that are genuinely serious and important" (59–60). Although I think that *Kanarie* is certainly able to indicate that which should be taken seriously—as noted above, the fantasy sequences at the border that explicitly acknowledge anti-Black violence, as well as the dance sequence in which Johan destroys the barracks and cuts himself up, are both very pronounced departures from earlier, more playful camp sequences—it is still the case that the film's overall emphasis on camp and style can indeed create comfort (even while depicting the violence of Afrikaner masculinity) when perhaps what is called for is discomfort. Or to put this another way, one can argue that this coming-out film creates (sexual) orientation when perhaps what is called for is is a bit of disorientation, or a type of cutting and rupture that leaves one undone, thrown.

Here, finally, *Kanarie* differs quite significantly from another queer Border War film: Oliver Hermanus's loose adaptation of André Carl van der Merwe's semiautobiographical novel *Moffie* (2006). Released internationally at the end of 2019 and in South Africa in 2020, the film *Moffie*, as Hermanus himself indicates, serves in some ways as a prequel to *Skoonheid*, in a sense giving some context as to how a man like François, who served as a pilot in the South African Defense Force, has come to be who he is (Germishuys 2020). *Moffie* is set earlier than *Kanarie:* it takes place in 1981, two years before the ECC, but it also follows the story of a young man, here Nicholas Van der Swart, who is conscripted into the army, where he begins to realize his desire for other men.[14] In the novel, Nicholas joins a particularly violent counterinsurgency unit of the South African Defense Force that was active in Namibia, and though his experience is intensely traumatizing, Nicholas makes lasting friendships with other gay men, falls in love, and eventually, like Johan, finds self-acceptance. But in his adaptation Hermanus strips the novel of its romantic plot and makes it less a coming-out story and more a deeply discomforting portrayal of what it means to come of age amid such racist and homophobic violence. In a discussion of the film at the Tromsø International Film Festival in Norway, Hermanus says that in order to establish the particular headspace of apartheid, to really depict the indoctrination of the system, he takes out "all the fun stuff" in the novel and makes it a much more brutal story. This leads to what Hermanus admits is a "triggering film"—one member of the press even had a panic attack during a South African screening—but also to one that opens old wounds in order to expose the fact that they have never healed (Lodge 2020).

Hermanus also adds scenes to the film that were not part of the book in order to give dimension and context to the way that white soldiers treat Black South Africans. In one of the earlier scenes in the movie, just after Nicholas boards the train that takes him to training, fellow conscripts taunt and insult a Black man who is waiting at a train station. The man has done nothing, he says nothing, and yet the soldiers are unrelenting. One even throws a bag of vomit at his face. In another scene, mid-movie, a Black family sits huddled in their compound while SADF soldiers discuss how they will "have their fun" with them later. And toward the end of the film, Nicholas and his fellow soldiers kill a young Black man in battle. None of these scenes is easy to watch—either for Nicholas or for the audience—and what makes them very different from the cuts away to Black bodies in *Kanarie* is that they don't just signal the "limitation of black representation in white Afrikaans narratives" (Pieterse 2019, 380); they make undeniable the horror of white violence against Black bodies. Here, a mixed-race director, one who emphasizes in interviews that he identifies more with the victims than with the perpetrators of this violence, forces viewers to confront this history.

The film version of *Moffie* therefore eschews the muted hope at the end of both *Kanarie* and the original novel. After Nicholas completes his years of service he sets off to find his friend Dylan with whom he had shared an intimate moment in the trenches, a rare moment of tenderness that provided a brief opening to an otherwise beyond the brutality of the army. But the self-assured and sensitive Dylan, hated and tormented by their masochistic sergeant, is not the same Dylan that Nicholas finds years later. During their service, Dylan had been sent off to Ward 22, the infamous military psychiatric hospital in Pretoria where gay men were subjected to shock therapy, chemical castration, and other abusive methods to supposedly cure them of homosexuality. The film does not dwell much on Ward 22 but it is clear that Dylan is forever altered by it. In the final scene of the film, the newly reunited Nicholas and Dylan go for a swim in the ocean. Underwater, Nicholas reaches out and brushes his hand against Dylan's arm. But this causes Dylan abruptly to leave the water, and the final image of the film is Nicholas sitting alone at the edge of the water with no sign of Dylan's return. Tenderness is no longer possible. Given what the army has done not only to Black bodies but to queer bodies, Hermanus, as he does in *Skoonheid*, seems to favor a final cut that, unlike *Kanarie*'s, cuts out the possibility for an otherwise and that dwells not on liberation but on the lasting psychological damage done by apartheid's multiple dehumanizations.

Compounding Violence

Though each of the films discussed in this chapter is very different in terms of style, content, and positionality, they all very deliberately demonstrate how systems of oppression combine, overlap, and compound in ways that uphold violent heteronormative structures. In this way, these films differ from those in previous chapters in that what seems to be resisted is neither a homophobic present nor an encroaching gay rights agenda, but rather a rosy vision of a rainbow nation that is safe and equal and free from trauma. Rather than opening up Afri-queer fugitive times or trying to change hearts and minds, queer male South African feature films seem to be focused on critiquing past and present inequalities and systems of patriarchal, racial, and homophobic violence.

In their preface to *Reclaiming Afrikan*, Matebeni and Pereira (2014) write about the need for creating spaces away from this compounded violence. They write:

> As sexual and gender non-conforming or queer persons, we have been alienated in Africa. We have been stripped of belonging and our connectedness. For these reasons, we have created our own version of Afrika—a space that *cuts across* the rigid borders and boundaries that have for so many years made us feel disconnected and fractured. . . . We break borders, and even beyond these borders—we share a sense of kinship—a belonging to a struggle for freedom and social justice. (7; my emphasis)

Here Matebeni and Pereira call for types of queer cutting across and breaking that can rupture forms of oppression and feelings of unworthiness that hinder freedom. To a certain extent, Hermanus, Trengove, and Olwagen each create films that participate in this type of breaking, in these various cuttings, especially as the films cut openings for previously occluded sexualities and for queer intimacies in institutions and spaces that are all too often presumed to be heterosexual. But what seems to be the case is that in the queer male South African cinema discussed here, the focus is more on the difficulty of achieving these ruptures in systems still dominated by different forms of violent and racist masculinity. In many ways, then, the kinship, belonging, and struggle for justice that Matebeni and Pereira describe above are, in fact, cut off or cut out of the narratives. Ultimately, then, I read these films as works of art, both powerful and imperfect, that present complicated and tangled characters—in equally complicated and tangled situations—who perhaps do not yet know how to rearrange the racial, gendered, and homophobic structures that define past and present South Africa.

4

Holding Space, Saving Joy

Queer Love and Critical Resilience
in East Africa

The film that closed out the opening day of the first-ever Queer Kampala International Film Festival (QKIFF) in 2016 was *Major!*, a documentary about the life of Miss Major Griffin-Gracy, a seventy-five-year-old African American transgender activist, former sex worker, and treasured community leader. The film discusses Miss Major's activism from the Stonewall Rebellion to her role fighting for the rights of Black trans prisoners. But as the filmmakers contend, *Major!* is not only a biographical film. It is a documentary that "seeks to create a living, breathing history of a community's struggle and resilience" ("Major!" 2019). Indeed, as the film ends, various members of Miss Major's queer community face the camera squarely and defiantly declare, "I'm still here." Or in another iteration: "I'm still fucking here." When the credits rolled during the Kampala screening where I was present, there was a huge round of applause. There were a few audible "wows" from the audience, and several members looked back at the screen, raised a fist, and echoed the film's call for resilience by claiming, loud enough for everyone to hear, "I'm still fucking here."

As was the case with the Out in Africa Film Festival in post-apartheid South Africa, queer film festivals in East Africa, and particularly in Kenya and Uganda, have been sites for constructing and promoting queer visibility. In both Kenya and Uganda, where, unlike South Africa, the production of queer cinema is relatively minimal and limited to a handful of feature and documentary films, queer film festivals become both an opportunity to celebrate the success of the queer community and occasions where the frustrations of censorship become evident. I begin this chapter, which focuses on the Kenyan music video "Same Love (Remix)" and on Wanuri Kahiu's feature *Rafiki*, with a discussion of QKIFF for precisely this reason: understanding films and videos in the regional contexts in which they circulate not only allows us to think about the resistance of the characters within the texts themselves but also forces us to acknowledge the way that even screening queer African stories is often itself a resistant and contested practice.

And indeed the screening of *Major!* at QKIFF was an inspiring finish to a day that had its ups and downs. The festival began on a Friday afternoon at a hotel slightly outside of the city center. Attendees had received information about the location via WhatsApp, a free messaging application, only the night before. The organizers had originally wanted QKIFF to be held in one of Kampala's movie theaters. However, the theaters that they approached attempted to charge four to five times what they normally charge for hosting a film festival, making it cost prohibitive.[1] Furthermore, the Ugandan Communication Board, which needs to give its permission for screenings in movie theaters, was charging QKIFF five dollars a minute to preview each film, and there were no guarantees that they would allow the film to be shown after they viewed it. The organizers tried contacting different embassies to see if they would host the festival as a private event. But the embassies were reluctant, for diplomatic reasons, and they said that if they were going to be involved then the police had to know in advance. When the festival's organizer, Kamoga Hassan, approached the police, he found himself in front of the very same officer who had arrested him and several others in a traumatizing raid during a Pride celebration a few months earlier. On the third night of Pride 2016, police raided Club Venom, where the queer community had gathered for a pageant to crown Mr./Ms./Mx. Uganda Pride. The police, claiming an illegal gay wedding was taking place, locked the gates of the club, arrested over a dozen people, and for more than ninety minutes detained, beat, and humiliated those in attendance, even threatening to release photos of the Pride celebrants, which would further endanger them.[2] The raid on Pride, coming just two years after the passage and subsequent overturning (based only on a technicality) of Uganda's Anti-homosexuality

Act, was a harsh reminder to the queer community that the state-sponsored threats to their safety—threats that had not existed before U.S. evangelicals came to Uganda in 2009 warning against homosexual recruitment—had not disappeared.[3] So when Hassan recognized these very same officers, he and the other organizers decided to find locations where they could hold the film festival underground, avoiding the police and the Ugandan Communication Board altogether. The small hotel where *Major!* played was one of three locations for the festival.

However, because the hotel was not a venue set up for film screening, the festival organizers had to procure and bring in their own projector and their own screen. But on the opening day when *Major!* was screened, the person from whom QKIFF was renting a screen was nowhere to be found. When the man did finally answer his phone, he threatened the organizers and told them he knew they did not have the proper permits for their festival and would call the police if they tried to get their deposit back. So the opening day's films were projected on a white wall. Unfortunately, this meant that the films were quite hard to see, as the wall was scuffed and dinged and the thin curtains in the room did not block out much of the sunlight. With so much light streaming in, the wall's blemishes were visible through each of the projected images, making evident the scars of all of the structural hurdles the organizers had to face.

Furthermore, the crowd itself was at first sparse. In addition to it being midday on a Friday, potential attendees were nervous. After the Pride raid people in the queer community were feeling especially vulnerable. But by the time *Major!* was shown, enough people seemed convinced that the police would not raid the festival that there was a fairly sizable crowd of about fifty. People were trickling in, gathering for drinks outside the screening room, and posing for professional photos in front of the QKIFF backdrop. Moreover, once the sun had gone down the white wall worked quite well in lieu of a screen, and the projected images covered up all of the wall's imperfections. Audience members were messaging the two hundred members of the WhatsApp group (a group that you could join only if you were prescreened by the organizers) and praising the film in real time while it was being shown. In fact, throughout the weekend the audience grew steadily. By Sunday, when *The Pearl of Africa*, a Swedish-made documentary about a Ugandan trans woman, closed out the festival, several hundred people were in the audience. The closing night venue had switched to RAM Bar, a bar that hosted gay nights every Sunday and had just a few days earlier hosted a fundraiser for the trans rights organization Rainbow Mirrors. The space, in other words, felt safe, and many people were excited to see Cleo, the subject of the film who was known to many in the community, on the big screen. In the film Cleo talks about her transition and her ability to finally show affection for her husband, Nelson, as an act of claiming and staking out space in a homophobic society. She says, "I so wanted to claim my space." I read this line, this insistence on existing and surviving and even thriving in a hostile environment, as another iteration of "I'm still fucking here," which proved to be an appropriate (albeit unofficial) mantra not just for Miss Major's community but also for the QKIFF organizers and attendees.

This chapter examines two different audiovisual texts in the context of two East African film festivals, the Queer Kampala International Film Festival, which lasted only two years, and the more established Out Film Festival (OFF) Nairobi. The first piece I discuss is Art Attack's "Same Love (Remix)," a music video that screened at QKIFF 2016 the day after *Major!* and that I include in a book on cinema, both because of the way it acts as a short film and because of the attention it drew from the Kenyan Film Classification Board. The second film I discuss here is Kahiu's *Rafiki*, the first Kenyan film ever to be screened at Cannes. *Rafiki* was famously unbanned for exactly seven days in Kenya so that it could be eligible for an Academy Award, and though it was then rebanned a handful of weeks before the OFF 2018 festival, where I was in attendance, it seeped into nearly every discussion and set the tone for the three-day festival. Setting my reading of these films next to the festivals in which they both showed and did not show enables me to elaborate and complicate Karl Schoonover and Rosalind Galt's (2016, 97) claim that queer film and queer film festivals "courageously turn public spaces into counterpublics." What I want to explore here is what it means to be "still fucking here," in light of the censorship and the constant erasure of queer African lives, and what it means to create what the directors of *Major!* call "a living, breathing history" of resilience that is also a testament of future lives. Ultimately, I argue that these queer East African films and film festivals demonstrate how resilience, when it is delinked from neoliberal imperatives and when it embraces rather than disavows vulnerability, tenderness, and defeat, can serve as a critical tool for political transformation.

Critical Resilience

As a number of scholars have argued, the word *resilience* has come to take on very specific meanings within the framework of neoliberalism. Though the term has shifted in meaning and has been used to apply to a wide range of contexts, Sarah Bracke (2016, 53) notes that its usage increases exponentially from the 1980s onward, a period that coincides with the solidification of neoliberal governments and conceptions of the self that prize individualistic competition over social and communal networks of care. Tracing *resilience* as a keyword, Bracke argues that what the different applications of the word have in common is "the ability of a substance or an object to bounce back and spring into prior shape" (54). The *Oxford English Dictionary* tells us that *resilience* can also mean "adaptable, robust, hardy" (54). Thus, whether one is talking about a resilient planet, a resilient economy, or a resilient individual, *resilience* refers to the ability to recover, to return to an original status or form, and to absorb shock (54). Critics like Bracke claim that within the context of neoliberalism, resilience takes the form of an "ethical imperative" (64): it is not just a neutral descriptive term; it is something that one must figure out how to achieve in order to be considered a good neoliberal subject. Bracke further argues that resilience, as a narrative of self-sufficiency and mastery, dismisses forms of vulnerability and dependence as shameful and as things to overcome rather than to acknowledge and embrace (58–59).

For Mark Neocleous (2013, 5), resilience is a narrative that prepares the subject for the precarity of neoliberalism. "Neoliberal citizenship," he writes, "is nothing but a training in resilience as the new technology of the self, a training to withstand whatever crisis capital undergoes and whatever political measures the state carries out to save it." Neocleous also notes that, in IMF (International Monetary Fund) literature, resilience is often promoted as a convenient solution to poverty alleviation. Thus, resilience as an ethos of modern social life tells an individual that he or she must cope, weather the storm alone (or perhaps with a therapist or self-help book), and emerge stronger. Resilience narratives do not call into question systems that lead to vulnerability, systematic oppression, or even environmental disaster because to be resilient, to be a good neoliberal subject, a person (or economy or ecology) actually needs forms of crisis.

In a fascinating book called *Resilience and Melancholy: Pop Music, Feminism, Neoliberalism* (2015), Robin James examines the way that this neoliberal ethos of resilience is integrated into contemporary musical practices, structures, and genres. She argues that when Black musical forms get appropriated into mainstream pop—her specific focus is on electronic dance music (EDM)—they are used for messages of resilience, mimicked in the music's soaring and dropping structures, rather than for messages of resistance. James argues that in popular music like EDM the singer is overcoming something dissonant—She refers to the "Look, I Overcame" narrative that has become the new ideal form of femininity (James 2015, 79). But she argues that this dissonance is no longer disruptive because it gets folded into narratives about "healthy," good subjects who have weathered their crises well rather than resisting or disturbing the system. Likewise, resilience does not call for forms of solidarity or intersectionality and, according to Bracke (2016, 63), "thwarts the skills of imagining an otherwise." According to this line of thinking, resilience is not at all about resistance (a term with which it is sometimes conflated) but about accepting the cards one is dealt and trying to figure out how to play the best hand. Resilient subjects submit themselves to the flexibility that defines late capitalism. By contrast, resistance, at least in its oppositional or transgressive mode, would require challenging the system and questioning why the cards were dealt in that particular manner.

For the queer Kenyan intellectual Keguro Macharia, who is riffing off of Audre Lorde's poem "A Litany of Survival," these neoliberal forms of resilience need to be distinguished from survival. "Survival," he writes in a blog post on the topic of tenderness,

> is the imaginative act of pursuing freedom amidst devastation. Resilience says, "I can handle it—do your worst." Survival says, "I can imagine beyond and work toward practicing freedom." Survival is also hard work, requiring daily practice. It is exhausting work: to resist being pulled out of your body and out of your unhome, to be present as the object of political homophobia. To imagine yourself elsewhere—in another body, another place, another mind, another spirit. Somewhere less vulnerable. (Macharia 2017)

For Macharia, resilience is both passive and individualistic, whereas survival is an imaginative labor that moves toward a "freedom rooted in care" (2017). He ends his poetic post with the following couplet: "Calluses form. / Is there space for tenderness?" (2017). A statement about the effects of what it means to be the object of political homophobia is here coupled with a question about whether the callus, the skin that thickens and hardens over a wound, leaves room for the type of tender care needed for survival.

What thinkers like Bracke, James, Neocleous, and Macharia object to, and rightly so, is that in resilience discourse social and political crises become naturalized. The resilient subject is told not to worry about the crisis but to be robust and hardy. Part of their critique is that the linear temporality of resilience narratives—first defeat, then a bouncing back—precludes imagining different, nonlinear alternatives, that a fantasy of future mastery replaces the present work of caring with and about others. But what I want to suggest in this chapter is that in the counterpublics and works of art created by queer African artists, activists, and allies, resilience is not always linear: it does not always dismiss vulnerability in the name of self-mastery but often tries to preserve it, to create space for it. The resilience in these films and in these spaces is, moreover, not one that celebrates robustness as a fundamental good; it is, rather, what I call a critical resilience, a form of resilience that works very much like the imaginative labor of survival Macharia describes, that—critically—creates space for the tenderness beneath the protective callus it needs.

I use the word *critical* here in two main senses. First, as with critical theory, critical resilience challenges capitalist modernity and seeks to transform society into one that is more equitable and less oppressive.[4] In other words, critical resilience may champion individual endurance, but it does so in a way that also challenges neoliberal narratives by seeking to upend hierarchal organization and reimagine social life. Second, I use the term *critical* as in a critical, or life-threatening, condition: in medical parlance a critical condition is an "uncertain prognosis, vital signs are unstable or abnormal, there are major complications, and death may be imminent" (Suellentrop 2009). In this way, I emphasize that resilience is often critical—essential for survival—and that, at the same time, the line between being alive and not is unstable. Moreover, critical resilience is often itself in a critical condition, with imminent death being just as possible an outcome as bouncing back. In critical modes of resilience, unlike neoliberal ones, death, defeat, and injury are not simply overcome. Most importantly, though, critical resilience is not opposed to resistance but a resource for it. In other words, to look back at a camera or a screen or another human being and declare, "I am claiming my space," or "I'm still fucking here," is an act of both resistance and critical resilience.

It would, of course, be tempting to toss out the word *resilience* altogether. In fact, as Bracke argues, resilience discourse, with its cruel promises of success and rejection of interdependence, comes at a price too high to pay. But *resilient* is often a self-descriptive adjective used by those engaging in the type of transformative survival work that Macharia, and Lorde before him, discuss, and it is a word that queer African activists and artists are using more and more. Dope Saint Jude, an unabashedly "queer grrrl" Capetonian hip-hop artist, has an EP called *Resilient*. There is, in fact, an entire Ugandan-made documentary about the Ugandan transgender community called *Resilience Diaries*, made by the LGBT-focused filmmakers collective East African Video Artists. And at the premiere of the film, Pepe Julian Onziema—a trans man, filmmaker, and program director at SMUG (Sexual Minorities of Uganda), Uganda's largest LGBTI rights organizations—underscored the idea's importance to him, stating that he has a tattoo of the word *resilience*.

Resilience Diaries, in fact, provides a perfect illustration of what I understand to be critical resilience. Throughout the film trans women, trans men, activists, and lawyers make statements that articulate a certain ongoingness and fortitude that are various versions of statements like "I am claiming my space" and "I'm still (fucking) here." But, at the same time and in the same breath, these subjects also articulate the sense of being in a vulnerable and critical/life-threatening situation. In each of the statements below, robustness and vulnerability coexist (italics added for emphasis):

1) In the opening monologue of the film, an unnamed trans woman states: "*We are hated, hurt, and killed, not even safe on our own street.* But remember: we are your children, friends, and neighbors. You don't see us simply because you have chosen not to see us. And we are here and *we will always be here.*"

2) The human rights lawyer Godiva Akullo states: "Sometimes you just have to grab what it is that you want. And I think that trans people are now doing that. They are saying, we are tired of waiting. *We are here and we are demanding.* And as long as that spirit continues there is nothing that can hold us back. *Of course there are losses that might be made along the way.*"

3) The legal scholar and activist Suzan Mirembe states: "*Trans and intersex people are here. We have been here for a long time.* . . . We need a government that is responsive. . . . We need the police to respond to us as Ugandans, not as special citizens. We need you to go out and investigate when *we tell you we have been violated.* For the judiciary, we want you to listen. Not with a biased ear, not with homophobia or transphobia. We want you to actually see us as human beings and ask yourself: If any other Ugandan walked in here and said that *we have been violated*, what would the courts do?"

Here, the subjects insist on their ability to adapt and endure: *we will always be here; we are here and we are demanding; we have been here for a long time.* And, at the same time, they articulate how exposed they are: *we are hated, hurt, and killed, not even safe on our own street; of course there are losses that might be made along the way; we tell you we have been violated.* I take these statements together to be indicative of the hard work and the daily, exhausting practice of survival, and also of the calluses that have formed that enable one to continue on. I read these words not as ones that say, "I can handle it—do your worst," or "Look, I Overcame," but rather as comments on the way that "we are here and we are demanding" is completely inseparable from "we tell you we have been violated." For Bracke, vulnerability and resilience "operate as political opponents." She writes, "Vulnerability here brings us to the question of social transformation, while resilience further separates us from it, even though transformation might be part of its cruel promise" (Bracke 2016, 70). But I see in recent East African cinema, and in the spaces that filmmakers and activists hold, a critical resilience in which vulnerability and the injuries that accompany it are resources for social change. And, as Judith Butler (2016, 26) writes in an essay in the same volume as Bracke's, "Under certain conditions, continuing to exist, to move, and to breathe are forms of resistance." What I wish to demonstrate in this chapter is the way that East African films and film festivals mobilize resilience not to submit subjects to neoliberal complacency but to participate in social transformation and to open spaces where one can continue "to exist, to move, and to breathe."

In both Kenya and Uganda this type of critical resilience has been especially important amid what Sylvia Tamale (2013, 33) calls "state-orchestrated 'moral panics'" that, like those mobilized in Nigeria, have been used by governments "as an effective decoy to distract attention from the more significant socioeconomic and political crises afflicting society." And though Uganda's antihomosexuality laws have received much more international attention than Kenya's, Macharia (2013a, 284) reminds us that, since 2005, when Kenyans began to debate the Sexual Offences Act, "Kenyans have passed a series of laws and policies that wed national belonging to heterosexuality and that pledge to protect the heteronormative family." He adds that while these laws are not explicitly antiqueer, they do very much resemble proposed antigay legislation in Uganda by asserting that "the heterosexually reproductive family must be protected against queers" (284). I want, then, to think about how "Same Love (Remix)" and *Rafiki*, very much like the earlier Kenyan film *Stories of Our Lives* (as discussed in the introduction to *Queer African Cinemas*), demonstrate the different ways that existing, moving, and even breathing are crucial to a project that ruptures the suffocating present of these moral panics while also acknowledging what it means to be overwhelmed and sometimes defeated by systems of oppression. Here, then, I return to thinking about Afri-queer fugitivity as a way to maneuver within spaces of confinement (spaces where one does not always have room to breathe) and to simultaneously imagine and create new freedoms. For me, critical resilience names some of these maneuvers and articulates the hard and sometimes defeating work of African, queer survival, work that requires active and imaginative adaptability and robustness as well as the tenderness beneath the callus.

Censoring Same Love in Kenya

The 2016 music video "Same Love (Remix)," a Kenyan remake of Macklemore and Ryan Lewis's famous 2012 song by the same name, illustrates the distinction between neoliberal, linear modes of resilience and the forms of critical resilience that I identify at the heart of queer East African counterpublics. In February 2016, the "Same Love (Remix)" aired twice on Kenyan television before the Kenya Film Classification Board (KFCB) tweeted out a link to the YouTube video and declared it banned. By the time it played at the Queer Kampala International Film Festival in November of that same year, it had, thanks to KFCB's free publicity, gained international attention and hundreds of thousands of views. Both the original Macklemore and Ryan Lewis video and the Kenyan remix video position themselves as activist pieces of art. Comparing the two, however, highlights the ways in which the Kenyan remix mobilizes narratives of resistance and critical resilience that do not always properly align with the neoliberal temporalities that are present in the original version. Like Karmen Geï, the remake of Merrimé's Carmen, the remake of "Same Love" re-arranges the original Western work and invites a listening for more improvisational, less linear structures and ways of being.

When Macklemore and Ryan Lewis released "Same Love" in 2012, they did so in part to support Referendum 74, which would legalize same-sex marriage in Washington State—since, at that time, the U.S. Supreme Court had not yet ruled in favor of same-sex marriage nationally. The song and music video were both hits and arguably assisted in the referendum's passage and in shifting the national cultural tide in favor of same-sex marriage in the United States, which was legalized in 2015. And their video makes the promarriage argument much more explicitly than the song itself. It opens with a high-angle shot of a hospital light over a bed, and a baby boy is born to a white father and Black mother. The video follows the life of the boy, who turns out to be gay, as he grapples with his sexuality, finds a (white) partner, and marries him in a church wedding. As the outro plays, the video repeats the high-angle shot of the hospital light, but this time the boy, now an ailing old man, sits in a hospital bed with his husband at his side. The two lock hands as the camera zooms in on their wedding rings. The men have overcome obstacles and live a happy, hetero-chronological life together.

Throughout the music video there are also cuts to archival footage of Martin Luther King Jr. and to other key images of the Black civil rights movement. Therefore, just as the song clearly positions the teleological passage from birth to marriage to death, it also seems to position a teleological passage from the

African American civil rights movement to the contemporary gay rights movement. As Cameron Crees (2014, 79) notes, this works sonically too:

The song opens with a tonal centre of E major and instantly introduces the theme of marriage. The sound is similar to that of a rotary organ sound, which is closely associated with Gospel music and therefore, Christian marriage. It is a wave of sound as individual notes of the chord are difficult to distinguish. Piano notes ring through the opening chord like wedding bells. There is a slight layered effect as the piano notes are individual samples. The vinyl crackle effect is added to the sampled piano notes to create a more vintage sound to the pre-introduction alluding to the Golden Age of Records, which was at the same time as the Black Civil Rights movement during the mid-twentieth century. . . . The pinging metallophones and idiophones play at the close of the song too; when combined with the video, the marriage of the two gay men provides a circularity and continuity to the song, as if the message of the song is everlasting (similar to a fairy tale marriage ending of "happily ever after").

And Crees suggests that because Macklemore and Lewis center their song on the hook in Curtis Mayfield's "People Get Ready," a song Mayfield composed after the 1963 March on Washington, DC, the music itself seems to carve out an overlapping movement from Black civil rights to gay rights.

But Thomas R. Dunn (2016) argues that the references to the civil rights movement in Macklemore and Lewis's song actually belies a neoliberal and anti-Black agenda that advances a progay marriage agenda by minimizing Black resistance and Black struggles. Dunn points out that the only images of Black resistance that are included in the video are from the 1960s, and, moreover, they are black-and-white images that contrast with the rich color images of the rest of the video, seemingly situating the struggle against racism as a thing of the past. He writes that this "deflects viewers' attention from both the structural racism that continues to be fought today and more radical forms of black empowerment that follow the 1960s" (277). Dunn also argues that the inclusion of the multiracial main character, rather than highlighting contemporary race issues, winds up foreclosing other forms of intersectionality. And the fact that Macklemore and Lewis, two successful white hip-hop musicians, seem to focus so much on the homophobia of the largely Black hip-hop community also, according to Dunn, adds to the problematic racial politics of the song and video and highlights how homonormative marriage can foreclose radical challenges to neoliberalism and white supremacy.

I argue that Art Attack's remix complicates the neoliberal temporality that dominates Macklemore and Ryan Lewis's song and puts forth an agenda that embraces gay marriage and provides a radical, antiprogressivist critique at the same time, allowing both to exist simultaneously as part of the ongoingness of queer African resistance. To this extent, it is interesting to look at what the remix keeps and what it dispenses of from the original. Macklemore's voice and the lyrics he sings are completely gone, replaced by Art Attack's colloquial rap flow that stylistically matches Macklemore's rhythmically free-form technique but recounts an entirely different narrative. Gone, too, is the framing device around marriage. Instead of a linear story of birth, marriage, and death rapped by a white, cisgender, heterosexual rapper, Art Attack provides a story about depression, resilience, suicide, activism, marriage, love, and rejection, all (re)mixed together. Progress, in other words, is not inevitable in Art Attack's version. Rather, time loops and interlocks, and bouncing back does not always follow the original crisis.

The Art Attack collective consists of seventeen East African artists—singers, dancers, movie producers, and socialites, many of whom identify as queer—who came together specifically to make the video, which is based on the life story of one of their members and one of the video's producers, George Barasa. Barasa is a queer gospel singer and activist who came out on Kenyan national television in 2013, two years after being outed by a newspaper in his hometown. After being subsequently disowned by his family, Barasa moved to Nairobi, where he became depressed and attempted suicide. When he woke up at the hospital after his suicide attempt, he learned that he was HIV positive. Though the news of his status sank him deeper into depression, eventually he was able to, in his own words, "start living life again." He enrolled in high school and founded an NGO called Out in Kenya. His career picked up when he started performing his music and modeling, and he gradually became a well-known social media activist. The "Same Love (Remix)" makes Barasa's suicide attempt its framing device and intersperses images of a young gay man, played by the Tanzanian model Dayon Monson, facing himself in the bathroom mirror and overdosing on pills and medications, with images of gay rights protests, gay couples falling in love, homophobic newspaper articles, and clips from television shows like Empire. In this way, the video positions Barasa's resilience and queer cultural and political gains alongside images that show the difficulty and sometimes impossibility of bouncing back.

The song begins with an intro as Art Attack's front man, Ken Kabuga, raps over the same soft piano chords and ambient organ sounds that begin Macklemore and Lewis's "Same Love": "This song is dedicated to the New Slaves, the New Blacks, the New Jews, the New Minorities for whom we need a civil rights movement, maybe a sex rights movement. Especially in Africa. Everywhere this goes out to you. I feel you." After an opening epigraph—"To love and to be loved is to feel the sun from both sides," a quote from the American psychotherapist and media personality David Viscott—the first images of the video are flags. First there is a rainbow flag being waved in a Pride march and then a South African flag, presumably in reference to the fact that South Africa is the only African country that has made gay marriage legal. The next images are of Kenyans going about their daily lives: one woman leaves her house in the morning; another walks down the street with her head covered and a small backpack in her arms. A man rides his bicycle; a group of teenagers play soccer. Then we see images of Ugandan tabloid newspapers like *Red Pepper* and *Rolling Stone*, which publish lists and sometimes even the addresses of what they call the country's "top homosexuals," juxtaposed with Pride marchers in Turkey shouting, "Don't be silent, be heard, gays exist" (figure 4.1). The screen then cuts to black and Kabuga begins singing over the familiar arrangement that Macklemore and Ryan Lewis adapt from Mayfield.

As Monson's character faces himself in the bathroom mirror, with bottles of medication coming in and out of focus, Kabuga raps, "This is my story yo, my

FIGURE 4.1. Still from "Same Love (Remix)" (2016). A man holds a copy of the Ugandan tabloid *Rolling Stone*, which publishes the names and addresses of queer people.

sorry story yo, this is me, this is you, this is us, this is the World, World war, Wild war, cold war, love war. . . . Years back I fell in love with a male kid in school. He was cool, he was funny, always true, always shining. My heart told me I was right, I could go ahead and love him, I could go ahead and have him. I could go ahead and hug him." We see images of Monson, the video's main character, with his boyfriend, hanging out at waterfalls, goofing around, holding hands, and taking selfies, again intercut with him in front of the mirror, contemplating suicide (figure 4.2).

Though Macklemore's voice and lyrics are absent from the song, the remix keeps the chorus by Mary Lambert who, like Barasa, is an out, queer gospel singer. And when Lambert sings the chorus—"And I can't change / Even if I tried / Even if I wanted to / My love, my love, my love / She keeps me warm / She keeps me warm"—the video brings in another couple, Kenyan rapper Noti Flow (Natalie Florence) and her girlfriend. Like Monson and his boyfriend, the lesbian couple walks around Nairobi holding hands, sharing ice cream cones, and hanging out on a park bench in Nairobi's National Arboretum. When the chorus ends, the story returns to Monson's character and we see a medium shot of George Barasa himself walking toward the camera in a royal-blue studded button-down shirt (figure 4.3). The lyrics, which echo Barasa's own experience, describe the moment when the main character comes out to his mother and is disowned.[5] In

FIGURE 4.2. Still from "Same Love (Remix)" (2016). The depressed protagonist of the video drinks in his bathroom.

FIGURE 4.3. Still from "Same Love (Remix)" (2016). George Barasa (aka Joji Baro).

the video, images of Barasa are intercut with scenes from Fox's show *Empire* when a young Jamal, the son of hip-hop mogul Lucious Lyon, walks to the dinner table in a pair of high heels. After Lucious throws Jamal in a trash can, bending forward to slam his son down, the video cuts to a match-on-action shot of Barasa collapsing to his knees, completing the downward motion of Jamal. But now Barasa has lost his blue button-down and is wearing a white tank top and carrying two plastic bags, which presumably carry the clothes he takes as he leaves home. And again, the video returns to Monson in the bathroom mirror, linking his depression to the lack of support from his family. But Art Attack also makes clear that the main character's personal experience is sanctioned by the state. The video shows images of tabloids outing gay people in Kenya and Uganda, as well as images of the Protect the Family march that took place in Nairobi on July 6, 2015, to protest Obama's visit to Kenya amid concerns (that turned out to be true) that he would ask president Uhuru Kenyatta to recognize the rights of Kenya's gay citizens.

When Mary Lambert's chorus resumes, the video returns to the Noti Flow story line, showing her proposing to her girlfriend on a park bench (figure 4.4). The rest of the video alternates images of the two women at home cooking, watching television, and caressing each other in bed, with more overtly political messages. Here, to paraphrase Tina Campt (2017, 32), the quotidian is mobilized as the site of resistance. And at the same time, Kabuga specifically

FIGURE 4.4. Still from "Same Love (Remix)" (2016). Noti Flow proposes to her girlfriend.

calls out Uganda and Nigeria for their homophobic laws, saying, "The hate is too much, all in the name of piety." The song also contains shout-outs to famous queer Africans, namely Binyavanga Wainaina, Joji Baro (George Barasa's stage name), Brenda Fassie (the famous bisexual South African singer who Barasa says is his role model), and Kasha Jacqueline Nabagesera, a Ugandan activist who founded the queer publication *Kuchu Times* and the organization Freedom and Roam Uganda. The visual juxtaposition of these political statements with the everyday acts of Noti Flow and her girlfriend going about their daily lives is echoed in Art Attack's lyrics: "It's a bedroom struggle and also a street struggle."

As the song ends, Kabuga's rapping is layered over Lambert's vocals. Kabuga raps, "Love is patient / Love is kind / Love is selfless / Love is faithful / Love is full of hope / Love is full of trust / Love is not proud / Love is God and God is Love," while Lambert softly repeats the lines and melody from the chorus, "Love is patient / Love is kind." But though the lyrics are hopeful, the image returns to Monson's character taking his life and collapsing on the floor with his head hanging over the threshold of the bathroom door. The final shaky image, the only one shot with a handheld camera, is a suicide note he leaves: "I am tired. Tired of the pressure. Tired of the pain. Tired of the stigmatization. Tired of the insults and the attacks and the hate. Goodbye world. Mummy, I love you. Wish I hadn't been born this way. Bye." The shakiness of the image of the note and the moments of silence that follow the end of the song speak to the often invisible, destabilizing effects of sanctioned homophobia. The resilient, happily-ever-after ending of Macklemore and Ryan Lewis's original hip-hop hit is completely reworked.

Because the video and the lyrics of the remix are so different, because they are framed around a suicide rather than a marriage, Art Attack's version foregrounds all the ways in which resilience is sometimes impossible. Robin James, in fact, argues that one of the ways to counter neoliberal narratives of resilience and overcoming is through death and melancholy. She writes,

> When power demands that you *live*, that you resiliently make more life for yourself, and, in turn, for society/capital, *death* seems like the obvious way to fight back. Or, alternatively, if power banks on your death, if it abandons you to die, what happens if you don't die in the *right way, at the right time*, if you don't decay *at the rate anticipated*? If resilience is a biopolitical technique for investing in life, *melancholy* is a dysfunctional, queerly biopolitical method of investing in and intensifying "death" (i.e., hegemonically unviable practices). (James 2015, 11)

The limits of such a strategy are, in many ways, obvious. Death and melancholy are not exactly inspiring options, and although intellectually and even artistically they might have some merit, they are not necessarily the most helpful emotional states for queer activists, queer subjects, or any other vulnerable groups that are trying to claim their space and lead functional, livable lives. And, indeed, it is understandable why queer Africans, still very much entrenched in fighting for their rights and their daily survival, do not typically espouse the type of queer negativity and antirelational stance that many Western queer theorists and academics take. This is why Art Attack's video, despite the suicide, is not about, to borrow Mari Ruti's (2017) phrasing, "the ethics of opting out." In the video, Noti Flow and her girlfriend get engaged, ignoring Kenya's antihomosexuality laws, and create a happy and erotic home life together. And Barasa's own story about finding life again after feeling that "his soul was crashed" is echoed in the video too. Even the epigraph of the video comes from David Viscott, an American psychiatrist and radio show host who was known for writing self-help books and whose last book was called *Emotional Resilience*. Indeed, there is much in the video and the song that encourages one to overcome and triumph even though the video acts as a documentary of hate, hurt, violation, and loss. Moreover, as Adriaan van Klinken (2019, 78) argues in his reading of the video, in the Christian and pan-African discourses that the video adopts, death is seen not as an end but as "beginning a new (after)life." Van Klinken likewise warns against reading the suicide in "Same Love (Remix)" as a queer injunction to give up on the future and instead reads the video as calling attention to the problem of suicide by queer young people "who are not recognized as fully human in the first place" (78). By detrivializing these deaths, van Klinken argues that the video opens up queer life to infinite possibilities, including divine love. Art Attack does not, therefore, champion melancholy as a way of resisting neoliberal resilience, nor does it offer a model for overcoming, bouncing back, or political progress.

What I am suggesting is that the "Same Love (Remix)" music video performs the type of critical resilience I describe above, a way of stating, "I'm still fucking here," that acknowledges the injustices of the system and the pain that persists even when one does bounce back. Rather than investing in and intensifying death as James suggests, this strategy—and it is oftentimes strategic—understands that damage and survival or brokenness and resistance are interlocked, an argument made brilliantly and much more elaborately by Darieck Scott in his book *Extravagant Abjection: Blackness, Power, and Sexuality in the African American Literary Imagination*. Scott argues that, typically, Black resistance thinkers—he specifically discusses Frantz Fanon and the way that Black Power intellectuals took him up—see the past as "an obstacle to imagining and building an empowered political position capable of effective liberation politics" (D. Scott 2010, 4). But Scott argues that there is another strategy to carry forward a project of resistance: to examine the deleterious effects of slavery, colonialism, and racial capitalism, not just to demonstrate that they were injurious but also to see that the injuries themselves can serve as tools or models of political transformation (9). In a wonderful reading of Scott's work, Robert McRuer (2018, 100) highlights Scott's attention to woundedness and muscular tension in Fanon's writing. McRuer writes, "Wounded, tense muscles, in Scott's readings of Fanon, are indicative and anticipatory, they *indicate* what colonialism and war have done and they *anticipate* an active resistance, by those same bodies."[6] Scott, in other words, focuses on the potential—the muscle that is tensed and about to activate—that Fanon sees in his wounded Algerian patients. And, for Scott, this active potential in brokenness or woundedness affords a liberating escape from linear time. Scott writes, "I find gestural and postural possibilities, which loop (rather than align or stick on a pyramid) the past, present, and future, an approach to time that I call interarticulated temporality; a state of death-in-life and life-in-death characteristic of the paradox of a being that experiences utter defeat yet that is not fully defeated"

(2010, 26). To me, these "gestural and postural possibilities" recall the calluses that Macharia writes about because they anticipate a future that is paradoxical, that is hardened but also protective of tenderness, that contains vulnerability but does not seek to disavow it.

And, in fact, when "Same Love (Remix)" screened at the Queer Kampala International Film Festival and Barasa was there for a postscreening panel, he made a point to discuss how the suicide of the main character in the video followed rather than preceded the image of Wainaina (whose coming out signified a momentous political triumph) and the blissful love life of the lesbian couple. Gains in the movement, he noted, are sometimes followed by depression, just as depression or pain is sometimes followed by a win. I read this as the very type of "interarticulated temporality" or "state of death-in-life and life-in-death" that Scott finds hidden in the margins of Fanon's thought. Or to put this differently, Barasa was painfully aware of the way that pain loops, and the remix—based on his life—emphasizes looping time over any narrative of defeat or overcoming.

In this way, "Same Love (Remix)" has more in common with Mayfield's 1965 "People Get Ready" than it does with Macklemore and Ryan Lewis's version of the song. In "People Get Ready"—one of the first gospel crossover hits in the United States—the people, collectively, are taken along for an uplifting (though not soaring or triumphant) ride to and through the civil rights movement:

People get ready, there's a train a-comin'
You don't need no baggage, you just get on board
All you need is faith to hear the diesels hummin'
Don't need no ticket, you just thank the Lord

As I argued above, the Macklemore and Ryan Lewis video, with its particular emphasis on the (gay) marriage plot, shows the protagonist overcoming homophobia and parallels this triumph to the way in which the Black civil rights movement supposedly overcame racism. But the melody and timbre of the song align themselves more with Mayfield's humming diesels—more steady and repetitive than soaring and dropping—as well as with Lambert's warm and haunting self-acceptance when she sings, "I can't change even if I wanted to," a chorus that is restrained and assured rather than triumphant. And though "People Get Ready" was inspired by the 1963 March on Washington, it was also written in the wake of the JFK assassination and the bombing of the Sixteenth Street Baptist Church in Birmingham, Alabama, that killed four young girls. Therefore, though the train that is a-comin' is symbolic of the social change that has, in a sense, already left the station, Mayfield's song channels the way that pain is always intertwined, or looped, with (divine) faith in potentiality. And as Crees writes, Mayfield's looping is repeated in "Same Love." But whereas the Macklemore and Lewis "Same Love" video repackages Mayfield's restrained message into one of triumph, in Art Attack's version, which keeps Lambert's chorus and Mayfield's structure, messages of hope are looped with notes (musical and handwritten) about being too tired or traumatized to move forward.

Moreover, whereas the Macklemore and Lewis version can be credited with shifting national sentiment on same-sex marriage, the legacy of "Same Love (Remix)" is itself much less unidirectional. Several members of Art Attack, including Monson and Barasa himself, have since fled Kenya and sought refugee status in Canada after being physically attacked or threatened. But at the Kampala Film Festival, Barasa also made a point that the "defeat," or censorship, of the video itself was, in a way, not fully a defeat. Though the Kenya Film Classification Board's decision to ban "Same Love (Remix)" prevented it from being shown on Kenyan television, it brought national and global attention to the video, enabling queer audiences in Africa and across the diaspora to see their lives and struggles reflected in popular art, perhaps for the first time. Moreover, the KFCB made Art Attack, whose seventeen members were all threatened with arrest, central to larger debates about online media and censorship. When the KFCB banned the video from television, it also tried to pressure Google to pull it down from YouTube. Ezekiel Mutua, the CEO of the KFCB, argued that because the video depicted graphic scenes of same-sex couples it could be classified as pornography and as promoting homosexuality. At a media briefing Mutua stated, "Kenya must not allow its people to become the Sodom and Gomorrah of the current age through psychological drive from such content. We have written to Google to remove the video from their platforms. We expect they will do it within one week from now to avoid further violation of the law" (quoted in Murumba 2016). Though Google refused to take down the video, they did add a content warning that appears only in Kenya. Kenyan viewers, or at least those with a Kenyan ISP, must click "continue" before they watch a video that has "been identified as potentially inappropriate." In response to the KFCB's attempt to regulate YouTube, which also led to the board's intensification of internet censorship, Art Attack added their own, sarcastic content warning that appears below the video on the YouTube page for viewers everywhere. It reads, "WARNING: This video contains imagery and a message that may be unnecessarily offensive to some." Art Attack's use of the word *unnecessarily* underscores the point of the video, which is to make homosexuality seem everyday and ordinary and to make homophobia seem cruel and inhumane. And, to a certain extent, Mutua's crusade against the video helped to spread the message, since about 175,000 people clicked the YouTube video in the three-week period after it was banned ("Google Refuses" 2016). It also brought the video to the attention of Kamoga Hassan and the other organizers of the Queer Kampala Film Festival, who brought Barasa to Uganda to screen his censored but readily available video to an underground film festival and to an audience who, even after experiencing the traumatic raid on their Pride celebration just months earlier, risked their safety to attend the festival and to insist on "still being here."

Unfortunately, though 2016 QKIFF was a huge success, especially considering the suppression of the 2016 Ugandan Pride, the following year QKIFF was not so fortunate and, in a sense, the complicated fallout from the "Same Love (Remix)" video seems to have been repeated for the festival at which it premiered. For the 2017 festival, the QKIFF organizers had found a new space, a hip, mixed-use warehouse space called Design Studio. Learning their lesson from the previous year, they built their own screen and spent hours covering all the holes in the warehouse roof where light might shine through and dilute the viewing experience. I was again in attendance at the opening night, which was a festive atmosphere with a huge crowd, food, soft drinks, and live music. But the next afternoon Hassan received a tip that the police were coming. He had just enough time to pack up his equipment and to erase evidence of any queer film festival. The organizers went into temporary hiding and were devastated, suspecting that someone from the community had informed on them. They canceled the rest of the festival and showed a few of the films weeks later at a private residence. Hassan has said that he will regroup and think about how to hold future festivals, but in the immediate aftermath of the 2017 festival he was, like the main character of "Same Love (Remix)," too tired and traumatized to move forward. Indeed, he was in a very critical condition.

"How Do We Save Our Joy?"

Unlike the Queer Kampala International Film Festival, run by independent filmmakers on a shoestring budget, the Out Film Festival (OFF) Nairobi has enjoyed institutional support and has been largely ignored by the Kenyan government even as it grows bigger and bigger each year. It began in 2011, with Johannes Hossfeld of the Goethe Institute and the queer writer and journalist Kevin Mwachiro as the organizers. The Goethe Institute has provided the screening venue since then and, because it is a private cultural center (not run by the German government, though it does receive German state funding), it enjoys relative autonomy. The festival has received financial support over the years from a range of African and international NGOs and has been able to make screenings free to the public. They also do HIV screenings, throw parties, and, beginning in 2015, organize the panel discussions that have become, according to some, the heart of the festival. Moreover, the organizers of OFF have found a legal way to obviate the Kenyan Film Classification Board: the festival is set up as a private film club for members age eighteen and older. Since the event is private rather than public, the government does not need to prescreen movies, and in order not to draw much attention to themselves the organizers keep the advertising of the festival to a minimum, circulating posters mostly in queer-friendly spaces. However, the festival may still not screen banned or illegal films, which means that it has been unable to screen Kenya's two queer feature films, *Stories of Our Lives* and *Rafiki*.

At the November 2018 Out Film Festival Nairobi, the absence of *Rafiki* was particularly palpable. When it was announced in April 2018 that the film would be screening at Cannes, Mutua initially praised and congratulated the director Wanuri Kahiu on public radio. But a few days later he did an about-face, banning the film that, in an April 27 tweet, he said went against "the law, culture, and the moral values of Kenyan people" and announced that anyone in possession of the film would be breaking the law. Kahiu herself was furious about the ban. She had followed proper procedures, learning from some of the mistakes made by the *Stories of Our Lives* crew who did not get proper permits. She submitted the script for preapproval to the KFCB (though Mutua claims that the script was altered and not properly resubmitted) and had police on set during the filming as required by law. She believed that the film should be viewed by mature audiences and had been hoping for and expecting an 18-and-over rating. When Mutua banned the film outright, Kahiu decided to sue the government both as a matter of principle and so that her film could be eligible for the Academy Awards, which requires entries to have screened in their home country for at least seven consecutive days. On September 21, 2018, Justice Wilfrida Okwany lifted the ban on *Rafiki* for exactly seven days, stating, "One of the reasons for artistic creativity is to stir the society's conscience even on very vexing topics such as homosexuality" (Bearak 2018). Though the queer community objected to being called a "vexing" topic, there was much jubilation around the announcement. Theaters in Nairobi, Mombasa, and Kisumu began to screen the film and kept needing to add more and more screenings to meet demand. By the end of the week, it had become the second-highest grossing Kenyan film of all time, and distributors say that the rush and excitement at the cinema had only been felt before at the *Black Panther* release earlier that same year ("*Rafiki* Tops" 2018). Though audiences at some screenings of the film, especially those screenings later in the week that were not filled with a primarily queer audience, snickered at some of the more intimate moments, most queer people writing, tweeting, or talking about the film felt that it was a revolutionary moment. As Holly-Nambi says in her review of the film on the *AfroQueer* podcast, "When the film ended, a large part of the audience stayed until the very last credit rolled. Some people were immobile because they were so moved, some because they wanted to see all the Kenyan names that were behind the production of this film, and some people, like me, sat still because they just didn't want this moment to be over. It really felt like a moment in history. The first time a queer Kenyan film has been shown in Kenyan cinemas" ("*Rafiki* Uncensored" 2018). Unfortunately, when the seven days were over, on September 30, the film was rebanned.

The 2018 Out Film Festival Nairobi was held on November 7, just five and a half weeks after the seven days of *Rafiki* ended. But the energy and momentum of the film were still demonstrable and, in a move that was deliberately meant to provoke and taunt Mutua and the KFCB, an image of a *Rafiki* ticket stub was used for the festival's promotional poster (figure 4.5). The curators of the 2018 festival, Jackie Karuti and Muthoni Ngige, addressed this decision in the opening paragraph of the festival's program. They wrote,

On behalf of the Out Film Festival Nairobi, we would like to congratulate the cast and crew behind the film *Rafiki*; the first Kenyan feature film to compete at the prestigious Cannes film festival. . . . We had all the plans to screen and cheer *Rafiki* at OFF this year but unfortunately we cannot. Fortunately for us we were all recently treated to numerous screenings thanks to the timeless efforts of people who ensured the temporary lifting of its ban for seven days. When the kickass team at the National Gay and Lesbian Human Rights Commission (NGLHRC) bought out the entire theater one afternoon and invited us to go watch for free one of us saved their ticket as future testament to a momentous ruling and gathering. We hereby present it to you as our OFF 2018 poster.

The ticket on the festival poster therefore occupies a fascinatingly looped temporality. It is at once an archival reminder that this momentous event did occur; an indication of the present state of the ban, which substitutes the ticket stub for a promotional photo of the film that surely would have been on the poster if *Rafiki* were showing; and, as Karuti and Ngige write, a "future testament." What they mean by a future testament becomes clear in the third paragraph of the program, when they discuss the film that they have chosen for the

OUT FILM FESTIVAL
NAIROBI 2018

RAFIKI

Cinema 2

ADMIT F-11
0

Seat. E-11
REGU2D Ksh550.0

*0 0 0 6 6 6 0 3 / 0 0 7 *

Image courtesy of: Jackie Karuti

WE DO NOT HAVE THE LUXURY OF SHAME
07/11/2018 - 10/11/2018

SCREENINGS + PANELS: WEEKDAYS 5PM / SATURDAY 4PM
Goethe-Institut Auditorium
Admission: free
Restricted +18

BRITISH COUNCIL   Hivos   HEINRICH BÖLL STIFTUNG EAST & HORN OF AFRICA   GOETHE INSTITUT

FIGURE 4.5. The cover of the 2018 program for Nairobi's Out Film Festival, depicting the stub of Karuti's *Rafiki* ticket.

opening night, Deepa Mehta's 1996 romantic lesbian drama *Fire*. When *Fire* was screened in India, cinemas in Bombay, Delhi, and Calcutta were attacked and vandalized, and the film was pulled from theaters. But Mehta, other activists, and members of the film community petitioned the government not only to rerelease the film but also to ensure moviegoers' security. Eventually, *Fire* was rereleased with no incidents of violence. By putting *Fire*, which Karuti and Ngige call "a film ahead of its time," in the coveted opening slot at OFF 2018, which otherwise would have gone to *Rafiki*, the curators intimate that *Rafiki* too will again have its day. But *Fire* was chosen not only because its backstory overlaps with *Rafiki*'s but also because the Indian Supreme Court, just a few weeks before *Rafiki*'s temporary unbanning, decriminalized homosexuality and declared, "History owes an apology to the members of the community for a delay in ensuring their rights" (Safi 2018). India's ruling was especially important for Kenyans who, at the time of OFF, were less than one hundred days away from a ruling on their own decriminalization case, though the original decision date, which had been scheduled for February 2019, was pushed back to May 24, 2019, when a three-judge panel ultimately ruled against decriminalization. But at the time of OFF 2018 there was much hope attached to what was referred to on social media as #Repeal162, as Section 162 of the penal code makes consensual sex deemed to be against the order of nature a criminal offense.[7] And, in fact, the National Gay and Lesbian Human Rights Commission (NGLHRC), the organization that bought out the screening of Rafiki on the day that the "future testament" ticket was acquired, was also the main plaintiff in the case. Because Kenya's and India's penal codes are both products of British colonial rule—the British imported into Kenya elements of the 1860 Indian Penal Code that outlawed homosexuality—the win in India held particular significance for NGLHRC's case.[8] It became harder for gay-rights opponents to claim that decriminalization was a Western phenomenon in the wake of the India ruling. The NGLHRC-sponsored Rafiki ticket on the festival poster is therefore a future testament not only in that it would, at a later date, remind queer Kenyans of the historical nature of the Rafiki screenings but also in the sense that it anticipates a future freedom that Fire and India embody. If, as Darieck Scott argues, past injuries can serve as models of political transformation, then the Rafiki ticket stub, which marks the absence of the film itself, is a way of understanding defeat as political potential.

My reading of Rafiki also underscores this imbrication of defeat and political potential and demonstrates the way the film is infused with an anticipatory hope that is deeply intertwined with a vulnerability and broken past it never tries to disavow or overcome. Rafiki is based on Monica Arac de Nyeko's Caine Prize–winning short story "Jambula Tree." Kahiu was drawn to the story because she was looking for hopeful African love stories, stories that would showcase the joy, frivolity, and tenderness of young Africans falling in love with each other.[9] "Jambula Tree" is a love story about two Ugandan girls, Anyango and Sanyu, who are from the same Kampala housing estate. However, the girls are separated after they are caught, by the neighborhood gossip Mama Atim, in an intimate moment under a purple jambula tree and Sanyu is sent off to London. The story begins when Anyango hears of Sanyu's return: "I heard of your return home from Mama Atim our next door neighbour. You remember her, don't you? We used to talk about her on our way to school, hand in hand, jumping, skipping, or playing run-and-catch-me" (Arac de Nyeko 2013, 91). Anyango then recounts the girls' extended courtship in the Kampala housing estate where many of the economically struggling characters are trapped in loveless relationships and where soldiers in green uniforms have become the new order. In the story, Anyango anticipates Sanyu's return, telling Sanyu where to find her and what to expect to see in the neighborhood that has not changed much at all. Though the reader never knows what becomes of the two lovers (the entire story is narrated the day before Sanyu's arrival), the ending is, almost literally, ripe with possibility. Anyango describes the picture of the purple jambula tree she has hanging in her room and says: "Sanyu, you rise like the sun and stand tall like the jambula tree in front of Mama Atim's house" (105). Anyango is therefore anticipating a moment that may very well be joyous but that will nevertheless be unable to erase past pain. The ending, to borrow Darieck Scott's verbiage, is full of "gestural and postural possibilities" that speak both to defeat (i.e., the neighborhood that has not changed, the jambula tree where they were caught) and to the fact that Sanyu's return indicates a future that "is not fully defeated," that might "rise like the sun."

The film *Rafiki* follows both the basic plot and the "gestural and postural possibilities" of "Jambula Tree": two girls, here Kena and Ziki, fall in love and are discovered by Mama Atim, with Ziki subsequently sent off to London. However, Kahiu makes a number of changes and additions to the story. First, the film is called *Rafiki*, which means "friend" in Swahili. During the shooting of the film, Kahiu and the crew did not want to draw attention to the fact they were making a lesbian love story. Though the script was in fact approved by the Kenya Film Classification Board before filming began, and police were on set as was required by law, they still wanted an inconspicuous title that would not be linked to the short story.[10] They settled on *Rafiki*, which, as Kahiu has stated in several public appearances and interviews, is how queer Kenyans need to introduce their partners in a society in which it is not yet safe to name their love directly. The title, then, has a double meaning: it both names the special friendship between Kena and Ziki and names the fact that the real nature of their relationship needs to be hidden.[11]

The second major change that Kahiu made to "Jambula Tree," which begins with the return of Sanyu and then tells the backstory, is to make the structure of *Rafiki* linear. Kahiu's film begins with the girls meeting and then falling in love, and it ends with the return of Ziki. But because, unlike in the original short story, the return is not known in advance, Kahiu finds other ways of keeping the hopeful yet hesitant expectation alive through a vibrant soundtrack, beautiful costuming, lighting, and color palettes. Kahiu also takes the very Ugandan short story, full of references to specific Kampala neighborhoods and Ugandan foods, and makes it a very Kenyan film. The soundtrack is performed almost entirely by Kenyan women under the age of thirty-five, and the setting and speech patterns are very Kenyan, with the characters often using Sheng, Nairobian slang that combines Swahili and English with a mixture of words from other local languages like Kikuyu and Luo. There are also, as Holly-Nambi points out in her review, recognizable Kenyan fashion labels like Chili Mango and Africa Suave and art by the famous Kenyan artist Wangechi Mutu. These inclusions are important not only because the film showcases Kenya's thriving creative community but also because it implicitly makes the argument that the queer love story is indeed a Kenyan one and resists any claims that it is un-African.

Rafiki is Kahiu's fourth film and with it she seems to have cemented her status as one of Kenya's most notable filmmakers. As Robin Steedman (2018) remarks, Nairobi-based female filmmakers like Kahiu, along with Judy Kibinge, Anne Mungai, Hawa Essuman, and Ng'endo Mukii, have become some of the most successful and acclaimed filmmakers in Kenya's small but growing film industry. Therefore, despite the fact that the Kenya Film Commission has focused on selling Kenya as a destination for non-Kenyan filmmakers rather than developing its own industry, filmmakers like Kahiu and her cohort have made use of Nairobi's vibrant creative scene and media market to deliver films that are putting twenty-first-century Kenyan cinema into a global spotlight (Steedman 2018, 316). Though Kahiu has worked in several different genres, her contribution to this creative scene has slowly transformed into what she calls Afro–Bubble Gum art, "fun, fierce, and frivolous" art that counters the images of poverty, sickness, and destitution that are so often associated with Africa.[12] To her, then, the idea of being frivolous and full of joy is indeed political, and *Rafiki*'s mise-en-scène reflects this politics.

The film begins with off-screen ambient sounds of Nairobi's cityscape, as the screen lists funders, the film's title and director, and the obligatory acknowledgment of "Jambula Tree." After a few seconds, Muthoni Drummer Queen's pulsing hip-hop song "Susie Nomo" begins to play. But the first image is not an establishing shot of Nairobi or Slopes, the middle-class neighborhood where the film takes place. Rather it is a tightly framed shot of eighteen of the windows of a two-tone pink apartment building, and it announces not the characters themselves but the main (bubblegum-influenced) color scheme of the film. The camera then cuts to three other images, all from different angles, of the same pink building before continuing with the opening credits. Throughout the opening montage, as "Susie Nomo" continues to play, whimsical drawings of the film's cast and crew are interspersed with images of the neighborhood's residents. We see Kena in one of her signature coral-colored V-neck T-shirts skateboarding down the street, kids playing soccer, girls hula-hooping, a man shaving, and friends playing checkers. And there are also many quick cuts to close-ups of the objects that make up daily life: knives being sharpened, peppers being chopped, bananas for sale, a sewing machine at work. Like "Same Love (Remix)," *Rafiki* begins by announcing that its story is very much a part of Nairobian everyday life. In this sense, *Rafiki* registers Nairobi as a city that, as Eddie Ombagi (2018, 106) argues, "is structured to allow queer, queering and queered flows by its queer users." Critics have compared *Rafiki* to early Spike Lee films like *Do the Right Thing*, but the fast-paced introduction recalls films like *City of God* and *Slumdog Millionaire* that capture the beauty and intensity of city life in the global South, and the whimsical depiction of a youthful African neighborhood has much in common with Jean-Pierre Bekolo's Cameroonian film *Quartier Mozart*. But the "fun, fierce, and frivolous" color palette of the film is in a class of its own. Kahiu takes the purple of Arac de Nyeko's jambula tree and the green accents in the original short story and blends them into a palette dominated by shades of pink, pink-orange, and red, accented not only by rich greens but also by bright blues and yellows.

The first half of the film is a joy-filled girl-meets-girl love story. Kena—who hangs out with a group of guys, including Blacksta, the *boda boda* (motorcycle) driver, who thinks she would make a good wife—sees pink-haired Ziki across the street with her friends. They exchange coy smiles but no words (figure 4.6). Since they move in different circles and there is no script for how they would approach each other, they communicate initially through tentative body language. As Neo Musangi (2014, 50) writes of their own gender-bending performance art in the streets of Nairobi:

> There is a language to be found in a visible silence. To stand in the streets and draw attention to oneself is a possible—but not the only—language. It is one among many. It is to tell one's story without uttering a word. It is also to own one's pain and to immerse oneself into the matrix of danger. It is to put oneself "out there" as it were. It is to reclaim one's place in both time and space.

And, likewise, Kena and Ziki, visibly silent, put themselves "out there," searching for a new language to express their desire within a matrix of danger, to reclaim a time and space that might be otherwise.

For the first part of the film Kahiu keeps the two girls cautiously circling around each other. The audience can only anticipate what the future will hold, what types of love, pleasure, violence, or fantasy their hesitations might lead to.[13] Kena and her friends play soccer or congregate around Mama Atim's restaurant and are served by her daughter Nduta, who is sleeping with Blacksta.

FIGURE 4.6. Still from *Rafiki* (2018). Kena (*left*) talks to Blacksta but is unable to take her eyes off Ziki, who is dancing with her friends.

Kena is also somewhat preoccupied by the news she has heard from the gossipy Mama Atim that her father, who left her mother and remarried, is now expecting a son. Ziki's life is comparably carefree. She comes from a wealthier family, and she is often seen dancing with her friends and wearing vibrant new outfits. Kahiu also thickens the plot by making Kena and Ziki the daughters of two rival politicians, and when Ziki's friends tear down campaign posters of Kena's dad, Kena chases Ziki and her crew. When she catches up and gets close to Ziki for the first time, she is at a loss for words and the two hold each other's glances for a moment before Ziki runs off. A few scenes later, Ziki approaches Kena to apologize for her friends' behavior, and Kena asks her if she would like to get a soda. But soon, the malicious chatter of Mama Atim and the dirty glares from Nduta encourage them to abandon the soda. They become fugitive and artfully escape to a nearby rooftop away from the constraints, gazes, and noises that threaten to make their love impossible.

Away from the noise of the city and against a pinkish-purple sky that perfectly matches Ziki's hair and lipstick, the two girls lay down a colorful blanket and begin their first conversation (figure 4.7). Kena tells Ziki that she is waiting for her test scores and wants to be a nurse. Ziki says she should be a doctor or a surgeon and then reveals that before university she wants to travel the world and go to places where they have never seen an African. She says, "I want to just show up there and be like, 'Yo, I'm here. And I'm a Kenyan. From Africa.'" Kena replies, "But you're not the typical Kenyan girl they'd be looking for." Ziki agrees and says that she does not want to be like her parents,

FIGURE 4.7. Still from *Rafiki* (2018). Kena (*left*) and Ziki (*right*) on the rooftop where they have fled to escape the world below.

staying at home doing typical Kenyan things like laundry, making babies, making *chapos* (Kenyan chapatis). As the sun shines in her face and makes her glow, Ziki holds up her pinky, painted with neon pink nail polish, and says to Kena, "Let's make a pact that we will never be like any of them down there. Instead we're going to be . . ." Kena fills in her sentence: "Something real." Ziki repeats "something real" as the two lock fingers, imagining a world that would look and feel different from the one they currently inhabit and feel trapped by, practicing resistance and a refusal to inhabit norms in the small gesture of interlocking fingers. But the pact the two girls make, the "something real" they imagine, has yet to take a concrete form: here, at this moment, as the girls gaze down at their city, they are just beginning to envision how to construct a life that breaks boxes, evades rules, and flees the constraints of heteronormativity. When she returns home, Kena's mother immediately notices something unusual about Kena but attributes Kena's new happiness to Blacksta. Ironically, Kena's mother encourages her to spend more time with Ziki, saying that people like the Okemis will lift her up, whereas everyone else, including Blacksta, is like a weight that will keep her stuck.

And Kena does indeed start spending more time with Ziki. When Ziki tries to join a soccer game Kena is playing with her friends, a downpour suddenly begins and Kena leads Ziki to an abandoned *matatu* (minibus used for collective transport in Kenya) that appears to be drenched in pink light. Though it seems that the two will finally kiss, Kena leaves abruptly, overcome with shyness. Soon afterward, however, the two go on an extended date throughout

Nairobi. As the beautiful acoustic love ballad "Ignited" by Mumbi Kasumba plays, they go paddleboating, dance at a nightclub, paint each other with neon paint, and finally kiss. Then, a few scenes later, when Kena finds out that she has received high enough marks on her exams to go to medical school, she and Ziki return to the abandoned matatu, celebrate with candles and cupcakes, and then finally spend the night together (figure 4.8).[14] Though the homophobia of the broader culture has been introduced through a pastor preaching in a church scene and a gay man who keeps getting harassed in the neighborhood, Kena and Ziki are able to live momentarily in a bubble of their own. Their scenes together are always quiet, filled with long silences or soft music that seems to contrast with the bustling noise of the rest of the city and that creates a space for them to be and find themselves, to experience emotional connections and tenderness. But eventually their quiet bubble is pierced with violence. Ziki's friends become jealous of the time she spends with Kena, and Mama Atim and her daughter Nduta, who resents the attention Kena receives from Blacksta, all take notice of the girls' closeness. When Ziki's friends confront Kena and call her a lesbian—the first and only time the word is used in the film—a fight ensues. Ziki pulls Kena away and tends to her wounds, but when Kena's mother walks in on them kissing and tells Kena to leave, they flee together, again seeking out a space away from the constraints of the suffocating present.

They escape once more to the abandoned matatu, but what before seemed like a secret hideout full of light and warmth now becomes a place where they are stuck. The minibus, which is now dark and cramped, cannot move or take

FIGURE 4.8. Still from *Rafiki* (2018). Kena and Ziki share an intimate moment in the abandoned minibus near the fields where Kena plays soccer.

them anywhere, so they begin to plan for the future. Ziki says that they can get their own place together once Kena becomes a doctor, but just as they smile and kiss, Mama Atim and Nduta burst in. Mama Atim looks at them in disgust. "Two politicians' daughters stuck together like dogs," she remarks before calling over a crowd of men that has been lying in wait. But even Mama Atim and Nduta look slightly astonished at the level of violence they have unleashed. Kena and Ziki are attacked and beaten, and they wind up blood-spattered and bruised on a bright green bench in the police station (figure 4.9). (There they are subject to the same probing questions about their gender roles as the two main characters in "Ask Me Nicely," the first vignette in *Stories of Our Lives*.) Ziki's parents are furious with her, but Kena's father becomes one of the film's unexpected heroes. He covers Kena in his coat and embraces her and complains to the police that the attackers should be arrested, not the girls.

After the beating, Kena's mother takes her to a pastor who tries to pray for her salvation. But Kena remains stoic during the ritual and the next morning goes to visit Ziki. There, she learns that Ziki's parents have taken more drastic measures than her own: they are sending her to London. There are many close-ups of the girls' bruised faces, but they barely look at each other. Their wounds are too overwhelming. Ziki keeps her back to Kena as she tells Kena that she wants to be sent away, that she wants her "normal life back." Calluses have formed. The girls have been exposed and feel exposed, and the secret future they had been planning suddenly feels like it is in the past. In the wake of the exposure, Ziki tries to toughen her damaged exterior. She tells Kena that they were being naive and asks, "What did you expect was going to happen

FIGURE 4.9. Still from *Rafiki* (2018). Kena and Ziki are seated in the police station after being beaten by a mob of angry men.

either way? Are you planning to marry me? Are we going to have this beautiful family?" And Kena responds, "Yes," but Ziki tells her to leave and then, as her mother holds her, begs not to be sent away. This is where Ezekial Mutua and the KFCB would have liked the film to end, with the space that the girls created for themselves cut off and with heteronormativity restored. Mutua, in fact, just after the Cannes announcement, insisted that if the film were to be permitted in Kenya, it had to have an ending that did not convey hope. He told Kahiu that if she could end on a shot of the girls looking remorseful then he could give the film a rating and allow it to screen in the country. It was not the kissing or the intimacy or the love, then, that bothered him—it was the fact that all of this could go unpunished (Kahiu 2019). Much like the Nigerian censors, the Kenyan censors believe that at issue is not the depiction of homosexuality but depicting it without sufficient condemnation. But Kahiu refused to change the ending, so that this scene of vulnerability, the penultimate in the film, becomes one that is, like "Jambula Tree," full of anticipation and potential precisely because there is indeed something next, something beyond. In this way, *Rafiki* shows how "vulnerability, reconceived as bodily exposure, is part of the very meaning and practice of resistance" (Butler, Gambetti, and Sabsay 2016, 8).

In the film's epilogue, Kena, who is now a doctor or medical student at a local hospital, encounters Mama Atim as a patient there. Mama Atim refuses to be treated by Kena but informs her that Ziki Okemi is back in Slopes. Kena silently heads to her locker and examines a postcard that says only "I miss you" with a z doodled underneath. (Readers of "Jambula Tree" will recognize this as containing the same message as the one postcard that Sanyu sends to Anyango from London.) Slowly and quietly, Kena heads home, glances over at Ziki's building, and then heads to a hill nearby. Moments later we hear Ziki's voice from off-screen call out Kena's name and see her hand—with bright orange nail polish—rest on Kena's shoulder. Though the film ends here, without a direct resolution and without showing their faces together, the lyrics to Njoki Karu's breathy song "Stay" certainly imply that what Ziki might be saying is "I'm here." As Karu croons, "Lay with me, we can put the stars to bed, watching me 'til the morning sun rises" (a reference, perhaps, to the rising sun in "Jambula Tree"), and the credits roll, it is hard not to see this film as imagining a new future for them. And I argue that one can see in this ending, especially with its attention to Ziki's hand and fingers, the fulfillment of the pinky promise the two girls made on the roof, that they will be real, that they will craft an otherwise, perhaps even marry and have a beautiful family—not a family that needs to be protected against queers but "a family that disrupts the neat gender binary that anchors the nation" (Macharia 2013a, 286). And yet the withholding of Ziki's face, and of the life they build after the reunion, indicates that this ending, as Ombagi (2019, 272) argues about *Stories of Our Lives*, exists not despite but because of the "various tensions and frictions that create a landscape of queer liveability" in Nairobi. Rather than seeing the ending as a triumph or an overcoming, I see it as an opening in which vulnerability, tenderness, and defeat are resources for resistant, queer life-building.

Here, then, I see the film not only as anticipatory, as holding open a future moment, but also as aspirational in the sense that Christina Sharpe describes in *In the Wake: On Blackness and Being*. Sharpe, thinking about aspiration as both ambition and inhalation, writes, "Aspiration is the word that I arrived at for keeping and putting breath in the Black Body," for imagining and transforming space through an ethics of care and an ethics of seeing (Sharpe 2016, 131). Sharpe's work examines the precarity of Black life in the United States in the wake of slavery and the centuries of violence in which the Black body has been subjected to "physical, social, and figurative death" in countless ways (17). But wake work, or living in the wake, is for Sharpe a way of accounting not only for that death but also for "the largeness that is Black life" (17). She describes being in the wake as recognizing "the ways that we are constituted through and by continued vulnerability to overwhelming force though not *only* known to ourselves and to each other *by* that force" (16). Like Darieck Scott, then, she finds it necessary to name and articulate injury and woundedness as a means of anticipating a resistance to it. She writes, "In short, I mean wake work to be a mode of inhabiting *and* rupturing this episteme with our known lived and un/imaginable lives. With that analytic we might imagine otherwise from what we know now in the wake of slavery" (18). Aspiration, then, is how she describes the rupturing of the suffocating present with other possible futures. Aspiration is about breathing and existing and creating and allowing the lungs to fill with air. But it is also a way of remembering pain. Aspiration, in this sense, is connected to the cut and to fugitivity and the artful way one deviates from something to which one nevertheless remains bound. But for Sharpe aspiration is also connected to the concept of the hold and to the many different meanings of *hold* that she mobilizes throughout her book. Primarily, for Sharpe, this refers to the suffocating hold of the slave ship and all the iterations of captivity that affect and negate Black lives (and that, as I have been suggesting throughout this book, are not limited to Black lives in the diaspora).[15] But there is also the hold, as in being held, as in the grip humans and bodies have on one another in a network of care when one beholds another, when people are beholden to each other, obliged to be concerned about the other's well-being (Sharpe 2016, 73, 99, 100). Aspiration, then, inhales from within the hold and also reaches for new ways of holding life and love.

I also understand the hold and holding to be forms of critical resilience that hold time and space for vulnerability, that say in the same *breath*: "we are here and we are demanding" and "we tell you we have been violated." Holding, as in a holding pattern or as in holding one's ground, has, in fact, a very different temporality than "I Overcame," but it is, I argue, no less resilient and in many ways even more resistant, more critical. And it is, I argue, these forms and modes of holding and of critical resilience that made *Rafiki* feel so revolutionary to the queer people who watched it in Kenyan theaters during the seven unbanned days. Here's what Stacy Kirui, a Kenyan student and storyteller who went to see the film each of the seven days it was banned, wrote of her experience:

> There, in that big cinema, women who ached the way I did held me, and I held them, as we experienced a story familiar to all of us. In the cinema, I was held by other Black queer women who resonated with the realities of loving other Black women under duress. We passed pocket tissues around and rested our heads on each other's shoulders. We squeezed each other's hands. We were vulnerable. We grieved mothers like Ziki's whose complexity we knew all too well. Mothers who held us while we were consumed by the pain of loving too differently while they simultaneously begged us to love a little less differently. Mothers like Kena's who could not fathom us, who left us to be our fathers' children because we loved too unfamiliarly. Mothers like Mama Atim who harmed us in ways they would never wish for their own children to be harmed. We also grieved fathers like Kena's who held their children and loved them back to safety.
>
> There, in the cinema, the noise quieted. For a moment we were neither the elephant in the room nor the spectacle. We watched these two queer women come of age together and some of us came of age with them. In *Rafiki* we saw ourselves, our lives, our joys, our struggles, our triumphs. We were real. (Kirui 2018)

The act of beholding those queer lives coming of age, of holding one another in the visible silence of the theater, of being held in one's seat after the credits roll was, to many, breathtaking, transformative, critically needed. Indeed, speaking about the film on a panel at OFF 2018, Holly-Nambi says, "Seeing people seeing themselves on screen during *Rafiki* felt otherworldly, like going to church. It felt life-saving. Films should be put in the hands of people whose lives need to be saved." In that sense, the coming of age enacted by Kena and Ziki, who own their pain, who reclaim their time and space, who find the language to write their own stories, was to many queer Kenyan viewers something to aspire to, something to hold on to.

Of course, *aspiration*, like *resilience*, is a keyword that has come to take on a very specific meaning in our neoliberal moment. As McRuer (2018, 176) writes, "Aspiration has basically been . . . codified as an individualist, libertarian concept oriented around personal achievement and merit," and he warns that it often forecloses meaningful class analysis. Here, then, one might note that parts of Kena's and Ziki's hopes and aspirations are indeed hitched to class mobility. Kena's high test scores and her potential career as a doctor signal to Ziki that the couple can move in together and sustain themselves economically without needing the approval of their parents. But though a doctor's salary would indeed make things easier for them, I also read their rooftop promise "to be real"—a phrase repeated by Kirui, who found a type of realness while watching the film—as one that resists heteronormative, heteropatriarchal aspirations based on personal achievement and merit. Ziki very much does not want to be a typical Kenyan girl, and though the aspirations she and Kena express might depend on economic independence and stability, I do also see them as gesturing toward, as Frieda Ekotto says in *Vibrancy of Silence*, ways of simply operating differently, ways that are inspirational to all types of queer Africans, and especially to queer youth who may have never seen queer African love and happiness modeled for them or held out as a real possibility.

But in order to more fully understand the spaces queer films like *Rafiki* hold open, I would like to return once more to the 2018 Out Film Festival Nairobi from which *Rafiki* was *withheld*. On the third night of the festival there was a panel called Pride and Protest in Uganda that focused largely on the queer movement in Uganda *in the wake* of the fateful Pride 2016 raid. The performance poet Gloria Kiconco moderated the session and described how many Ugandans had dropped out of the movement or hibernated after the raid because they were so traumatized. But she also noted that new parties and spaces were popping up because, as fellow panelist Godiva Akullo (also featured in *Resilience Diaries)* articulated, queer people are "resilient." When Kiconco asked the panelists to comment specifically on what types of queer organizing and socializing were occurring in Kampala, the queer artist and organizer of feminist utopias Mildred Apenyo took the mic. "How do we save our joy?" she asked Kiconco and the audience. She continued, "That is how I am interpreting this question. I am absolutely militant about making my safety joyful, but I know that wouldn't have helped when we were holding each other on the ground [at Pride 2016]. But the moment they let us go, we kept organizing [our events]. . . . And me, I am flourishing." Even though Apenyo was talking about the need for militancy and organization, she was also articulating a way of mobilizing and resisting from a position of vulnerability and defeat, from the hold. Vulnerability, in other words, "is part of the very meaning and practice of resistance" (Butler, Gambetti, and Sabsay 2016, 8), but so are joy and frivolity. *How do we save our joy? When we were holding each other on the ground. In the cinema, I was held by other Black queer women. I'm still here.* All of these statements articulate the interarticulatedness of care, flourishing, and trauma.

The Pride and Protest panel that night, and in fact all of the panels at the Nairobi festival, had very little to do with the films being screened at the festival. And festival organizers Karuti and Ngige made it clear that this was intentional, that the panels were about a radicalness and openness and defiance that were not only connected to the films being shown. The festival to them was just as much about watching films collectively as it was, in Karuti's words, about *"holding space* to congregate."[16] Of course, sometimes one holds space and that space is violated (as in the case of Ugandan Pride 2016 and QKIFF 2017), or that space is censored by those attempting to resist queer rights, queer bodies, and queer existence. But at other times holding space can mean creating resistance by saving joy, savoring joy, and carving it out within spaces of defeat. Here's what Kahiu herself says about joy in relation to the violence depicted in *Rafiki*:

> We have to be really very clear that we are joyful, radiant people. And the way I think of joy is not like happiness. Happiness is sometimes fleeting, but I think joy is almost a bowl that contains all of our experiences. And some of those experiences are hard but that does not mean that we are any less joyful. . . . And [in the film] that moment of hardship is within the context of love, and within the context of a joyful space, and within the context of radiance. (Kahiu 2019)

The violence, she says, "needed to be *held*" but she did not want it to be the emphasis of the film (2019). Kahiu holds this violence within her bowl of joy, within her space of rebelliousness and radiance.

And this was also precisely the type of joyful, defiant space that OFF 2018—taking its cue in part from the mood created by the seven days of *Rafiki*—created and fiercely held open. The previous year, the theme of OFF Nairobi had been "A Quiet Revolution," and Kahiu had been there for a filmmakers' panel talking about a film that, in 2017, no one had yet seen, that had not yet been selected for Cannes or been banned or temporarily unbanned. Quietness held open a space for being "out there," as Musangi says. But the theme of OFF 2018 was "We Do Not Have the Luxury of Shame," a phrase that comes from a line in the first episode of the television series *Pose* about the 1980s–1990s underground ball scene in New York City, where queer and trans people of color joined houses, created chosen families, and competed against each other in dancing, fashion, and vogueing categories. The line is spoken by Blanca, a new housemother, who is taking her previously homeless "son," Damien, to audition for dance school despite the fact that a lack of self-worth caused Damien to hold back, to miss the deadline. Shame, or at least shame alone, Blanca intimates, does not create space for other possible futures, for aspiration, for critical, life-saving resilience. What Blanca asks of Damien, which is what the 2018 OFF organizers seemed to be asking of the attendees, is to harness vulnerability for its potential to transform.[17] "We Do Not Have the Luxury of Shame" was therefore a theme that, in the *wake* of *Rafiki* and in anticipation of #Repeal162, redacted the "quiet" in "a quiet revolution," while also paying respect to the quiet hold of *Rafiki* and a film like *Fire*.[18] It led to frank discussions about queer sex, and to Apenyo's descriptions of punching a man who threatened her safety at a queer party, and to Jim Chuchu's declaration that queer African films should not have to be downloaded illegally and watched alone on laptops because queerness is not explosive to those who live it every day. And it led to an after-party where Samantha Mugatsia, the actress who played Kena, drummed with her band Yellow Light Machine (which was how she was originally discovered by Kahiu, who thought she had the exact look of Kena) and where the Ugandan DJ Rachael Ray Kungu, East Africa's first female DJ, who was repeatedly outed in tabloids like *Red Pepper*, played tunes until four in the morning because space was being held and no one wanted it to end. The organizers and attendees of OFF created a moment in which joy was indeed saved, in which calluses were exposed, in which a community of people experiencing both the defeat of *Rafiki*'s censorship *and also* the exuberance of its existence and the hopeful anticipation of decriminalization were able to say proudly and defiantly, "I'm still fucking here."

Coda

Queer African Cinema's Destiny

I want to conclude *Queer African Cinemas* by looping back to the beginning, back to a foundational queer African film, the 1997 Guinean movie *Dakan*, that, like Deepa Mehta's *Fire*, speaks to past injuries while also serving as a future testament of what could be. In the fall of 2019, about a year after OFF 2018, None on Record released an *AfroQueer* podcast episode on *Dakan*, a film I have mentioned several times now throughout this book. In her introduction to the episode, host Selly Thiam begins by discussing how relatively few cinematic or televisual representations of queer Africans exist and how stunned she was when, a few years earlier, she had discovered the existence of a beautiful 1997 queer African love story that she had never heard of and whose director seems to have disappeared from public life. To promote the episode of the podcast, *AfroQueer* posted an image on their Facebook page that featured Kena and Ziki from *Rafiki* on one side and Manga and Sory, the two male protagonists of *Dakan*, on the other side (figure C.1). Then they posted a quote—"Nobody wanted to fund my film. They said that Africa was not ready for a gay film"—and asked people to guess who the quote was from. In a way,

FIGURE C.1. Teaser image posted on social media to advertise the *Dakan* episode of the *AfroQueer* podcast, featuring Manga and Sory *(left)* and Kena and Ziki *(right)*. © AfroQueer Podcast.

it was a trick question. Though the image did have the word *destiny* written over the top, and though *Dakan* does mean "destiny" in Mandinka, Kena and Ziki are clearly more recognizable than Sory and Manga—and indeed, the first commenter guessed that the quotation came from the director of *Rafiki*, Wanuri Kahiu. *AfroQueer* responded, however, that the quotation in fact came from Mohamed Camara, the director of *Dakan*, who would be the subject of their next episode.

As *AfroQueer* seemed to intimate in its promotion of the podcast, there are indeed many similarities between *Dakan* and *Rafiki*, despite the fact that they are separated by over two decades in time and an entire continent geographically, as well as by a number of other gendered, linguistic, and religious differences. *Dakan* begins with a scene of high school boys Manga and Sory making out at night in Sory's red convertible, a scene that was completely unprecedented in African cinema at the time. Like the abandoned matatu that Kena and Ziki escape to, this private automotive space provides them with just enough cover to express their love. And, like Kena and Ziki, they face a host of people around them who do not think this love should exist, in addition to an important few who are supportive. Manga and Sory also face parental pressures to abandon their love. Manga, like Kena, is subjected to spiritual intervention, though it involves a traditional healing process and not a Christian one. And Sory, like Ziki, is sent away by a wealthy parent trying to protect the family's respectability and financial success. But again, like Kena and

Ziki, the separated lovers do come back to each other and indicate that queer life-building—perhaps even flourishing—is possible, despite all the attempts to thwart it. Manga, who is married off to a white woman, tells his wife as they are making love that he cannot get Sory out of his head. He goes out in search of Sory and eventually finds him in a village with his own wife and a baby. The film ends defiantly yet quietly, with the same vague hopefulness as *Rafiki*, albeit a hopefulness complicated by the wives and child left behind, as Manga and Sory drive off together in Sory's SUV without saying a word. The two films are, to my knowledge, the only two feature films to end with the possibility of two Black and African same-sex lovers staying together and registering hope for the durability of queer African love.

Dakan, like *Rafiki*, premiered at the Cannes Film Festival and was much more widely viewed outside its country of origin than within it, and it was also a film that felt revolutionary to queer Africans who had never seen themselves on screen before and had certainly never seen a film in which queer African lovers were allowed to stay together. Beti Ellerson recounts a moment during a screening of *Dakan* at Howard University in 1999:

> In one instance a gay Senegalese man came to the open microphone to express his pride in being a homosexual from Senegal and stated that it was the second time he had seen the film and was overwhelmed by it. Receiving applause from the audience, he further stated that the entire gay population of Africa thanked Camara and that by making the film, he had pulled back the curtains of hypocrisy and this was the first time that he had seen this done. (Ellerson 2005, 62)

And though Ellerson notes that the audience seemed frustrated that Camara, as a straight man, could not give them any details about gay life in Guinea or give them a sense of whether the ending was realistic, she notes the profound sense of affirmation the audience derived from seeing Sory and Manga drive away together.

However, on the African continent *Dakan* did not enjoy the same love that *Rafiki* received. In his interview with Thiam, Camara recounts how when the film was screened at FESPACO—the famous pan-African film festival held in Ouagadougou, Burkina Faso (and where Samantha Mugatsia received an award for her portrayal of Kena)—he had to change hotels every day and leave each screening five minutes early to avoid being beaten up.[1] When *Dakan* was screened in Guinea at the Franco-Guinea cultural center, Camara decided to hide behind the door rather than leave and barely escaped angry crowds looking for him. Moreover, after *Dakan* was released, Camara was also ostracized from African filmmaking circles. He tells Thiam that the famous Senegalese filmmaker Djibril Diop Mambety approached him after the Cannes screening to tell him that his career as a filmmaker was over, a prediction that turned out to be true. When Thiam finds Camara twenty-two years after *Dakan* was made, he is living with his wife in Guinea and has not made another film.

And yet Camara did not at all seem to regret making *Dakan*. He repeats to Thiam the origin story that he told Ellerson in 1999. Though several of the details have shifted over the two decades, in both accounts he describes how the idea to make *Dakan* had come to him when he was in Burkina Faso working on an earlier film. There, he saw two men kissing, something he had never before witnessed in Africa and something he thought happened only in Europe, where he had lived for a brief period of time. When he asked about the men, locals told Camara that it was fine, "They're just women," indicating, as Thiam suggests, that the community had a much more fluid and customary understanding of gender than Camara knew was possible. Intrigued, Camara immediately began to write the script, taking extra care to show that homosexuality could be both commonplace in African communities and, at the same time, something shameful. He had trouble funding the film, trouble casting actors (he eventually persuaded his younger brother to play Manga), was constantly accused of being gay himself, and angered local imams so much that they issued a fatwa against him. He didn't mind this, however, and even, as Thiam reports, debated the imams on local television, insisting that God loves all his creations. In his 1999 interview with Ellerson, Camara says that the ending of the film could be interpreted in many ways, with many possible scenarios for what might happen to Sory and Manga after they leave Sory's village. But in his 2019 interview with Thiam, he seems to have a more positive spin on the ending, stating that they are "going toward freedom" and adding that "the world belongs to those who refuse to give up."

Dakan (or "Destiny") was a film that—over two decades ago—held space for a queer African love story to exist on screen, a film that for many years served as an anomalous reminder of what did once exist and a future testament of what could exist.[2] With *Rafiki*, and its similarly hopeful ending for two queer African lovers, that space has been held yet again; but unlike with *Dakan*, which ended Camara's career, *Rafiki* seems to have opened up many new possibilities for Kahiu (who is now slated to make a new Disney film), for Kenyan cinema, and for queer African cinema more broadly. To be clear, I am not suggesting a teleological sketching of African cinema in which *Rafiki* finally fulfills the destiny of *Dakan*, or in which queer African cinema has achieved a certain evolutionary stage. Nor am I suggesting that queer African films need to be happy. Indeed, almost all of the films discussed in this book, even those without happy endings, register practices of tenderness, care, and freedom that can be resources for resistance and queer life-building. Rather, by closing my book with the beginning of queer African cinema and with a film that was in many ways ahead of its time, I am suggesting that one may read the trajectory of queer African cinema through a looped, interarticulated temporality in which defeat and triumph always coexist, where escape and confinement—cutting away from and being contained by—are always entangled in multiple Afri-queer, fugitive ways.[3]

On the one hand, as I write this in the spring of 2021, there is certainly much to celebrate about how queer African cinema has transformed over the past several decades. One might point not only to the success of *Rafiki* but also to the ability of TIERS and The Equality Hub to open up the types of stories Nollywood tells, or to the proliferation of complex queer films that challenge hegemonic masculinities in South Africa, or to the ability of the internet and YouTube in particular to provide a platform for queer expression, as in the case of "Same Love (Remix)."[4] Moreover, at the time of writing, there has been talk of adapting African literary works with overt queer subtexts to global television screens. The network FX has announced the adaptation of Akwaeke Emezi's novel *Freshwater*, which reflects many of the nonbinary transgender author's own experiences, into a series, and Netflix has recently signed a deal with the prolific Nigerian producer Mo Abudu to create a series based on Lola Shoneyin's novel *The Secret Lives of Baba Segi's Wives*, which includes the story of a lesbian woman. (These announcements also reflect a continuation of the trend of adapting queer African fiction like *Walking with Shadows*, *Moffie*, and "Under the Jambula Tree" to the screen.) And, at the same time, producers and directors, writers, podcasters, musicians, vloggers, photographers, and artists—including more and more women and transgender and nonbinary people—across Africa are continuing to create queer content that pushes and expands the boundaries of queer storytelling, while African actors and celebrities are increasingly defending queer life in public. Decriminalization in Botswana, Gabon, and Angola, as well as the recognition of same-sex marriage in Tunisia, have also bolstered hopes of queer Africans across the continent.

On the other hand, queer African cinema, like queer African citizens, has been hit with many setbacks over the past two decades: the censorship of *Rafiki* that was followed by the disappointment of Kenyan courts deciding against decriminalization; the need for Barasa and Monson and many other queer and gender-nonconforming Africans to flee the continent in order to feel physically safe; the local protests against *Inxeba*; and the cancellation of QKIFF after police raids. The year 2020 saw the first trials of gay men arrested in Nigeria under the SSMPA (though the case against the forty-seven men arrested together was eventually struck down for "lack of diligent prosecution"), and that same year many queer Africans were cut off from their chosen families, support systems, and queer-friendly spaces (including film festivals) because of the COVID-19 pandemic. In a live Instagram interview in May 2021, posted as I was completing the final edits of this book, Jim Chuchu noted that with the recent arrests of queer activists in Ghana and trans women in Cameroon and a sexual offenses bill passing through parliament in Uganda, the situation for queer Africans felt very much like it did back in 2013, when he and the Nest Collective were making *Stories of Our Lives*.[5] What I have been suggesting throughout *Queer African Cinemas*, beginning with the Nest Collective's film, is that queer African films and videos register these stalemates and document the painfulness of the present just as much as they open up new spaces, new times, and new possibilities for surviving and flourishing.

And so I close this book about the various registers of resistance in queer African cinemas with *Dakan*, a film that records a beginning full of hurt and vulnerability and also maps out ways of quietly inventing new beginnings. But what I also want to emphasize here is that if *Dakan* was a resistant film, ahead of its time, it is not just because it was the first film to show two African men falling in love, resisting heteronormative expectations, and setting out on their own, unknown path. It was also ahead of its time—and, of course, very much in its own time—because it showed that this type of resistance would have consequences, that audiences might reject it, and that because queers do not love each other in isolation, parents, wives, and children would also be affected, would be called upon to either support their love or, as was often the case, mount their own resistance to it. *Dakan*, in this sense, was a film that made waves of its own, registering in both visible and subtle ways across the African continent, across the globe, and across decades. It signaled many of the ways that the queer African cinemas that followed in its wake would be simultaneously resisted by those who want to erase queer African existence and held up as a model of resistance and critical resilience for those who, in the words of Camara, "refuse to give up." In this way, *Dakan* can be read not only as a film about the *dakan*, or destiny, of Manga and Sory but also as a film that gestures to the destiny of queer African cinema as a collective body of films and videos: it registers the unpredictable, fugitive escape routes to an otherwise time and place, and, at the same time, it indicates the various ways queer love and life-building can be blocked or damaged when those escape routes are cut off, when violence is enacted. But I want to end this book like *Dakan* and *Rafiki*, whose loose endings full of potential gesture toward hopeful itineraries without articulating any fixed or known path, and suggest that queer African cinemas anticipate a destination that holds space to imagine new stories, new freedoms, and new joys even within the confines of the present.

INTRODUCTION. REGISTERING RESISTANCE

1   "Gayism" is a neologism that began circulating in some Anglophone African coun-
    tries in the early 2000s. It is used in this context almost exclusively as a derogatory
    term in public discussions.
2   These production history details come from Jim Chuchu and Njoki Ngumi, interview
    with the author, December 5, 2017, Nairobi, Kenya.
3   I use the acronym LGBTQ throughout this book to refer to the lesbian, gay, bisexual,
    transgender, and queer communities. However, when an organization or person uses
    a different iteration of the acronym, I use the acronym that they have chosen.
4   The myth recounts the story of Wacici, a herd boy who was beaten by his father
    because he failed to look after his father's cattle. After learning of a girl who walked
    around the Mūgumo and became a man, Wacici does the same and happily becomes
    a girl who no longer has to tend the cattle (Karangi 2008).
5   Chuchu and Ngumi, interview with the author, December 5, 2017, Nairobi, Kenya.
6   On their website, the Nest Collective (2015) discusses the censorship of the film
    and provides the following information: "On 30th September 2014, we applied for a
    classification of *Stories of Our Lives* from the Kenya Film Classification Board in line
    with legislation regarding the public screening of films in Kenya. On 3rd October,
    we received communication that the Kenya Film Classification Board has restricted
    the distribution and exhibition of *Stories of Our Lives* to the public in line with
    section 16(c) of the Film and Stage Plays Act. This, because the film 'has obscenity,
    explicit scenes of sexual activities and it promotes homosexuality which is contrary
    to our national norms and values.' This means that there will be NO further screen-
    ings, sale and/or distribution of *Stories of Our Lives* in Kenya." The Nest Collective
    then states their intention of complying with the ban but also adds an aspirational
    comment, saying, "We hope Kenyans will get to see this film one day, because we
    made it for Kenyans."
7   The release of *Rafiki* in early 2020 on the South Africa–based satellite service DStv,
    which broadcasts throughout the continent, might signal a future in which queer

African films, not just queer South African films, are more available. Unfortunately, though, the announcement that *Rafiki* would be available on Dstv in January 2020 did stipulate that it would not be available in Kenya because of the ban.

8 In "Showing the Unshowable: The Negotiation of Homosexuality through Video Films in Tanzania," Claudia Böhme also discusses two Swahili-language films that, she argues, borrow much from gay-themed Nollywood but that are unique in the Tanzanian context in that they represent the only locally made films on the topic. She writes, "The first visual representation of homosexual practices in Tanzanian film appeared in *Popobawa*, by Haji Dilunga in 2009, which treated the myth of an evil spirit called Popobawa (Batwing) that originated in Zanzibar in the 1960s. Popobawa is a batlike creature, said to appear at night and anally penetrate his victims" (Böhme 2015, 68). The second film she discusses is *Shoga Yangu*, which was censored in Tanzania in 2011. She describes *Shoga Yangu* as "a stereotypically negative representation of homosexuality as a bad, family-destroying behavior, the consequences of greed (*tamaa*), and the desire for quick money, as well as the use of the occult" (74).

9 It should be noted that I use the term *colored* here (as well as in chapter 3) in its specific South African context. As Livermon points out, "During apartheid, there were four designated racial categories: white/European, Coloured, Indian/Asian, and black/African. Blackness took on a political dimension during the fight against apartheid. This political blackness, perhaps akin to the US terminology 'people of color,' developed out of the black consciousness movement and encompassed Coloured and Indian identities" (Livermon 2012, 317n9). However, like Livermon, I use the term *Black*, as most use it in South Africa, to refer to Black/African and not to Indian and Colored South Africans.

10 For more on Adie's films, see my two film reviews "Nigeria's First Lesbian Documentary" (Green-Simms 2019) and "A Rare Cinematic Portrait of Queer Women's Intimacy in Nigeria" (Green-Simms 2020), both on the blog *Africa Is a Country*.

11 For a discussion of the None on Record video series "Seeking Asylum," see A. B. Brown's (2021) article "Lawful Performance and the Representational Politics of Queer African Refugees in Documentary Film."

12 In its final year, in fact, rather than holding a festival, Out in Africa decided to put its funding into the production of the film *While You Weren't Looking* (dir. Catherine Stewart, 2015), which toured nationally and internationally.

13 I therefore situate this project within feminist discussions that seek to dismantle the binary framework that posits an agential and autonomous resistance against subordination. Postcolonial feminists like Lila Abu-Lughod, for instance, challenge the tendency, including her own, to romanticize resistance, arguing instead for understandings of resistance that attend to its complexity. Saba Mahmood (2005) pushes Abu-Lughod's claims one step further, asking whether it is even possible to identify universal acts of resistance and arguing that the category of resistance imposes a "teleology of progressive politics . . . that makes it hard for us to see and understand forms of being and action that are not necessarily encapsulated by the narrative of subversion and reinscription of norms" (9). Mahmood suggests that we should

not be reducing forms of "being and action" to categories of resistance. But many feminist thinkers still see the usefulness and power of resistance and have argued instead for a rethinking of resistance outside of liberal categories and progressivist politics by expanding our understanding of what might constitute resistance, and it is precisely this orientation that I advocate in this book.

14 Here I am also thinking of Kevin Quashie's important work on quiet, *The Sovereignty of Quiet: Beyond Resistance in Black Culture*. Quashie urges that instead of focusing only on the "political meaningfulness" of Black culture, attention also be paid to the interiority of Black subjects and in particular to capacities for quiet, where quiet acts as "a metaphor for the full range of one's inner life—one's desires, ambitions, hungers, vulnerabilities, fears" (2012, 6). Quietness, vulnerability, and interiority are all, to Quashie, ways of moving beyond the "all encompassing reach" of resistance to search for what else exists (5). Though I am certainly influenced by Quashie's work, my own position is that rather than understanding quiet as something beyond resistance, we can understand quiet moments, or practices of stillness, or grace, or surrender, as resources for resistance and as part of what it can mean to be resistant in certain circumstances.

15 Building on the work of James Scott, who sees resistance as a "dress rehearsal," Puri (2004, 111) argues that resistance is best understood as a prelude to concrete political opposition rather than something superior to it, and she emphasizes that one can avoid the pitfalls of a teleological presumption by focusing on the labor necessary to transform resistance into opposition.

16 As Bobby Benedicto (2014, 17) argues, in queer studies a general emphasis on resistance often erases the way that complicity operates, especially when one considers the fact that gay subjects on the margins of the global order might also, simultaneously, hold class privilege, and that "local agency . . . can be mobilized to reproduce the center in the margins." Others, too, have made the case that queerness is not inherently oppositional. Jasbir Puar's (2007) work on homonationalism, for instance, sheds light on the ways in which queerness can be used in the service of xenophobia. And in her article "African Queer, African Digital: Reflections on Zanele Muholi's Films4peace and Other Works," Naminata Diabate (2018) discusses the ways that an artist like Muholi creates work that can be co-opted and put to the service of neoliberal capitalism.

17 The Nigerian psychologist Augustine Nwoye has a useful discussion of the distinction between the *Afri-* prefix and the *Afro-* prefix in his article "An Africentric Theory of Human Personhood." Nwoye, thinking in particular about the term *Afro-American*, writes that, given the American "association of the root term, 'Afro,' in making reference to the identifiable Americans of African descent," he prefers "the term Africentric, for making reference to the psycho-cultural frame of reference of the continental African peoples" (Nwoye 2017, 43).

18 Msibi was a lesbian HIV/AIDS activist, writer, and mother who passed away from AIDS in 2005 at the age of 26.

19 It should be noted, too, that the films examined here do not include the several queer films made in North Africa. As Taiwo Osinubi (2018) points out, "North

African countries have been overlooked within African studies because of linguistic, cultural, historical, and political differences from sub-Saharan Africa" (603). Though my study repeats this exclusion, it is also the case that it is precisely because of these linguistic, cultural, historical, and political differences that North Africa is beyond my field of expertise and that most studies of African cinema focus either on North Africa or on what is commonly, though often arbitrarily, referred to as sub-Saharan Africa. A study of queer African cinema that gives North Africa its proper due would also require a much more nuanced parsing of what Gibson Ncube (2018) describes as North Africa's and "the Maghreb's own conflicted relationship with its African-ness" than I am able to give (624). It would also need to address the well-established field of queer Maghrebian studies, as well as the complex and regionally specific ways that queerness has been historically accepted and practiced in North Africa. However, Ncube's own discussion of queer North African cinema in the *Journal of African Cultural Studies*, "Skin and Silence in Selected Maghrebian Queer Films" (2021), begins this work in important ways.

CHAPTER 1. MAKING WAVES

1 After independence, former French and British colonies took very different tracks when it came to the development of cinema. In an effort to form binding ties with its ex-colonies, the French Ministry of Cooperation actively funded films in Francophone West Africa and in 1963 formed the Bureau of Cinema to facilitate technological and financial support. This support, along with the cultural influence of the French New Wave filmmakers, led to a robust art film culture, and many filmmakers from Francophone colonies traveled to study filmmaking in France or Russia and toured their films at international film festivals. The Anglophone postcolonies, devoid of such support, produced fewer films at first and did not develop their own industries until the 1990s, when video technology became available and entrepreneurs began making films geared toward local audiences.

2 In order to make the Carmen story more specifically Senegalese, Ramaka spells the name *Karmen*, which is more in line with Wolof names and spelling (Dovey 2009, 248), and gives his Karmen the last name *Geï*. As a few critics have noted, Karmen's last name—pronounced the same as the word *gay*—could be a pun, but Ramaka (who also bears the name) states a different reason. He says, "I thought of the rhythm of the *sabar* [drums] called 'Ndèye Guèye.' The person who gave her name to this particular rhythm was a beautiful and exceptional dancer. She was a Carmen. So the title of my film is *Karmen Geï*" (quoted in Powrie 2004, 286).

3 The film features songs by Yandé Coudu Sène, a famous griot who, playing herself in the film, sings the story of both Ndèye Guèye and, at the end of the film, Karmen Geï. And the film also features songs by Massigi (El Hadj N'diaye), including a controversial holy song sung during Angelique's funeral procession, and by Karmen herself, who sings with a strained and sometimes shaky voice. Moreover, the rhythm of the sabar drums—often led by the famous Doudou N'Diaye Rose, head of Dakar's National Ballet—heard throughout the film is joined with a jazz score composed

by American jazz musician David Murray, who has a history of collaborating with Senegalese musicians including Rose, and who himself appears in the film to play his saxophone. But Ramaka himself rejects any categorization of the film and says, "I do not make a difference between that which is said, that which is movement, and that which is sung. . . . Everything is a question of tempo: the emotion that we express determines the need either to sing or speak it" (quoted in Powrie 2004, 285).

4   *Women in Love* was in fact released around the same time as another Ghanaian lesbian-themed video film, *Supi: The Real Woman to Woman*, which tells the story of a young woman who is seduced by an older female trader and who loses both her boyfriend and her fertility as a result.

5   Carla Peterson (2001, xii) argues that the term *eccentric* connotes "a double meaning: the first evokes a circle not concentric with another, an axis not centrally placed (according to the dominant system), whereas the second extends the notion of off-centeredness to suggest freedom of movement stemming from the lack of central control and hence new possibilities of difference conceived as empowering oddness."

6   For a detailed reading of the gorjigeen in Sembene's *Xala* as well as in other Senegalese films and novels, see Babacar M'Baye's (2019) excellent essay "Representations of the *Gôr Djiguène* [Man Woman] in Senegalese Culture, Films, and Literature."

7   One might also look at Jean-Pierre Bekolo's Cameroonian *Quartier Mozart*—a film about a girl who magically and temporarily transforms into a teenage boy and successfully courts the police chief's daughter—as another example of an African Francophone film that critiques the state and the heterosexual economy through a type of queerness that does not depict same-sex intimacy. For a discussion of *Quartier Mozart* and its queer time and space, see Green-Simms (2011).

8   According to Dovey (2009, 245), "The opening sequence of *Karmen Geï* is fashioned as a sabar, in which it is conventional to have six male sabar drummers (known as *géwëls*) pounding out rhythms that initiate the sabar dancing, the most popular and pervasive kind of dancing in Dakar. The dancing is characterized by its circular formation, with women moving in a provocative, energetic way very close to one another." Women often dance in duets, and because the more skilled dancers tend to be more risqué and explicit, the Senegalese audience will know that Karmen has "earned the social right to behave as she does in public" (245).

9   Though historians now refute claims that Gorée was a major site in the transatlantic slave trade—plaques on the wall at Gorée claim that millions of slaves passed through Gorée, while historians estimate it was around thirty-three thousand—the House of Slaves still stands as a powerful visual symbol of the horrors of captivity (Fisher 2013).

10 Of course, *lesbian* does not seem to be the most accurate word here. The category fits neither Karmen, who sleeps with men, nor Angelique, who, as Cheryl Stobie (2016) points out, wears a wedding ring that indicates that she is likely married to a man.

11 As Nelson points out, however, film critics and filmmakers (including Ramaka) argued that film is often not supposed to be realistic and that art does not often coincide with realities.

12   According to Beth Packer, who examines the way gender-nonconforming Senega-
     lese women articulate their rebelliousness as a way of following Cheikh Amadou
     Bamba's spiritual teaching, queer resistance by young people in Senegal today is
     shaped by "a religious-political subjectivity based on a Sufi model of resistance
     which frames emancipation as inner moral power" (Packer 2019, 62). According to
     Packer, for those queer women who follow Bamba, suffering and marginalization
     are often "seen as a test of faith for which [victims of oppression] will be rewarded,
     if not in this life, then in the next" (62).

13   I have been unable to ascertain whether *Women in Love* was released before the film
     Supi: The Real Woman to Woman. For a discussion of an earlier Afrikaans film depict-
     ing lesbianism, *Quest for Love*, see chapter 3.

14   Unoma Azuah, personal communication, July 18, 2019.

15   There also seems to be evidence that Yemonja, a Yoruba mermaid spirit, was also associ-
     ated with queerness, at least in the Americas and the Caribbean. In the very first volume
     of the journal *Yemonja* published in 1982 by the Blackheart Collective, a New York–
     based collective of Black gay artists, an explanation for the journal's name is given in the
     front matter: "In the 'New World' among Cubans and Brazilians, it has been the *adodis*
     (homosexuals), women and men, priests and priestesses who have been outstanding in
     the preservation" of Yemonja. They describe how in one myth "it is told how Yemonja
     came to a land or kingdom called Lado where only adodis (homosexuals) lived. She fell
     passionately in love with a male adodi and since then has been the protectress of all the
     adodis or homosexuals." I thank Kevin C. Quin for making me aware of this journal.

16   On video film and the "infrastructure of piracy," see Larkin 2008.

17   In the film that sparked the Ghanaian video boom, William Akuffo's *Zinabu* (1987),
     a poor auto mechanic named Kofi enters into a deal with a beautiful, wealthy witch,
     Zinabu, who promises to make Kofi wealthy if he refrains from sleeping with her
     or any other women. Kofi agrees and becomes wealthy, but when he is unable to
     keep his promise, Zinabu kills him (Garritano 2013, 2, 73). In 1992, Nigeria's first
     big hit, Kenneth Nnebue's *Living in Bondage*, was an occult and Faustian melodrama
     about an upwardly mobile businessman in Lagos who sacrifices his wife for wealth.
     Though, as Garritano notes, many Ghanaian video films, even many of the early
     hits, did not focus on the occult, and though Ghanaian video makers did indeed
     make efforts to "professionalize" and leave occult stories behind, occult films were
     one of the earliest popular video film genres.

18   For a further discussion of Pentecostalism's influence on video-film culture and its
     mode of visuality, see Meyer 2004, 2006a, 2006b, 2008, and 2015.

19   Similarly, as Lucas Hilderbrand (2009) points out, video has a unique aesthetics
     of failure that is produced through its continual use and duplication. Images drop
     out, develop lines of distortion (or noise bars), and become jerky or exaggerated.
     Even digitized video skips entire frames, is subjected to scratches and marring, and
     has its own interference patterns. Hilderbrand adds that viewing an image on TV
     means that the image one sees is never entirely complete because the colored pixels
     alternate at a different rate than they do in film (thirty "frames" per second instead
     of twenty-four).

20 However, it should be noted that while Marks, like other media scholars of video in the Euro-American context, focuses her analysis on experimental video art, on images that *invite* an embodied spectatorship, Nollywood and Ghallywood practitioners use video in different ways and for different reasons—and they certainly do not intentionally produce unfulfilling or "insufficiently visual" images in the same way that experimental artists do. The production gaffes, out-of-focus images, lighting difficulties, and low-resolution images that were especially prominent in the first two decades of video film production were not intended to solicit an affective response from the audience. Early practitioners turned to video because economic circumstances made celluloid out of reach, not because they felt attached to the grainy quality of video.

21 See Lee Edelman's *No Future* (2004, 11), in which he argues that "the Child has come to embody for us the telos of the social order and come to be seen as the one for whom that order is held in perpetual trust." Against the teleological time of the Child, Edelman posits a queer temporality, marked by a spectral, "haunting excess" and the pleasures of the death drive (31).

CHAPTER 2. TOUCHING NOLLYWOOD

1 The 2001 film *Girls Hostel* is likely the first Nollywood film to have a lesbian character—here, a hypersexual, abusive college roommate.

2 Emem Isong, interview with the author, June 6, 2010, Lagos, Nigeria.

3 This discussion of *Emotional Crack* derives largely from an article I wrote with Unoma Azuah in 2010 based on interviews I conducted on my own with filmmakers and on research Azuah and I did together with the Nigerian National Film and Video Censors Board (NFVCB), with local Nollywood vendors in Lagos, and with queer audiences in Lagos and Abuja. Discussions of *Women's Affair, My School Mother, Girls Cot, Rude Girls, Before the War, Sexy Girls,* and *Mr. Ibu and Keziah* in this chapter are also based on the piece I coauthored with Azuah (Green-Simms and Azuah 2012). I thank Azuah not only for watching and discussing (and even enjoying!) many of these films with me but for her permission to use in this chapter the parts of the article that I originally wrote (though the argument has been significantly updated). I have been careful to indicate in the body of this chapter when I am using information that Azuah and I gathered together. When not specifically indicated, I am using my own independent write-ups of the films and my own notes from interviews I conducted without Azuah. Of course, my understandings of the films are deeply indebted to my discussions with Azuah and with the queer audiences she helped to gather. I also want to thank Rudolf Gaudio for his help in assembling and hosting our audience in Abuja.

4 Olumide Makanjuola, interview with the author, May 30, 2019, Lagos, Nigeria. Otherwise unattributed comments from Makanjuola come from the same interview.

5 *Nollywood*, it should be stated, does not refer to all Nigerian cinema. It is a term coined by the *New York Times* in 2002 that specifically refers to the films of southern Nigeria, where the dominant ethnic groups are Yoruba and Igbo, the main religion

is Christianity, and the majority of films are made in English. While Nollywood does sometimes refer to Yoruba films, Ghanaian coproductions, or films made by Nollywood directors in the diaspora, it typically excludes the Hausa-language films made in the predominantly Muslim city of Kano in northern Nigeria—which are referred to as Kannywood.

6   In 2009, UNESCO reported that Nollywood was the world's second-largest film industry, falling behind India and ahead of Hollywood. The report, widely cited in studies of Nollywood, helped generate global interest in the industry and an upturn in investment. However, because UNESCO simply gathered data from countries and did not conduct its own research, it did not account for different ways each country counted its films. Alexander Bud (2014) reports that "when it comes to defining what can be counted as a film, the key criterion used by every major film board other than the Nigerian National Film and Video Censors Board (NFVCB) is distribution through cinema exhibition. By adding the proviso that the Nigerian statistics relate only to 'video films,' the UNESCO report lost the main basis of comparability with the likes of India, the UK and US." However, Nollywood is still an industry with an impressively sizable cinematic output: depending on the year, statistics place the annual number of films between 1,500 and 2,500.

7   When I conducted research on gay-themed Nollywood films with Azuah in 2010, we often found it difficult to get audiences, distributors, and directors to acknowledge the existence of films about homosexuality, despite the fact that we were able to find close to twenty gay-themed films, many of which had been quite successful. People kept insisting that films on such a taboo topic would not sell in Nigeria or that the censors would never approve of them, because homosexuality—and even discussions or representations of it—were "un-Nigerian."

8   For a more detailed reading of *Beautiful Faces* and a more complete discussion about the overlap between representations of prostitution and lesbianism, see my discussion in "Hustlers, Home-Wreckers and Homoeroticism" (Green-Simms 2012a).

9   Kabat Esosa Egbon, interview with the author, June 5, 2010, Lagos, Nigeria.

10   Campus groups known as confraternities have been present on university campuses in Nigeria since the 1950s, when Wole Soyinka founded the Pyrates at the University of Ibadan as an organization for the intellectual elite. However, the emergence of campus cults as violent organizations, filled primarily by members from wealthy families, began in the 1980s and 1990s during the era of militarization, structural adjustment, and post–oil boom corruption, a time when economic collapse had a devastating effect on Nigerian universities. It is estimated that in the late 1990s, several hundred students died in cult-related activities, and hundreds more suffered physical injuries; in 2004, the year *Beautiful Faces* was released, thirty-three students from three Nigerian universities died in the first two weeks of the semester (Popoola and Alao 2006, 74).

11   Andy Chukwu, interview with the author, June 20, 2010, Lagos, Nigeria.

12   Much thanks to Onookome Okome for bringing *Mabel* to my attention.

13   For instance, one commentator on the YouTube trailer for *Beautiful Faces* claims to "hate Nollywood movies with [homosexual] characters" because she believes that

Nollywood should focus on issues like AIDS or government corruption rather than "gay rights issues." Another person takes Stephanie Okereke to task for agreeing to play a lesbian. The commentator believes that Okereke is "out [for] revenge against her father or men in general" because she tends to take on "annoying" and "boring" feminist roles. This video (and, with it, these comments) have since been removed from YouTube.

14 There were a few Nollywood films, such as Kenneth Nnebue's *End Time* (1999) and Emem Isong's *Reloaded* (2009), that contained minor subplots dealing with male homosexuality but none that made it a central subject until the 2010 films. It should also be noted that Kannywood has typically avoided queer material, though as early as 2002 the Kano-based production company Sarauniya Studios did release a film called *Ibro Dan Daudu*, a film that caricatures the 'yan daudu in northern Nigeria (Gaudio 2009, 143). As Rudolf Gaudio writes, it would be a misnomer to call 'yan daudu gay or transgender—he describes them "as men who are said to talk and act 'like women' . . . are widely perceived to be witty and clever . . . [and] are perse-cuted for their presumed involvement in heterosexual and homosexual prostitution" (3). In *Ibro Dan Daudu*, starring Rabilu Musa Danlasan, whose Ibro character has many iterations, 'yan daudu are portrayed in an exaggerated manner, acting in a slapstick or feminine manner in social situations where that behavior would be unlikely, inaccurate, and inappropriate (143). The film, however, does not address their sexuality per se.

15 Dickson Iroegbu, interview with the author, June 8, 2010, Lagos, Nigeria.

16 Human Rights Watch (2016a) reports that, a month after the SSMPA law was signed, "in Abuja, a group of approximately 50 people armed with machetes, clubs, whips, and metal wires dragged people from their homes and severely beat at least 14 men whom they suspected of being gay. Three victims told Human Rights Watch that their attackers chanted: 'We are doing [President Goodluck] Jonathan's work: cleansing the community of gays.' Another victim said that the attackers also shouted: 'Jungle justice! No more gays!'"

17 Asurf Oluseyi, interview with the author, May 28, 2019, Lagos, Nigeria. Otherwise unattributed comments from Oluseyi come from the same interview.

18 For instance, in a segment of "On the Carpet with Bolinto" that covered the *Hell or High Water* premiere, host Bolanle Olukanni says that the film is talking about "gay rights in Nigeria," which, she notes enthusiastically, is a "big deal." See "*Hell or High Water* Nigerian Gay Rights Film Premiere," YouTube, June 8, 2016, https://www.youtube.com/watch?v=zOVhYc5qaQo. *Pulse Nigeria* also includes *Hell or High Water* in a list of five Nigerian films that "advocate for gay rights" (Izuzu 2018). The list includes three other TIERs films, as well as *Unspoken* (2013), Sunny King's short film (that takes place and was produced in the UK) about homosexuality in the Nigerian diaspora.

19 Or, as Eve Sedgwick articulates in her introduction to *Touching Feeling*, the film can be seen as one that plays to the "particular intimacy [that] seems to subsist between textures and emotions" (2003, 17). Rather than positioning itself outside of or as opposed to dominant culture, the film operates in what Sedgwick calls "a middle

range of agency that offers space for effectual creativity and change" (13), especially as it avoids any overt political argument to move audiences.

20 Tope Oshin, interview with the author, May 29, 2019, Lagos, Nigeria. Otherwise unattributed comments from Oshin come from the same interview.

21 See "Untold Facts S2 E9—The Role of Nollywood in LGBT+ Narratives," January 25, 2018, https://www.youtube.com/watch?v=aCgJEQmNXTU.

22 Noni Salma, interview with the author, July 17, 2019, telephone. Subsequent quotes in this section are from the same interview.

23 A full video of the discussion between Dibia, Graeme Reid, and Sarojini Nadar can be found at "'Africa Writing Queer Identity' at the 16th Time of the Writer 2013," YouTube, February 12, 2014, https://www.youtube.com/watch?v=wuLIri1BGJY.

24 In the context of the novel, Zabus (2013, 102) critiques the focus on the upper class, claiming, "Gayness is thus portrayed as a class phenomenon, which is confined to specific, privileged groups as if they only could afford such a luxurious imported product." Her point is an important one, but it also downplays that the goal of the film and the novel is to show homosexuality to be something innate, something that Adrian can't chose to put on or take off, at least without hurting himself and those around him. In this way, *Walking with Shadows* seems to be claiming that gayness is not in fact a luxury and that even those people whom society holds in high esteem—who appear to be doing well on the outside—might be suffering inside.

25 It is possible that *Gay Pastors* is actually an earlier film that was only uploaded to a Nollywood YouTube site in 2016. The video, however, has since been removed from YouTube and I have been unable to find any bibliographic details on it.

26 When I spoke with Oluseyi, he told me that actor Jussie Smollett's gay character Jamal is so popular that, when Smollet was attacked in a homophobic assault in the spring of 2019 and then accused of faking the attack, Nigerian Twitter vigorously defended Smollett. Oshin also emphasized the popularity of *Empire*.

27 Lisa Onu, personal communication, June 10, 2019, email.

CHAPTER 3. CUTTING MASCULINITIES

1 *Shot Down* was not explicitly a queer film as Worsdale wanted, above all, to make an anti-apartheid film. Tymon Smith (2021) calls it "a wildly anarchic minestrone soup of all the different aspects of white, anti-apartheid cultural production that was happening in Johannesburg at the time." *Shot Down* also incorporated a banned play, *Famous Dead Men*, that Krouse cowrote with Robert Colman.

2 Krouse kept a few silent rushes of the film that were only digitized and screened in 2021 as part of a retrospective on Krouse curated by the South African artist Adam Broomberg for the Kunsthallo gallery in London. The show also featured art, writing, and a filmed version of *Famous Dead Men*.

3 Ricardo Peach (2005, 148) writes, "*Out in Africa* was organised around a manifesto developed by a voluntary film festival committee, keen to see the development of a not-for-profit association which would support gay and lesbian equality and visibility and promote gay and lesbian film-makers in South Africa. The committee included

key people from ABIGALE (The Association of Bisexuals, Gays and Lesbians), GLOW (The Gay and Lesbian Organisation of the Witwatersrand) and the Gay Persons Health Forum. Representing these organisations were people such as Simon Nkoli who also later established TAP (Township AIDS Project) and Zackie Achmat, activist, film-maker and co-founder of the National Gay and Lesbian Coalition and TAC [Treatment Action Campaign]."

4   These films, along with all other films that Out in Africa screened, are now housed at the GALA archive in Johannesburg.

5   See "The History of Gay Television Kisses," *News 24*, March 5, 2017, https://www .news24.com/news24/xarchive/voices/the-history-of-gay-kisses-on-south-african-tv -20180719. In *Prismatic Performances*, Sizemore-Barber also has a chapter devoted to South Africans' reactions to the queer story line on the soap opera *Generations*.

6   I learned of the feature film and its much truncated run from Makgano Mamabolo, one of the producers and writers of both the television show and feature film. Makgano Mamabolo, interview with the author, May 31, 2021. Zoom.

7   It does, however, seem likely that this is slowly beginning to change. In April 2021, Athi Petela directed *Trapped,* a short film about a Black lesbian who has been hiding her identity from her mother. The film aired on SABC1 and was notable in that it was directed by a queer Black woman and also starred many out queer actors of color like Thishiwe Ziqubu, the nonbinary actor who played Shado in *While You Weren't Looking.* Ziqubu, who also has a robust directing and producing résumé, also recently indicated in a panel hosted by the National Film and Video Foundation that they would like to begin making films with queer story lines. And Makgano Mamabolo, who is a queer-identified Black actress as well as a producer on *Society* and *While You Weren't Looking,* has scripted a lesbian art film that she is now trying to fund.

8   Many thanks to Makgano Mamabolo for bringing this point to my attention. Makgano Mamabolo, interview with the author, May 31, 2021. Zoom.

9   Theo Sonnekus (2013, 28) writes, "In conversation with Lin Sampson from the *Sunday Times,* [Hermanus] says that after undertaking revealing research he discovered that 'Bloemfontein . . . has the highest rate of homosexuality in [South Africa and that there] is an element of secrecy. . . . Behind the rugby stadium [for example] is a gay cruising ground, flash your lights twice, that sort of stuff.'"

10 During one interview, for instance, Hermanus responds to a question about the implications and historical reversal of "a Coloured or Black director" telling a "White Afrikaner story." Hermanus responds, "We are definitely experiencing the reaction to that. I had two well-known South African gay socialites, no names mentioned (laughs); hustled their way into a press screening of the film, and they reacted very badly to it. They called a journalist who I know very well to try and influence her review of the film. . . . When I met with her I realized that the biggest problem they had with the film was that I was telling that story. However they had no problem with me making *Shirley Adams* (in which the lead character is Cape Coloured.) They really appreciated *Shirley Adams* because it was 'those people over there.' I think ownership over content is a big South African issue. People want context,

they want to know what connects you to the story. The first question I've been getting all week is 'where does this story come from?' What that question really means is 'are you Afrikaans?'" (Valley 2011).

11 For instance, Gqola (2007, 156) writes that there was a public outcry against a proposed circumcision village near Cape Town, suggested as a way to keep initiation safe, in part because "the village would be a permanent fixture, thereby breaking one of the most central tenets of the ritual: the *amabhoma*, used as temporary shelter for the initiates, would remain unburnt and be left standing. . . . Criticism of this pointed to the spiritual and symbolic meanings of leaving a certain life behind." All of this reveals that the burning of the huts was well-known and not a detail that had been kept secret.

12 I reproduce quotes from the unaired conversation between Holly-Nambi and Trengove with permission from Holly-Nambi.

13 And though South African songs about political resistance were certainly available at the time—in fact, in 1985 the ECC released a compilation of antiwar songs by South African musicians—they notably do not find their way into the arrangement.

14 As one queer viewer, who was conscripted into the army around the same time as *Moffie*'s protagonist, writes, "There was no End Conscription Campaign back then, so you got on that train and you were turned into a number. Every memory I have of that dehumanising experience returned to me while watching *Moffie*. Terrible people behaving savagely towards young boys who were dragooned into a drawn-out conflict that claimed many lives, and left hundreds of thousands scarred for life, on both sides" (van der Walt 2020).

CHAPTER 4. HOLDING SPACE, SAVING JOY

1 One of the organizers told me that he thinks that the theaters made the price so high because they felt bad turning away QKIFF but also did not want the hassle and attention of hosting a queer film festival. He also told me that they may have assumed the festival was being bankrolled by international gay rights organizations.

2 According to Human Rights Watch, police were also "taking pictures of lesbian, gay, bisexual, transgender, and intersex (LGBTI) Ugandans and threatening to publish them; and confiscating cameras. Witnesses reported that the police assaulted many participants, in particular transgender women and men, in some cases groping and fondling them. One person jumped from a sixth-floor window to avoid police abuse" (Human Rights Watch 2016b).

3 As Sylvia Tamale (2013, 34) notes, "Key among the U.S. conservative organizations supporting antihomosexuality sentiments in Africa is the Institute on Religion and Democracy (IRD), a Christian conservative think tank. Ironically, this group was instrumental in opposing the twentieth-century African liberation struggles . . . and these organizations now work hand in glove with African religious and political leaders to oppose progress in the rights of LGBTI persons." For a cinematic representation of American evangelicals' role in pushing for the Ugandan bill to make

homosexuality punishable by death, see Roger Ross Williams's documentary *God Loves Uganda* (2013).

4   For Max Horkheimer and members of the Frankfurt school, critical theory, which is distinct from traditional theory based on empiricism, was one that critiqued society, exposed its contradictions, and sought out possibilities for emancipation and change in a capitalist society.

5   As Barasa narrates to Kabuga, who was then blogging on Facebook under the name Cabu Gah: "My parents were outraged. My family was revolted. And my whole clan was in pure shock. And because of that, I was rejected by my family, my parents and my people. It crashed my soul" (Kabuga 2013).

6   McRuer (2018, 100) also points out that Scott unintentionally "excavates an ableism that is inherent in Fanon's theory" because Fanon, who is talking about soldiers who are literally wounded, "cannot locate value in woundedness and brokenness." McRuer finds in Scott's work and in his attention to wounded bodies and minds an important model for disability studies, a field that indeed makes space for the type of critical resilience—one not attached to linear models of overcoming—that I outline here.

7   The editor of the *Kuchu Times*, a Uganda-based queer publication, writes, "In essence, these clauses make any adult, who has consensual sex deemed to be against the order of nature, with another adult a criminal before the law. While the penal code encompasses even heterosexual relationships as seen in Section 162 (a) below, these clauses are never applied outside of LGBTQ relations even though it is no secret that hetero relations indulge in anal sex, or sexual acts that may be referred to as being against the order of nature" ("History in the Making" 2019).

8   As Rahul Rao (2020, 7–8) points out: "Legal histories of anti-sodomy law inform us that while sodomy was sporadically prosecuted in England under the common law, its first codification in the British Empire as 'carnal intercourse against the order of nature' occurred in section 377 of the [Indian Penal Code], which was enacted in 1860. The IPC was exported to the other colonies and also influenced codification in England itself, with section 377 providing the model for the reformed punishment of 'buggery' in the 1861 Offences against the Person Act. The 1899 criminal code of the Australian colony of Queensland provided a second influential model in the empire. Reflecting legislative changes that had taken place in England in the intervening period, its anti-sodomy provision was more expansive than section 377 in criminalizing passive and active partners, as well as attempts to commit the offences it defined. The Queensland model was exported to Britain's African colonies, including Nigeria, Kenya, Tanzania, and Uganda."

9   Wanuri Kahiu, interview with the author, December 5, 2017, Nairobi, Kenya.

10 Wanuri Kahiu, interview with the author, December 5, 2017, Nairobi, Kenya.

11 Here, I am reminded too of the work of Serena Dankwa, who examines intimate female friendships in Ghana and thinks about friendship as a more expansive category, one which avoids some of the pitfalls of the language of sexual identity that does not fully capture the nature of same-sex desires and relationships in postcolonial Africa. Dankwa writes, "Though the female friendships I chose to focus on

are indeed sexually intimate and engender certain erotic subjectivities, they span a range of shared, intimate practices that cannot be understood adequately through concepts of sexuality. The context of postcolonial precariousness in Ghana requires that many things are shared that would be considered intimate or private in middle-class Europe. Inevitably, practices of sharing shoes, beds, or mobile phones and the exigencies of everyday survival bring into close proximity the lives of people who are neither married nor partnered. The close bonds emerging between neighbors, friends, or family members are instigated through economically and emotionally significant practices such as sharing food or bath water. I understand intimacy through the emotional rifts, the passions, and the fragilities engendering same-sex relationships that are inspired by both material and affective needs and desires" (Dankwa 2021, 21). Though Kena and Ziki both have access to many of the things that would be considered private—their own bedrooms, for instance—the point Dankwa makes about the porousness between intimate practices of friendship and the sexual or erotic intimacy is captured in the title *Rafiki*.

12   See Kahiu's 2017 TED talk, https://www.ted.com/talks/wanuri_kahiu_fun_fierce _and_fantastical_african_art/.

13   For a discussion of *Rafiki* as a story of queer potentiality and world-making, see Lyn Johnstone's "Queer Worldmaking in Wanuri Kahiu's Film *Rafiki*" (2021).

14   Many Kenyan audience members I spoke with in Nairobi said that they were surprised that this scene contained no nudity, as they were expecting something much more explicit based on the KFCB's ban on the film.

15   As Omise'eke Natasha Tinsley (2010, 7) points out, the sex-segregated hold of the slave ship was also a space where women created erotic bonds with one another. Tinsley explains that in Suriname, the term *mati*, which refers to a woman's female friends as well as her lovers, comes from the word for "shipmate."

16   Indeed, as Lindiwe Dovey (2015, 177) argues, African film festivals are often dynamic sites of meaning making. She describes them as "multi-authored entities, influenced equally by their organizers, their curators, and their 'professional' and 'ordinary' participants."

17   As many readers are no doubt aware, Western queer theory has much to say about shame, with many theorists arguing for its usefulness and recuperation, suggesting shame as a less normative and more radical alternative to gay pride. While I do not think that Blanca or the OFF organizers are directing their comments about the luxury of shame to these theorists, I do nevertheless understand them to mean that shame, and negativity more broadly, is a luxury that only certain privileged bodies in certain privileged spaces can afford. Or to put this differently and again to paraphrase Mari Ruti, bodies that are still left out, and left out in multiple ways, do not have the same freedom to opt out. This is not at all an argument in favor of homonormativity but rather, in many ways, a rallying cry for the type of critical resilience I have been outlining.

18   As Sharpe (2016, 123–24) argues, redaction is one strategy for making Black lives visible and imagining otherwise.

1   See "Dakan" 2019. Further references to Thiam's interview with Camara are all taken from this episode.

2   See, too, Kwame Edwin Otu's (2021, 11) discussion of *Dakan*, in which he argues that, in challenging the "myths of heterosexual success and permanence," the film "sets the stage for an 'afro-queer' future that overcomes the anticipations of heteronormativity."

3   In this sense, I am also echoing the argument made by Osinubi that queer African stories are proleptic. He writes that these stories overcome the way subjects are silenced and marginalized in order to "live on or critique the foundational narratives or *proleptic designations* that would foreclose the possibility of 'happy' queers" (Osinubi 2016, xviii).

4   See also Grant Andrews's "YouTube Queer Communities as Heterotopias" (2021), which discusses the proliferation of queer South African vloggers.

5   The interview was conducted on May 28, 2021, with the Gay and Lesbian Coalition of Kenya and streamed on their Instagram page, https://www.instagram.com/p /CPXzhzXFy5b.

And Still We Rise. 2015. Dir. Nancy Nicol and Richard Lusimbo. Canada/Uganda. Social Sciences and Humanities Research Council of Canada.

Apostles of Civilised Vice. 1999. Dir. Zackie Achmat and Jack Lewis. South Africa.

Beautiful Faces. 2004. Dir. Kabat Esosa Egbon. Nigeria. Kas-Vid.

Before the War 1–2. 2007. Dir. Rahim Cas Chidiebere. Nigeria. World Choice Movies.

Boetie Gaan Border Toe. 1984. Dir. Regardt van den Bergh. South Africa. Philo Pieterse Productions.

Born This Way. 2013. Dir. Shaun Kadlec and Deb Tullman. United States/Cameroon. Kinonation.

Breaking Out of the Box. 2011. Dir. Busi Kheswa and Zethu Matebeni. South Africa. Left Hand Films.

Busted. 2018. Dir. Pat Oghre and Damijo Efe-Young. Nigeria. Lisa Onu.

Call Me Kuchu. 2012. Dir. Malika Zouhali-Worrall and Katherine Fairfax Wright. United States/Uganda. Chicken and Egg Pictures/Lindy Hop Pictures.

The Commission: From Silence to Resistance. 2017. Dir. Beverley Ditsie. South Africa. Ditsie Media.

Corporate Maid. 2008. Dir. Ikechukwu Onyeka. Nigeria. Chimezie Emellonwu.

Dakan. 1997. Dir. Mohamed Camara. Guinea. Film du 20ème Créations Cinématographiques.

Defiance: Voices of a New Generation. 2020. Dir. Harry Itie. Nigeria. The Rustin Times.

Difficult Love. 2010. Dir. Zanele Muholi. South Africa. Canadian Filmmakers Distribution Centre.

Dirty Secret. 2010. Dir. Theodore Anyanji. Nigeria. Divine Touch Productions.

Emotional Crack. 2003. Dir. Lancelot Oduwa Imasuen. Nigeria. Reemmy Jes.

Empire (TV series). 2015–20. United States. Fox Broadcasting Company.

End Time 1–2. 1999. Dir. Kenneth Nnebue. Nigeria. Nek Video Links.

Enraged by a Picture. 2005. Dir. Zanele Muholi. South Africa. Out in Africa Workshops.

Everything In Between (web series). 2017. Nigeria. TIERS.

Fifty. 2015. Dir. Biyi Bandele. Nigeria. EbonyLife Films.

Fire. 1996. Dir. Deepa Mehta. Trial by Fire Films.

Generations. (TV series). 1993–. South Africa. Morula Pictures.

Girls Cot. 2006. Dir. Afam Okereke. Nigeria. Simony/Sanga.

Girls Hostel 1–2. 2001. Dir. Ndubuisi Okoh. Nigeria. Christian Dior and Catwalk Pictures.

God Loves Uganda. 2013. Dir. Roger Ross Williams. First Run Features.

The Harvesters. 2018. Dir. Etienne Kallos. South Africa. Spier Films.

Hell or High Water. 2016. Dir. Asurf Oluseyi. Nigeria. Asurf Films/TIERS.

Hideous Affair. 2010. Dir. Ikenna Ezeugwu. Nigeria. World Choice Movies.

Hyenas. 1992. Dir. Djibril Diop Mambety. Senegal/Switzerland. Thelma Film AG.

I Am Samuel. 2020. Dir. Peter Murimi. Kenya. We Are Not the Machine.

I Am Sheriff. 2017. Dir. Teboho Edkins. Lesotho/South Africa. STEPS.

Ibro Dan Daudu. 2002. Sarauniya Studios. Nigeria. Yoko Films Productions.

Ifé. 2020. Dir. Uyaiedu Ikpe-Etim. Nigeria. Equality Hub.

Inxeba. 2017. Dir. John Trengove. South Africa. Riva Filmproduktion.

Isidingo (TV series). 1998–. South Africa. Endemol Entertainment.

Jezebel 1–4. 2007–8. Dir. Socrate Safo. Ghana. Movie Africa Productions.

Johnny Is Nie Dood Nie. 2015. Dir. Christiaan Olwagen. South Africa. Marche Media.

Kanarie. 2018. Dir. Christiaan Olwagen. South Africa. Marche Media.

Karmen Geï. 2001. Dir. Joseph Gaï Ramaka. France/Senegal. ARTE France Cinéma.

Kenyan, Christian, Queer. 2020. Dir. Aiwan Obinyan. Kenya. AiAi Studios.

Last Wedding. 2004. Dir. Dickson Iroegbu. Nigeria. Amaco Investments.

Law 58. 2012. Dir. Dickson Iroegbu. Nigeria. Samcivic Investment.

Lesbians Free Everyone: The Beijing Retrospective. 2020. Dir. Beverley Ditsie. South Africa. Ditsie Media.

Little Secret. 2010. Dir. Theodore Anyanji. Nigeria. Divine Touch Productions.

Living in Bondage (parts 1–2). 1992–93. Dir. Chris Obi Rapu. Nigeria. Kenneth Nnebue.

Major! 2015. Dir. Annalise Ophelian. United States. Floating Ophelia Productions.

Men in Love. 2010. Dir. Moses Ebere. Nigeria. Divine Touch Production.

Mirage Eskader. 1975. Dir. Bertrand Retief. South Africa. Kavalier Films.

Moffie. 2019. Dir. Oliver Hermanus. South Africa/United Kingdom. Portobello Productions.

A Moffie Called Simon. 1987. Dir. John Greyson. Canada/South Africa. Frameline.

Moonlight. 2016. Dir. Barry Jenkins. United States. A24.

Mr. Ibu and Keziah. 2010. Dir. Stanley Anekwe. Nigeria. Executive Image African Movies.

My Gay Husband. 2016. Dir. Eric Stevenson. Nigeria. Chrismighty Movies.

My School Mother. 2005. Dir. Ndubuisi Okoh. Nigeria. Mantex Nigeria.

October 1st. 2014. Dir. Kunle Afolayan. Nigeria. Golden Effects Pictures.

Outed. 2015. Dir. Kamoga Hassan. Uganda.

Out in Africa. 1988. Dir. Melanie Chait. South Africa.

The Pearl of Africa. 2016. Dir. Jonny von Wallström. Sweden/Uganda/Kenya/Thailand. Rough Studios AB.

Popobawa. 2009. Dir. Haji Dilunga. Tanzania. Wanachi Wote.

Pose (TV series). 2018–2021. United States. FX Network.

Pregnant Hawkers. 2013. Dir. Tony Iyke. Nigeria. Tony Iyke Sight and Sound.

Property of the State: Gay Men in the Apartheid Military. 2003. Dir. Gerald Kraak. South Africa. Stargate Distribution International.

Proteus. 2003. Dir. John Greyson. South Africa/Canada. Big World Cinema/Pluck Productions.

Quartier Mozart. 1992. Dir. Jean-Pierre Bekolo. Cameroon/France. Margo Films.

Quest for Love. 1988. Dir. Helena Nogueira. South Africa. Distant Horizon.

Rafiki. 2018. Dir. Wanuri Kahiu. Kenya/South Africa. Big World Cinema.

Rag Tag. 2006. Dir. Adaora Nwandu. United Kingdom. Muka Flicks.

Reloaded. 2009. Dir. Lancelot Oduwa Imasuen. Nigeria. Emem Isong.

Reluctantly Queer. 2016. Dir. Akosua Adoma Owusu. United States. Obibini Pictures.

Resilience Diaries. 2018. Dir. Vincent Kyabayinze. Uganda. East African Visual Artists.

Rude Girls. 2007. Dir. Saint Collins. Nigeria. Ache Links Production.

"Same Love (Remix)" by Art Attack. 2016. Dir. Sam B. Kenya.

See Me As. 2017. Dir. Tim McCarthy, Pepe Julian Onziema, Deus Kiriisa. Uganda. Voices Combatting Homophobia Uganda.

Seuns van die Wolke. 1975. Dir. Franz Marx. South Africa. Brigadiers Films.

Sex, Okra and Salted Butter. 2008. Dir. Mahamat-Saleh Haroun. France. AGAT Films and Cie.

Sexy Girls. 2009. Dir. Rahim Caz Chidiebere. Nigeria. Nigerian Movies.

The Shadowed Mind. 1988. Dir. Cedric Sundstrom. David Hannay Productions.

Shoga Yangu. 2011. Dir. Hissan Muya. Tanzania. Al-Riyamy.

Shot Down. 1987. Dir. Andrew Worsdale. South Africa. Condor Releasing.

Simon and I. 2001. Dir. Beverley Ditsie. South Africa. See Thru Media.

Skoonheid. 2011. Dir. Oliver Hermanus. South Africa. Swift Productions.

Society. (TV series). 2007–. South Africa. Puo Pha Productions.

The Soldier. 1988. Dir. Matthew Krouse. South Africa.

Stories of Our Lives. 2014. Dir. Jim Chuchu. Kenya/South Africa. Nest Collective/Big World Cinema.

Supi: The Real Woman to Woman. 1996. Dir. Ashiagbar Akwetey-Kanyi. Ghana. Cobvision Productions.

There Is Power in the Collar. 2020. Dir. Lodi Matsetela and Vincent Moloi. Botswana. Iranti Media.

Touki Bouki. 1973. Dir. Djibril Diop Mambety. Senegal. Cinegrit.

Trapped. 2021. Dir. Athi Petela. South Africa. Zinc Pictures.

Under the Rainbow. 2019. Dir. Pamela Adie. Nigeria. Equality Hub.

Unspoken. 2013. Dir. Sunny King. United Kingdom. Oakman Film.

Veil of Silence. 2013. Dir. Habeeb Lawal. Nigeria. TIERs.

Vibrancy of Silence: A Discussion with My Sisters. 2018. Dir. Marthe Djilo Kamga. Cameroon/Belgium/United States. University of Michigan.

Walking with Shadows. 2019. Dir. Aoife O'Kelly. Nigeria/United Kingdom. Oya Media/TIERs.

The Wedding Party. 2016. Dir. Kemi Adetiba. Nigeria. EbonyLife Films.

The Wedding Party 2. 2017. Dir. Niyi Akinmolayan. FilmOne Distribution.

We Don't Live Here Anymore. 2018. Dir. Tope Oshin. Nigeria. Sunbow Productions/TIERS.

We Must Free Our Imaginations (parts 1–6). 2014. Dir. Binyavanga Wainaina. Kenya.

While You Weren't Looking. 2015. Dir. Catherine Stewart. South Africa. Phat Free Films.

Women in Love (parts 1–2). 1996. Dir. Socrate Safo. Ghana. Movie Africa Productions.

Women's Affair. 2003. Dir. Andy Chukwu. Nigeria. Nwafor Anayo.

The World's Worst Place to Be Gay. 2011. Dir. Chris Alcock. United Kingdom/Uganda. BBC Three.

The World Unseen. 2007. Dir. Shamim Sarif. South Africa/United Kingdom. Enlightenment Productions.

Woubi Cheri. 1998. Dir. Philip Brooks and Laurent Bocahut. Ivory Coast/France. Dominant 7.

Yizo Yizo (TV series). 1999–. South Africa. Bomb.

Xala. 1975. Dir. Ousmane Sembene. Senegal. Filmi Doomireew.

Zinabu. 1987. Dir. William Akuffo. Ghana. World Wide Pictures.

Abu-Lughod, Lila. 1990. "The Romance of Resistance: Tracing Transformations of Power through Bedouin Women." *American Ethnologist* 17, no. 1: 41–55.

Adejunmobi, Moradewun. 2010. "Charting Nollywood's Appeal Locally and Globally." *Film in African Literature Today* 28: 106–21.

Adejunmobi, Moradewun. 2019. "Streaming Quality, Streaming Cinema." In Harrow and Garritano, *A Companion to African Cinema*, 219–43.

"African LGBTI Manifesto/Declaration." 2013. In Ekine and Abbas, *Queer African Reader*, 52–53.

Ahmed, Sara. 2006. *Queer Phenomenology: Orientations, Objects, Others*. Durham, NC: Duke University Press.

Ahmed, Sara. 2015. *The Cultural Politics of Emotion*. 2nd ed. New York: Routledge.

Andrews, Grant. 2018a. "The Boundaries of Desire and Intimacy in Post-Apartheid South African Queer Film: Oliver Hermanus's *Skoonheid*." *Image and Text* 31: 30–47.

Andrews, Grant. 2018b. "Liminal Spaces and Conflicts of Culture in South African Queer Films: *Inxeba* (The Wound)." In Emenyonu and Hawley, ALT 36, 52–66.

Andrews, Grant. 2021. "YouTube Queer Communities as Heterotopias: Space, Identity and 'Realness' in Queer South African Vlogs." *Journal of African Cultural Studies* 33, no. 1: 84–100.

Arac de Nyeko, Monica. 2013. "Jambula Tree." In *Queer Africa: New and Collected Fiction*, edited by Karen Martin and Makhosazana Xaba, 91–105. Cape Town: MaThoko's Books.

Azuah, Unoma. 2018. "Visual Activism: A Look at the Documentary *Born This Way*." In Emenyonu and Hawley, ALT 36, 7–16.

Azuah, Unoma. 2020. *Embracing My Shadow: Growing Up Lesbian in Nigeria*. Burscough, UK: Beaten Track Publishing.

Barber, Karin, ed. 1997. *Readings in African Popular Culture*. Bloomington: Indiana University Press.

Barber, Karin. 1997. "Views of the Field." In Barber, *Readings in African Popular Culture*, 1–11.

Bearak, Max. 2018. "Paving Way for Oscar Bid, Kenyan Court Overturns Ban on Film Featuring Lesbian Love." *Washington Post*. September 21. https://www.washingtonpost.com/world/2018/09/21/paving-way-oscar-bid-kenyan-court-overturns-ban-film-featuring-lesbian-love/.

Benedicto, Bobby. 2014. *Under Bright Lights: Gay Manila and the Global Scene*. Minneapolis: University of Minnesota Press.

Berlant, Lauren. 2015. "Structures of Unfeeling: 'Mysterious Skin.'" *International Journal of Politics, Culture, and Society* 28, no. 3: 191–213.

Böhme, Claudia. 2015. "Showing the Unshowable: The Negotiation of Homosexuality through Video Films in Tanzania." *Africa Today* 61, no. 4: 62–82.

Botha, Martin. 2012. *South African Cinema 1896–2010*. Chicago: Intellect.

Bracke, Sarah. 2016. "Bouncing Back: Vulnerability and Resistance in Times of Resilience." In Butler, Gambetti, and Sabsay, *Vulnerability in Resistance*, 52–75.

Brooks, Peter. 1985. *The Melodramatic Imagination: Balzac, Henry James, Melodrama and the Mode of Excess*. New York: Columbia University Press.

Brown, A. B. 2021. "Lawful Performance and the Representational Politics of Queer African Refugees in Documentary Film." *Journal of African Cultural Studies* 33, no. 1: 67–83.

Bud, Alexander. 2014. "Hooray for Nollywood? Nigeria Isn't the World's Second Biggest Film Industry After All." The Conversation. April 11. https://theconversation.com/hooray-for-nollywood-nigeria-isnt-the-worlds-second-biggest-film-industry-after-all-25527.

Butler, Judith. 2016. "Rethinking Vulnerability and Resistance." In Butler, Gambetti, and Sabsay, *Vulnerability in Resistance*, 12–27.

Butler, Judith, Zeynep Gambetti, and Leticia Sabsay, eds. 2016. *Vulnerability in Resistance*. Durham, NC: Duke University Press.

Campt, Tina M. 2017. *Listening to Images*. Durham, NC: Duke University Press.

Collison, Carl. 2017. "Actor Nakhane Touré Fends Off Hate Speech over Controversial New Film." *Mail and Guardian*. March 1. https://mg.co.za/article/2017-02-28-actor-nakhane-toure-fends-off-hate-speech-over-controversial-new-film/.

Coly, Ayo. 2016. "*Carmen* Goes Postcolonial, *Carmen* Goes Queer: Thinking the Postcolonial as Queer." *Culture, Theory and Critique* 57, no. 3: 391–407.

Coly, Ayo A. 2019. "The Invention of the Homosexual: The Politics of Homophobia in Senegal." In M'Baye and Muhonja, *Gender and Sexuality in Senegalese Societies*, 27–51.

Comaroff, Jean, and John Comaroff. 2000. "Millennial Capitalism: First Thoughts on a Second Coming." *Public Culture* 12, no. 2: 291–343.

Crawley, Ashon. T. 2017. *Blackpentecostal Breath: The Aesthetics of Possibility*. New York: Fordham University Press.

Crees, Cameron. 2014. "'Thinkin Bout Same Love': An Exploration of Homosexuality in Hip-Hop and R&B." *Kaleidoscope* 6, no. 2: 77–88.

"Dakan." 2019. *AfroQueer* Podcast. Produced by None on Record. November 7. https://afroqueerpodcast.com/2019/11/07/dakan/.

Dankwa, Serena Owusua. 2009. "'It's a Silent Trade': Female Same-Sex Intimacies in Post-colonial Ghana." *NORA: Nordic Journal of Feminist and Gender Research* 17, no. 3: 192–205.

Dankwa, Serena Owusua. 2021. *Knowing Women: Same-Sex Intimacy, Gender, and Identity in Postcolonial Ghana.* Cambridge, UK: Cambridge University Press.

Dercksen, Daniel. 2018. "Charl-Johan Lingenfelder Talks about the Astounding New South African Film *Kanarie.*" The Writing Studio. October 16. https://writingstudio.co.za/charl -johan-lingenfelder-talks-about-the-astounding-new-south-african-film-kanarie/.

Diabate, Naminata. 2018. "African Queer, African Digital: Reflections on Zanele Muholi's Films4peace and Other Works." In Emenyonu and Hawley, ALT 36, 17–37.

Dibia, Jude. 2005. *Walking with Shadows.* Lagos, Nigeria: BlackSands Books.

Dovey, Lindiwe. 2009. *African Film and Literature: Adapting Violence to the Screen.* New York: Columbia University Press.

Dovey, Lindiwe. 2015. *Curating Africa in the Age of Film Festivals.* New York: Palgrave Macmillan.

Drewal, Henry John, ed. 2008. *Sacred Waters: Arts for Mami Wata and Other Divinities in Africa and the Diaspora.* Bloomington: Indiana University Press.

Dunn, Thomas R. 2016. "Playing Neoliberal Politics: Post-racial and Post-racist Strategies in 'Same Love.'" *Communication and Critical/Cultural Studies* 13, no. 3: 269–86.

Dyer, Richard. 2002. *The Culture of Queers.* East Sussex, UK: Psychology Press.

Edelman, Lee. 2004. *No Future: Queer Theory and the Death Drive.* Durham, NC: Duke University Press.

Ekine, Sokari, and Hakima Abbas, eds. 2013. *Queer African Reader.* Nairobi: Pambazuka Press.

Ekotto, Frieda. 2007. "The Erotic Tale of *Karmen Geï* : The Taboo of Female Homosexuality in Senegal." *Xavier Review* 27, no. 1: 74–80.

Ellerson, Beti. 2005. "Visualizing Homosexualities in Africa—*Dakan*: An Interview with Filmmaker Mohamed Camara." In *African Masculinities: Men in Africa from the Late Nineteenth Century to the Present*, edited by Lahoucine Ouzgane and Robert Morrell, 61–73. New York: Palgrave Macmillan.

Emenyonu, Ernest N., and John C. Hawley, eds. 2018. ALT *36: Queer Theory in Film and Fiction.* Rochester, NY: Boydell and Brewer.

Evans, Gavin. 2009. "Hell No, We Wouldn't Go." Rootless Cosmopolitan. November 3. http://tonykaron.com/2009/11/03/hell-no-we-wouldnt-go/.

Fabian, Johannes. 1997. "Popular Culture in Africa: Findings and Conjectures." In Barber, *Readings in African Popular Culture*, 18–28.

Falkof, Nicky. 2016. "ENG/AFR: White Masculinity in Two Contemporary South African Films." *Critical Arts* 30, no. 1: 15–30.

Fisher, Max. 2013. "What Obama Really Saw at the 'Door of No Return,' a Disputed Memorial to the Slave Trade." *Washington Post.* June 28. https://www.washingtonpost.com /news/worldviews/wp/2013/06/28/what-obama-really-saw-at-the-door-of-no-return-a -debunked-memorial-to-the-slave-trade/.

Ford, James Edward, III. 2014. "Fugitivity and the Filmic Imagination." Call for Papers, University of Pennsylvania. January 4. https://call-for-papers.sas.upenn.edu/node /54723/.

Ford, James Edward, III. 2015. "Close-Up: Fugitivity and the Filmic Imagination: Introduction." *Black Camera, An International Film Journal* 7, no. 1: 110–14.

Frank, Barbara. 2008. "Mami Wata, Wealth-Owning Spirits, and Changing Economic Morals in West Africa." In Drewal, *Sacred Waters*, 115–24.

Garritano, Carmela. 2003. "Troubled Men and the Women Who Create Havoc: Four Recent Films by West African Filmmakers." *Research in African Literatures* 34, no. 3: 159–65.

Garritano, Carmela. 2013. *African Video Movies and Global Desires: A Ghanaian History.* Athens: Ohio University Press.

Gaudio, Rudolf. 2009. *Allah Made Us: Sexual Outlaws in an Islamic African City.* Malden, MA: Wiley-Blackwell.

"Gay Movie: Dickson Iroegbu in Trouble." 2012. Vanguard. March 24. https://www .vanguardngr.com/2012/03/gay-movie-dickson-iroegbu-in-trouble/.

Germishuys, Andrew. 2020. "Interview with Oliver Hermanus." SMDB News. March 12. http://www.samdb.co.za/blogs/blog/2020/03/12/moffie-review/.

"Google Refuses Kenyan Film Board's Demand to Remove Gay Music Video." 2016. *African Independent.* March 23. https://www.africanindy.com/culture/google-refuses -kenyan-film-boards-demand-to-remove-gay-music-video-5061960/.

Gqola, Pumla. 2001. "Defining People: Analysing Power, Language and Representation in Metaphors of the New South Africa." *Transformation*, no. 47: 94–106.

Gqola, Pumla. 2007. "'A Woman Cannot Marry a Boy': Rescue, Spectacle, and Transitional Xhosa Masculinities." In *From Boys to Men: Social Constructions of Masculinity in Contemporary Society*, edited by Tamara Shefer, Kopano Ratele, Nokuthla Shabalala, and Rosemarie Buikema, 145–59. Cape Town: University of Cape Town Press.

Gray, Chantelle. 2021. "The Spectre-Image: A Hauntology of *Skoonheid* and *Kanarie*." *Image and Text*, no. 35: 1–21.

Green-Simms, Lindsey. 2011. "'Just to See': Fanon, National Consciousness, and the Indiscreet Look in Post–Third Cinema." In *Indiscretions*, edited by Murat Aydemir, 203–24. Leiden, Netherlands: Brill/Rodopi.

Green-Simms, Lindsey. 2012a. "Hustlers, Home-Wreckers and Homoeroticism: Nollywood's *Beautiful Faces*." *Journal of African Cinemas* 4, no. 1: 59–79.

Green-Simms, Lindsey. 2012b. "Occult Melodramas: Spectral Affect and West African Video-Film." *Camera Obscura: Feminism, Culture, and Media Studies* 27, no. 2 (80): 25–59.

Green-Simms, Lindsey. 2019. "Nigeria's First Lesbian Documentary." *Africa Is a Country.* July 24. https://africasacountry.com/2019/07/nigerias-first-lesbian-documentary.

Green-Simms, Lindsey. 2020. "A Rare Cinematic Portrait of Queer Women's Intimacy in Nigeria." *Africa Is a Country.* September 30. https://africasacountry.com/2020/09/a -rare-cinematic-portrait-of-queer-womens-intimacy-in-nigeria.

Green-Simms, Lindsey. 2021. "*Walking with Shadows*: Jude Dibia and Olumide Makanjuola in Conversation with Lindsey Green-Simms." *Journal of African Cultural Studies* 33, no. 1: 101–8.

Green-Simms, Lindsey, and Unoma Azuah. 2012. "The Video Closet: Nollywood's Gay-Themed Movies." *Transition* 107, no. 1: 32–49.

Green-Simms, Lindsey, and Z'étoile Imma. 2021. "The Possibilities and Intimacies of Queer African Screen Cultures." *Journal of African Cultural Studies* 33, no. 1: 1–9.

Harrow, Kenneth. 2001. "The Queer Thing about Djibril Diop Mambety: A Counter-hegemonic Discourse Meets the Heterosexual Economy." *Paragraph* 24, no. 3: 76–91.

Harrow, Kenneth, and Carmela Garritano, eds. 2019. *A Companion to African Cinema*. Hoboken, NJ: Wiley-Blackwell.

Hartman, Saidiya. 1997. *Scenes of Subjection: Terror, Slavery, and Self-Making in Nineteenth-Century America*. Oxford: Oxford University Press.

Hartman, Saidiya. 2019. *Wayward Lives, Beautiful Experiments: Intimate Histories of Social Upheaval*. New York: Norton.

Haynes, Jonathan. 2016. *Nollywood: The Creation of Nigerian Film Genres*. Chicago: University of Chicago Press.

Hilderbrand, Lucas. 2009. *Inherent Vice: Bootleg Histories of Videotape and Copyright*. Durham, NC: Duke University Press.

"History in the Making: Kenya's LGBT Movement Seeks to Have Criminalization Clauses Repealed." 2019. *Kuchu Times*. January 23. https://www.kuchutimes.com/2019/01/history-in-the-making-kenyas-lgbt-movement-seeks-to-have-criminalization-clauses-repealed/.

Hoad, Neville. 2007. *African Intimacies: Race, Homosexuality, and Globalization*. Minneapolis: University of Minnesota Press.

Hoad, Neville. 2016. "Queer Customs against the Law." *Research in African Literature* 47, no. 2: 1–19.

Holland, Sharon Patricia. 2012. *The Erotic Life of Racism*. Durham, NC: Duke University Press.

Human Rights Watch. 2016a. "Tell Me Where I Can Be Safe: The Impact of Nigeria's Same-Sex Marriage (Prohibition) Act." October 20. https://www.hrw.org/report/2016/10/20/tell-me-where-i-can-be-safe/impact-nigerias-same-sex-marriage-prohibition-act/.

Human Rights Watch. 2016b. "Uganda: Police Attack LGBTI Pride Event." August 5. https://www.hrw.org/news/2016/08/05/uganda-police-attack-lgbti-pride-event/.

Izuzu, Chibumga. 2017a. "'Hell or Highwater' Starts a Necessary Conversation about Homosexuality in Nigeria." *Pulse*, April 5. https://www.pulse.ng/entertainment/movies/pulse-movie-review-hell-or-high-water-starts-a-necessary-conversation-about/9t7nfeg/.

Izuzu, Chibumga. 2017b. "Nollywood Tackles Homosexuality in a Tacky Way." *Pulse*, January 31. https://www.pulse.ng/entertainment/movies/motion-pictures-with-chidumga-nollywood-tackles-homosexuality-in-a-tacky-way/em489kn/.

Izuzu, Chibumga. 2018. "Five Nigerian Films That Advocate for Gay Rights." *Pulse*, May 9. https://www.pulse.ng/entertainment/movies/pulse-list-5-nigerian-films-that-advocate-for-gay-rights/pmseovm/.

James, Robin. 2015. *Resilience and Melancholy: Pop Music, Feminism, Neoliberalism*. Winchester, UK: Zero Books.

Jewkes, Rachel, Robert Morrell, Jeff Hearn, Emma Lundqvist, David Blackbeard, Graham Lindegger, Michael Quayle, Yandisa Sikweyiya, and Lucas Gottzén. 2015. "Hegemonic Masculinity: Combining Theory and Practice in Gender Interventions." *Culture, Health and Sexuality* 17, suppl. 2: s112–27.

Joffe, Taryn. 2018. Interview with John Trengove. *"The Wound* Director: 'To Be Out and Proud Is Still a Middle-Class Privilege in Our Society.'" BFI: Film Forever. April 20. https://www.bfi.org.uk/news-opinion/news-bfi/interviews/wound-john-trengove -interview/.

Johnstone, Lyn. 2021. "Queer Worldmaking in Wanuri Kahiu's Film *Rafiki*." *Journal of African Cultural Studies* 33, no. 1: 39–50.

Kabuga, Ken. 2013. "The Story of Joji Baro: The Gay Gospel Artist." *Nairobi Wire.* September 18. http://nairobiwire.com/2013/09/the-story-of-joji-baro-gay-gospel-artist .html.

Kahiu, Wanuri. 2019. "In Person: Director Wanuri Kahiu." *Rafiki* screening at Filmfest DC, Washington, DC, April 26.

Karangi, Matthew M. 2008. "Revisiting the Roots of Gĩkũyũ Culture through the Sacred Mũgumo Tree." *Journal of African Cultural Studies* 20, no. 1: 117–32.

Kirui, Stacy. 2018. "*Rafiki*: On What It Means to Watch an Unbanned Film Seven Days in a Row, Every Single Day the Ban Was Lifted." *Popula.* November 27. https://popula .com/2018/11/27/rafiki/.

Kumalo, Siseko H., and Lindokuhle Gama. 2018. "Interrogating Conceptions of Manhood, Sexuality and Cultural Identity." *Image and Text,* no. 32: 1–19.

Larkin, Brian. 2008. *Signal and Noise: Media, Infrastructure, and Urban Culture in Nigeria.* Durham, NC: Duke University Press.

Levine, Caroline. 2015. *Forms: Whole, Rhythm, Hierarchy, Network.* Princeton, NJ: Princeton University Press.

Lim, Bliss Cua. 2009. *Translating Time: Cinema, the Fantastic, and Temporal Critique.* Durham, NC: Duke University Press.

Livermon, Xavier. 2012. "Queer(y)ing Freedom: Black Queer Visibilities in Postapartheid South Africa." GLQ 18, nos. 2–3: 297–324.

Lodge, Guy. 2020. "'It's a Triggering Film': Visceral South African Drama *Moffie*." *Guardian.* April 15. https://www.theguardian.com/film/2020/apr/15/moffie-triggering-film -south-africa-toxic-masculinity-oliver-hermanus/.

Loizidou, Elena. 2016. "Dreams and the Political Subject." In Butler, Gambetti, and Sabsay, *Vulnerability in Resistance,* 122–45.

Maasilta, Mari. 2007. "African Carmen: Transnational Cinema as an Arena for Cultural Contradictions." PhD diss., University of Tampere, Finland.

Macharia, Keguro. 2013a. "Queer Kenya in Law and Policy." In Ekine and Abbas, *Queer African Reader,* 273–89.

Macharia, Keguro. 2013b. "Fugitivity." Gukira. July 2. https://gukira.wordpress.com/2013 /07/02/fugitivity/.

Macharia, Keguro. 2017. "tender(ness)." Gukira. November 10. https://gukira.wordpress .com/2017/11/10/tenderness/.

Mahmood, Saba. 2005. *Politics of Piety: The Islamic Revival and the Feminist Subject.* Princeton, NJ: Princeton University Press.

"Major!" 2019. Official website for *Major!* https://www.missmajorfilm.com.

Marks, Laura. 2002. *Touch: Sensuous Theory and Multisensory Media.* Minneapolis: University of Minnesota Press.

Matebeni, Zethu, ed. 2014. *Reclaiming Afrikan: Queer Perspectives on Sexual and Gender Identities*. Athlone, South Africa: Modjaji Books.

Matebeni, Zethu, and Jabu Pereira. 2014. Preface to Matebeni, *Reclaiming Afrikan*, 7–9.

M'Baye, Babacar. 2011. "Variant Sexualities and African Modernity in Joseph Gaye Ramaka's *Karmen Geï*." *Black Camera* 2, no. 2: 114–29.

M'Baye, Babacar. 2019. "Representations of the *Gôr Djiguène* [Man Woman] in Senegalese Culture, Films, and Literature." In M'Baye and Muhonja, *Gender and Sexuality in Senegalese Societies*, 77–106.

M'Baye, Babacar, and Besi Brillian Muhonja, eds. 2019. *Gender and Sexuality in Senegalese Societies: Critical Perspectives and Methods*. Lanham, MD: Lexington Books.

McRuer, Robert. 2018. *Crip Times: Disability, Globalization, and Resistance*. New York: New York University Press.

Meyer, Birgit. 2004. "'Praise the Lord': Popular Cinema and Pentecostalite Style in Ghana's New Public Sphere." *American Ethnologist* 31, no. 1: 92–110.

Meyer, Birgit. 2006a. "Impossible Representations: Pentecostalism, Vision, and Video Technology in Ghana." In *Religion, Media, and the Public Sphere*, edited by Birgit Meyer and Annelies Moors, 290–312. Bloomington: Indiana University Press.

Meyer, Birgit. 2006b. "Religious Revelation, Secrecy, and the Limits of Visual Representation." *Anthropological Theory* 6, no. 4: 431–35.

Meyer, Birgit. 2008. "Mami Wata as a Christian Demon: The Eroticism of Forbidden Pleasures in Southern Ghana." In Drewal, *Sacred Waters*, 383–98. Bloomington: Indiana University Press.

Meyer, Birgit. 2015. *Sensational Movies: Video, Vision, and Christianity in Ghana*. Berkeley: University of California Press.

Mgqolozana, Thando. 2020. *A Man Who Is Not a Man*. Abuja, Nigeria: Cassava Republic Press.

Mills, Ivy. 2019. "The Queer Thing about Djibril Diop Mambety Revisited: Hyena Iconographies in Senegalese Cinema." Paper delivered at the 45th Annual African Literature Association Meeting, Columbus, OH, May 16.

Mohammed, Azeenarh, Chitra Nagarajan, and Rafeeat Aliyu. 2018. Introduction to *She Called Me Woman: Nigeria's Queer Women Speak*, edited by Azeenarh Mohammed, Chitra Nagarajan, and Rafeeat Aliyu, 1–20. Abuja, Nigeria: Cassava Republic Press.

Moten, Fred. 2003. *In the Break: The Aesthetics of the Black Radical Tradition*. Minneapolis: University of Minnesota Press.

Moten, Fred. 2007. "The New International of Rhythmic Feeling(s)." In *Sonic Interventions* 18, edited by Sylvia Mieszkowski, Joy Smith, and Marijke De Valck, 31–56. Amsterdam: Rodopi Press.

Muholi, Zanele. 2013. "Faces and Phases." In Ekine and Abbas, *Queer African Reader*, 169–72.

Mulvey, Laura. 1975. "Visual Pleasure and Narrative Cinema." *Screen* 16, no. 3: 6–18.

Mulvey, Laura. 2006. *Death 24x a Second: Stillness and the Moving Image*. London: Reaktion Books.

Muñoz, José Esteban. 2009. *Cruising Utopia: The Then and There of Queer Futurity*. New York: New York University Press.

Munro, Brenna M. 2012. *South Africa and the Dream of Love to Come: Queer Sexuality and the Struggle for Freedom*. Minneapolis: University of Minnesota Press.

Munro, Brenna M. 2018. "Pleasure in Queer African Studies: Screenshots of the Present." *College Literature: A Journal of Critical Literary Studies* 45, no. 4: 657–65.

Murumba, Stellar. 2016. "Films Board Gives Google a Week to Take Down Gay Song Video." *Business Daily Africa*. February 24. http://www.businessdailyafrica.com /corporate/Films-board-gives-Google-a-week-to-take-down-gay-song-video/539550 -3089994-as8todz/index.html.

Musangi, Neo. 2014. "Time and Space." In Matebeni, *Reclaiming Afrikan*, 49–56.

Ncube, Gibson. 2018. "Renegotiating the Marginality of the Maghreb in Queer African Studies." *College Literature: A Journal of Critical Literary Studies* 45, no. 4: 623–31.

Ncube, Gibson. 2021. "Skin and Silence in Selected Maghrebian Queer Films." *Journal of African Cultural Studies* 33, no. 1: 51–66.

Nelson, Steven. 2011. "*Karmen Geï*: Sex, the State, and Censorship in Dakar." *African Arts* 44, no. 1: 74–81.

Neocleous, Mark. 2013. "Resisting Resilience." *Radical Philosophy* 178, no. 6: 2–7.

Nest Collective. 2015. "*Stories of Our Lives*: Not in Kenya." January 13. http://www .thisisthenest.com/news/2015/1/13/stories-of-our-lives-not-in-kenya/.

Newell, Stephanie. 2002. Introduction to *Readings in African Popular Fiction*, edited by Stephanie Newell, 1–10. Bloomington: James Currey/Indiana University Press for the International African Institute.

Newell, Stephanie. 2006. *The Forger's Tale: The Search for Odeziaku*. Athens: Ohio University Press.

Ngai, Sianne. 2005. *Ugly Feelings*. Cambridge, MA: Harvard University Press.

Njoku, Benjamin. 2012. "BOMBSHELL! Dickson Iroegbu Releases Gay Movie." *Vanguard*. January 28. https://www.vanguardngr.com/2012/01/bombshell-dickson-iroegbu -releases-gay-movie/.

Nnaemeka, Obioma. 2004. "Nego-Feminism: Theorizing, Practicing, and Pruning Africa's Way." *Signs* 29, no. 2: 357–85.

Nwaubani, Adaobi Tricia. 2017. "LGBT Acceptance Slowly Grows in Nigeria, Despite Anti-gay Laws." Reuters. May 16. https://www.reuters.com/article/us-nigeria-lgbt-survey/lgbt -acceptance-slowly-grows-in-nigeria-despite-anti-gay-laws-idUSKCN18C2T8/.

Nwoye, Augustine. 2017. "An Africentric Theory of Human Personhood." *Psychology in Society* 54: 42–66.

Nyanzi, Stella. 2014. "Queer Pride and Protest: A Reading of the Bodies at Uganda's First Gay Beach Pride." *Signs* 40, no. 1: 36–40.

Nyanzi, Stella. 2015a. "Knowledge Is Requisite Power: Making a Case for Queer African Scholarship." In *Boldly Queer: African Perspectives on Same-Sex Sexuality and Gender Diversity*, edited by Theo Sandfort, Fabeinne Simenel, Kevin Mwachiro, and Vasu Reddy, 125–35. The Hague: HIVOS.

Nyanzi, Stella. 2015b. "When the State Produces Hate: Re-thinking the Global Queer Movement through Silence in the Gambia." In *The Global Trajectories of Queerness*, edited by Ashley Tellis and Sruti Bala, 179–93. Leiden, Netherlands: Brill/Rodopi.

Nyeck, S. N. 2008. "Impossible Africans." *Outliers* 1, no. 1: 5–7.

Nyong'o, Tavia. 2018. *Afro-Fabulations: The Queer Drama of Black Life.* New York: New York University Press.

Obadare, Ebenezer, and Wendy Willems. 2014. Introduction to *Civic Agency in Africa: Arts of Resistance in the 21st Century,* edited by Ebenezer Obadare and Wendy Willems, 1–24. Rochester, NY: Boydell and Brewer.

Okanlawon, Kehinde. 2018. "Cultures of Public Intervention regarding LGBTQ Issues after Nigeria's Same-Sex Marriage Prohibition Act (SSMPA)." *College Literature* 45, no. 4: 641–51.

Okorafor, Nnedi. 2019. "Africanfuturism Defined." *Nnedi's Wahala Zone Blog.* October 19. http://nnedi.blogspot.com/2019/10/africanfuturism-defined.html.

O'Mara, Kathleen. 2013. "LGBTI Community and Citizenship Practices in Urban Ghana." In *Sexuality Diversity in Africa: Politics, Theory, Citizenship,* edited by S. N. Nyeck and Marc Epprecht, 188–207. Montreal: McGill-Queen's University Press.

Ombagi, Eddie. 2018. "Nairobi Is a Shot of Whisky: Queer (Ob)Scenes in the City." *Journal of African Cultural Studies* 31, no. 1: 106–19.

Ombagi, Eddie. 2019. "Filming the Invisible: Rubrics of Ordinary Life in *Stories of Our Lives* (2014)." *Journal of African Cinemas* 11, no. 3: 261–76.

Omelsky, Matthew. 2020. "African Fugitivities." *Black Scholar* 50, no. 1: 56–69.

Osinubi, Taiwo Adetunji. 2016. "Queer Prolepsis and the Sexual Commons: An Introduction." *Research in African Literatures* 47, no. 2: vii–xxiii.

Osinubi, Taiwo Adetunji. 2018. "Denormativising Imperatives in African Queer Scholarship." *College Literature: A Journal of Critical Literary Studies* 45, no. 4: 596–612.

Otu, Kwame Edwin. 2017. "LGBT Human Rights Expeditions in Homophobic Safaris: Racialized Neoliberalism and Post-traumatic White Disorder in the BBC's *The World's Worst Place to Be Gay.*" *Journal of Critical Ethnic Studies* 3, no. 2: 126–50.

Otu, Kwame Edwin. 2021. "Heteroerotic Failure and 'Afro-Queer Futurity' in Mohamed Camara's *Dakan.*" *Journal of African Cultural Studies* 33, no. 1: 10–25.

Packer, Beth. 2019. "Queering the 'Greater Jihad': Sufi Resistance and Disruptive Morality in Senegalese Women's Soccer." In M'Baye and Muhonja, *Gender and Sexuality in Senegalese Societies,* 53–76.

Peach, Ricardo. 2005. *Queer Cinema as a Fifth Cinema in South Africa and Australia.* PhD diss., University of Technology, Sydney.

Peterson, Carla L. 2001. "Foreword: Eccentric Bodies." In *Recovering the Black Female Body: Self-Representations by African American Women,* edited by Michael Bennett and Vanessa D. Dickerson, ix–xvi. New Brunswick, NJ: Rutgers University Press.

Phillips, Richard. 2012. Interview with Oliver Hermanus. "Filmmaker Oliver Hermanus Discusses Beauty." World Socialist Website. August 4. https://www.wsws.org/en/articles/2012/08/sfoh-a04.html.

Pieterse, Annel. 2019. "Film Notes: Masculinity, Violence, and Queer Identity in Recent South African Films." *Safundi* 20, no. 3: 375–81.

Popoola, B. I., and K. A. Alao. 2006. "Secret Cults in Nigerian Institutions of Higher Learning: Need for a Radical Intervention Programme." *Journal of School Violence* 5, no. 2: 74–85.

Powrie, Phil. 2004. "Politics and Embodiment in *Karmen Geï*." *Quarterly Review of Film and Video* 21, no. 4: 283–91.

Puar, Jasbir K. 2007. *Terrorist Assemblages: Homonationalism in Queer Times*. Durham, NC: Duke University Press.

Puri, Shalini. 2004. *The Caribbean Postcolonial: Social Equality, Post-Nationalism, and Cultural Hybridity*. New York: Palgrave Macmillan.

Qintu Collab. 2019. *Meanwhile . . . Graphic Short Stories about Everyday Queer Life in Southern and East Africa*. Braamfontein, South Africa: MaThoko's Books.

Quashie, Kevin. 2012. *The Sovereignty of Quiet: Beyond Resistance in Black Culture*. New Brunswick, NJ: Rutgers University Press.

"*Rafiki* Tops Kenyan Box Office before Being Banned Again." 2018. Channel 24. October 3. https://www.news24.com/channel/movies/news/rafiki-tops-kenyan-box-office -before-being-banned-again-20181003-2.

"*Rafiki* Uncensored." 2018. *AfroQueer* Podcast. Produced by None on Record. June 30. https://afroqueerpodcast.com/2018/06/30/rafiki-uncensored/.

Rao, Rahul. 2020. *Out of Time: The Queer Politics of Postcoloniality*. Oxford: Oxford University Press.

Royster, Francesca T. 2012. *Sounding like a No-No: Queer Sounds and Eccentric Acts in the Post-soul Era*. Ann Arbor: University of Michigan Press.

Ruti, Mari. 2017. *The Ethics of Opting Out: Queer Theory's Defiant Subjects*. New York: Columbia University Press.

Safi, Michael. 2018. "Campaigners Celebrate as India Decriminalises Homosexuality." *Guardian*. September 6. https://www.theguardian.com/world/2018/sep/06/indian -supreme-court-decriminalises-homosexuality/.

Salami, Minna. 2020. *Sensuous Knowledge: A Black Feminist Approach for Everyone*. New York: HarperCollins.

Schoonover, Karl, and Rosalind Galt. 2016. *Queer Cinema in the World*. Durham, NC: Duke University Press.

Scott, Darieck. 2010. *Extravagant Abjection: Blackness, Power, and Sexuality in the African American Literary Imagination*. New York: New York University Press.

Scott, Lwando. 2021. "*Inxeba* (The Wound), Queerness and Xhosa Culture." *Journal of African Cultural Studies* 33, no. 1: 26–38.

Sedgwick, Eve Kosofsky. 2003. *Touching Feeling: Affect, Pedagogy, Performativity*. Durham, NC: Duke University Press.

Sharpe, Christina. 2016. *In the Wake: On Blackness and Being*. Durham, NC: Duke University Press.

Sizemore-Barber, April. 2020. *Prismatic Performances: Queer South Africa and the Fragmentation of the Rainbow Nation*. Ann Arbor: University of Michigan Press.

Smith, Tymon. 2021. "Matthew Krouse's Anti-authoritarian Past Lives Again." *New Frame*. June 4. https://www.newframe.com/matthew-krouses-anti-authoritarian-past-lives-again/ ?fbclid=IwAR2NUKGUF6gAzc28IB25KFmI12exhniB1mzf8ZlO9O64actWxpaYH5EYBqU.

Snead, James A. 1992. "Repetition as a Figure of Black Culture." In *Out There: Marginalization and Contemporary Culture*, edited by Russell Ferguson, Martha Gever, Trinh T. Min-ha, and Cornell West, 213–32. Cambridge, MA: MIT Press.

Sonnekus, Theo. 2013. "'We're Not Faggots!': Masculinity, Homosexuality and the Representation of Afrikaner Men Who Have Sex with Men in the Film *Skoonheid* and Online." *South African Review of Sociology* 44, no. 1: 22–39.

Steedman, Robin. 2018. "Nairobi-Based Female Filmmakers: Screen Media Production between the Local and the Transnational." In Harrow and Garritano, *A Companion to African Cinema*, 315–35.

Steele, Samantha. 2011. "Beauty and the Beast Within." *Mail and Guardian*. July 15. https://mg.co.za/article/2011–07–15-beauty-and-the-beast-within/.

Stobie, Cheryl. 2016. "'She Who Creates Havoc Is Here': A Queer Bisexual Reading of Sexuality, Dance, and Social Critique in *Karmen Geï*." *Research in African Literatures* 47, no. 2: 84–103.

Suellentrop, Chris. 2009. "What Does 'Stable' Condition Mean? How Can Someone Be 'Critical but Stable?'" *Slate*. November 6. https://slate.com/news-and-politics/2009/11/what-do-stable-critical-and-other-medical-conditions-mean.html.

Tamale, Sylvia. 2013. "Confronting the Politics of Nonconforming Sexualities in Africa." *African Studies Review* 56, no. 2: 31–45.

Tamale, Sylvia. 2020. *Decolonization and Afro-Feminism*. Ottawa, ON: Daraja Press.

Taylor, Adam. 2014. "The Simple Reason Nigeria Just Banned Gay Marriage and Gay Meetings." *Business Insider*, January 14. https://www.businessinsider.com/why-nigeria-banned-gay-marriage-and-gay-meetings-2014–1/.

Tettey, Wisdom John. 2016. "Homosexuality, Moral Panic, and Politicized Homophobia in Ghana: Interrogating Discourses of Moral Entrepreneurship in Ghanaian Media." *Communication, Culture and Critique* 9, no. 1: 86–106.

Thamm, Marianne. 2018. "*Kanarie*: The Redemptive Power of Music and Finding Solace in a Violent White World." Maverick Life. October 22. https://www.dailymaverick.co.za/article/2018-10-22-kanarie-the-redemptive-power-of-music-and-finding-solace-in-a-violent-white-world/.

Tinsley, Omise'eke Natasha. 2010. *Thiefing Sugar: Eroticism between Women in Caribbean Literature*. Durham, NC: Duke University Press.

Tinubu, Aramide. 2017. Interview with John Trengove. "Interview: Director John Trengove Talks South African Coming-of-Age Drama, *The Wound*." *Shadow and Act*. April 17. https://shadowandact.com/interview-director-john-trengove-talks-south-african-coming-of-age-drama-the-wound/.

Tsika, Noah A. 2016. *Pink 2.0: Encoding Queer Cinema on the Internet*. Bloomington: Indiana University Press.

Ugor, Paul. 2007. "Censorship and the Content of Nigerian Home Video Films." *Postcolonial Text* 3, no. 2: 1–22.

Valley, Dylan. 2011. "Interview with Director Oliver Hermanus." *Africa Is a Country*, August 5. http://africasacountry.com/2011/08/interview-with-film-director-oliver-hermanus/.

van der Merwe, André Carl. (2006) 2011. *Moffie*. New York: Europa Editions.

Van der Walt, Terry. 2020. "Moffie Reopens Wounds of Border War Suffering." *IOL News*. March 22. https://www.iol.co.za/weekend-argus/opinion/moffie-reopens-wounds-of-border-war-suffering-45350956/.

van Dijk, Rijk. 2001. "Time and Transcultural Technologies of the Self in the Ghanaian Diaspora." In *Between Babel and Pentecost*, edited by André Corten and Ruth Marshall, 216–34. Bloomington: Indiana University Press.

van Klinken, Adriaan. 2019. *Kenyan, Christian, Queer: Religion, LGBT Activism, and Arts of Resistance in Africa*. University Park: Pennsylvania State University Press.

Wainaina, Binyavanga. 2015. "I Am a Homosexual, Mum." *Africa Is a Country*, January 19. https://africasacountry.com/2014/01/i-am-a-homosexual-mum/.

Weheliye, Alexander G. 2005. *Phonographies: Grooves in Sonic Afro-Modernity*. Durham, NC: Duke University Press.

Wendl, Tobias. 2001. "Visions of Modernity in Ghana: Mami Wata Shrines, Photo Studios and Horror Films." *Visual Anthropology* 14, no. 3: 269–92.

Williams, Linda. 2002. *Playing the Race Card: Melodramas of Black and White from Uncle Tom to O. J. Simpson*. Princeton, NJ: Princeton University Press.

Wilson, Jake. 2012. "'Frightening' Gay Outsider Tale." *Sydney Morning Herald*. July 26. https://www.smh.com.au/entertainment/movies/frightening-gay-outsider-tale-20120725-22qj3.html.

Zabus, Chantal J. 2013. *Out in Africa: Same-Sex Desire in Sub-Saharan Literatures and Cultures*. Rochester, NY: Boydell and Brewer.

Page numbers followed by *f* indicate figures.

video films, popular: aesthetics of failure in, 216n19; as category, 14–15; haptics of, 61; occult melodramas and video boom in Ghana and Nigeria, 59–62; small screens, effect of, 66. *See also* Nollywood
Viscott, David, 177, 181
visual activism, 16, 130–31
vulnerability: in *Breaking Out of the Box* (Matebeni and Kheswa), 29; in *Dakan* (Camara), 208; exposure and, 196–97; potential and, 197; quietness and, 213n14; *Rafiki* (Kahiu) and, 189, 197–99, 202; resilience and, 33, 168–73, 199; resistance and, 7, 21, 197–98, 201; "Same Love (Remix)" and, 183; silence and, 22; in *Stories of Our Lives* (Chuchu), 2, 6–7; *ulwaluko*, masculinity, and, 144
Vundla, Batana, 129, 142

Wainaina, Binyavanga, 1, 27, 180
Walking with Shadows (film; O'Kelly), 17, 113–17, 115f, 118
Walking with Shadows (novel; Dibia), 113–16
Wallström, Jonny von, 15
water spirits: *Jezebel* (Safo) and, 63–65; Kumba Kastel in *Karmen Geï* (Ramaka), 38–39, 47, 51, 53–54; Kumba Kastel in *Women in Love* (Safo), 58; Mami Wata, 31, 54–59, 63–65; in *Women in Love* (Safo), 39, 58; Yemonja (Yoruba mermaid spirit), 216n15
waywardness: about, 41–42; in *Jezebel* (Safo), 41; in *Karmen Geï* (Ramaka), 41–42, 46, 48, 53–55; Mami Wata and, 59, 69
Wedding Party, The (Adetiba), 101
Wedding Party 2, The (Akinmolayan), 105
We Don't Live Here Anymore (Oshin), 105–12, 108f–11f, 117–18
Weheliye, Alexander, 49
We Must Free Our Imaginations (Wainaina), 27

Wendl, Tobias, 56
West African cinema: Anglophone and Francophone traditions, 38, 214n1; FESPACO (Panafrican Film and Television Festival of Ouagadougou), 12, 205; impossible queer eroticism and, 37–38. *See also* Ghana and Ghanaian cinema; Nollywood; Senegal and Senegalese cinema
While You Weren't Looking (Stewart), 128–30, 212n12, 221n7
Williams, Linda, 67, 82
Williams, Raymond, 139
Women in Love (Safo), 39, 40, 58, 65, 216n13
Women's Affair (Chukwu), 79, 83–84, 89
worlding, 11–12
World's Worst Place to Be Gay, The (Alcock), 15
World Unseen, The (Sarif), 13, 130
Worsdale, Andrew, 125, 220n1
Woubi Cheri (Bocahut and Brooks), 15
Wright, Katherine Fairfax, 15

Xala (Sembene), 42

Yizo Yizo (Bomb), 128
Youngman, Caine, 18
YouTube: *Beautiful Faces* (Egbon), 218n13; *Everything In Between* (TIERS), 117–18; *Hell or High Water* (Oluseyi), 104, 106; Kenyan efforts to censor, 18, 174, 184–85; Nollywood on, 119, 218n13, 220n25; *Pregnant Hawkers* (Iyke), 98; queer cinema and, 11, 14–15, 34, 207; *We Must Free Our Imaginations* (Wainaina), 27

Zabus, Chantal, 116, 220n24
Zinabu (Akuffo), 216n17
Ziqubu, Thishiwe, 221n7
Zouhali-Worrall, Malika, 15